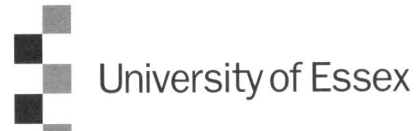University of Essex   Library

Date Due Back

Human remains and identification

MANCHESTER
1824

Manchester University Press

HUMAN REMAINS AND VIOLENCE

Human remains and violence aims to question the social legacy of mass violence by studying how different societies have coped with the dead bodies resulting from war, genocide and state sponsored brutality. However, rather paradoxically, given the large volume of work devoted to the body on the one hand, and to mass violence on the other, the question of the body in the context of mass violence remains a largely unexplored area and even an academic blind spot. Interdisciplinary in nature, *Human remains and violence* intends to show how various social and cultural treatments of the dead body simultaneously challenge common representations, legal practices and morality. This series aims to provide proper intellectual and theoretical tools for a better understanding of mass violence's aftermaths.

Series editors

Jean-Marc Dreyfus and Élisabeth Anstett

ALSO AVAILABLE IN THIS SERIES

Destruction and human remains: disposal and concealment in genocide and mass violence
Edited by Élisabeth Anstett and Jean-Marc Dreyfus

Human remains and mass violence: methodological approaches
Edited by Jean-Marc Dreyfus and Élisabeth Anstett

Governing the dead: sovereignty and the politics of dead bodies
Edited by Finn Stepputat

Human remains and identification

Mass violence, genocide, and the 'forensic turn'

Edited by

Élisabeth Anstett and Jean-Marc Dreyfus

Manchester University Press

Published by Manchester University Press
Altrincham Street, Manchester M1 7JA
www.manchesteruniversitypress.co.uk

British Library Cataloguing-in-Publication Data
A catalogue record for this book is available from the British Library

Library of Congress Cataloging-in-Publication Data applied for

ISBN 978 07190 97560 hardback

First published 2015

Typeset by Out of House Publishing
Printed in Great Britain by
TJ International Ltd, Padstow

Contents

Illustrations

Contributors

Élisabeth Anstett has been a researcher in social anthropology at the National Centre for Scientific Research (CNRS) in Paris since October 2009, and is a member of IRIS (*Interdisciplinary Research Institute on Social issues*). Her area of expertise covers Europe and the post-socialist world, on which she has published extensively. Her recent works focus on the way post-Soviet societies are dealing with the traces left by the Soviet concentration camp system, among which are mass graves, and more broadly on the legacies of mass violence in Eastern Europe, especially in Russia and Byelorussia. She has published, among other works, *Une Atlantide russe, anthropologie de la mémoire en Russie postsoviétique* (Paris: La Découverte, 2007) and co-edited with Luba Jurgenson *Le Goulag en héritage, pour une anthropologie de la trace* (Paris: Pétra, 2009).

Karel C. Berkhoff is Senior Researcher at the NIOD Institute for War, Holocaust and Genocide Studies at the Royal Netherlands Academy of Sciences. He has published *Harvest of Despair: Life and Death in Ukraine under Nazi Rule* (2004; 2008; Ukrainian translation 2011) and *Motherland in Danger: Soviet Propaganda during World War II* (2012), both with Harvard University Press. He is working on a book about the history and remembrance of Babi Yar, site of the largest single Nazi shooting of Soviet Jews.

Viacheslav Bitiutckii was one of the founders of Voronezh Memorial in 1988 and remains the chairman to this day. Between 1990 and 1993 he was a deputy in the Voronezh Regional Council and from 1992 to 1997 was deputy chair of the commission for the restitution of rights for the rehabilitated victims of political repression. Since 1994 he has been a member of the executive committee of the international society Memorial and has, from 1998, been a legal consultant for the Migration and Law programme of the Memorial educational centre. Viacheslav is an advisor to the Voronezh regional public office of the Russian Human Rights Commissioner and his sphere of interest includes not only the history of political justice and repression in the USSR, but also raising public awareness of these issues. His recent publications include *Stalin's Lists in Voronezh: The Book of Remembrance for the Victims of Political Repression in the Voronezh Region* (Voronezh, 2007) and *Political Repressions in Voronezh* (Krasnoyarsk, 2011). Viacheslav is also a regular contributor to the *Voronezh Courier* with articles such as 'The victims of terror' (2012) and 'Dubovka in 2012: no name, no border, no fence' (2012/2013).

Jean-Marc Dreyfus is Reader in Holocaust Studies within the Department of History at the University of Manchester. His research interests include: Holocaust studies; genocide studies/anthropology of genocide; the history of the Jews in Europe in the nineteenth and twentieth centuries; the history of the Jews in France in the nineteenth and twentieth centuries; economic history of France and Germany; Holocaust memory/politics of memory; the modern history of Alsace; and rebuilding post-war societies. He is the author of five monographs, including *Pillages sur ordonnances: la confiscation des banques juives en France et leur restitution, 1940–1953* (Paris: Fayard, 2003) and, with Sarah Gensburger, *Nazi Labor Camps in Paris* (New York, Oxford: Berghahn Books, 2012) and *Il m'appelait Pikolo: un compagnon de Primo Levi raconte* (*He Called Me Pikolo: A Companion of Primo Levi Tells His Story*) (Robert Laffont, 2007) and *L'impossible Réparation* (Flammarion, 2015). He is the co-editor of the *Dictionnaire de la Shoah* (*Dictionary of the Holocaust*) (Paris: Larousse, 2009).

Gabriel N. Finder is an associate professor in the Department of Germanic Languages and Literatures at the University of Virginia and director of the university's Jewish Studies Program. He received a JD from the University of Pennsylvania and his PhD from the University of Chicago. He practised law in both Israel and the US before embarking on a university career. He has various scholarly interests, which are reflected in his teaching as well as his research. He teaches the Holocaust, post-Holocaust trials, German Jewish history and culture, East European Jewish history and culture, and Yiddish language along with other courses. His research interests lie in Central and East European Jewish history and culture, the Holocaust, memory of the Holocaust, the reconstruction of Jewish life after 1945, and relations between Jews and non-Jews in Central and Eastern Europe with an emphasis on Poland, especially under communism. His publications in these areas have appeared in several scholarly journals and edited volumes. He is contributing co-editor of volume 20 (2008) of *Polin*, the theme of which is the construction of Holocaust memory in Poland. He is currently co-authoring a book on the trials of Nazi war criminals in communist Poland, and he is the co-editor of two forthcoming volumes: one on post-war Jewish honour courts; the other on humour in Jewish culture in the twentieth and twenty-first centuries for volume 29 of the yearbook *Studies in Contemporary Jewry*.

Gillian Fowler is a Senior Lecturer in Forensic Anthropology and Archaeology in the School of Life Sciences at the University of Lincoln in the UK. She is a forensic anthropologist and archaeologist with extensive experience working in post-conflict mass-grave exhumations in Guatemala and more recently in Afghanistan, where she is a consulting forensic anthropologist for Physicians for Human Rights (PHR). In addition to international consultancy, Gillian undertakes casework for UK police forces and is a member of UKDVI. She is a fellow of the Royal Anthropological Institute and is also a member of the British Association for Forensic Anthropology (BAFA).

Admir Jugo worked as a forensic archaeologist and anthropologist on exhuming human remains from mass graves and other exhumation sites in the territory of the Former Yugoslavia, primarily Bosnia and Herzegovina. His research focuses on biological anthropology of human remains, but also on the process of transitional justice in Bosnia and Herzegovina and Spain, forensic archaeology and scientific and social aspects of exhumations and mass graves. Admir holds a degree in Biology from the University of Sarajevo and is currently working towards his master's in Genetics from the same university. He has also helped in the development of training programmes for the Archaeology and Anthropology Department of ICMP, and has provided training for both ICMP and non-ICMP staff, and was a research assistant and forensic consultant on the four-year ERC-funded project 'Bosnian Bones, Spanish Ghosts: "Transitional Justice" and the Legal Shaping of Memory after Two Modern Conflicts'.

Rémi Korman is a doctoral candidate in history at EHESS, Paris. His PhD focuses on the politics of memory of the Tutsi genocide in Rwanda and more particularly on memorial processes. Through working on his PhD he has also developed a strong interest in preserving the archives of the genocide, and in order to promote the knowledge related to these places of memory and knowledge he has recently established the website www.rwanda.hypotheses.org. He is currently working for the 'Reseau Memorha' in Lyon, an organization focused on museums and memory issues and is the author of 'La politique de mémoire du génocide des Tutsi au Rwanda: enjeux et évolutions', *Droit et Cultures: Revue Internationale Interdisciplinaire* (2013).

José López Mazz is a Professor at the Anthropological Institute of the University of the Republic of Uruguay (UdelaR) and a Senior Researcher at the Sistema Nacional de Investigadores (ANII). He was until 2014 the head of the Anthropological Forensic Team (GIAF) which searches for the bodies of missing people from the military dictatorship (1973–84). His area of expertise covers archaeological methods and techniques for forensic researches, and the archaeology of the social conflict in Latin America (from prehistory to the present). He has published, among others works, *Investigaciones arqueológicas sobre Detenidos Desaparecidos* (Montevideo: Presidencia de la República/IMPO, 2006); 'An archaeological view of political repression in Uruguay (1971–1985)', in *Memory from the Darkness* (New York: Springer, 2010); and is co-editor with Mónica Beron of *Indicadores arqueológicos de guerra, conflicto y violencia* (Montevideo: Universidad de la Repúbica, 2014).

Tony Platt is the author of ten books and 150 essays and articles dealing with issues of race, inequality, and social justice in American history. Platt has taught at the University of Chicago, University of California (Berkeley), and California State University (Sacramento). He is a Distinguished Affiliated Scholar at the University of California, Berkeley. His publications have been translated into German, Spanish, Italian, and Japanese. His latest book – *Grave Matters: Excavating California's Buried Past* – was published by

Heyday in 2011. He lives in Berkeley and Big Lagoon, California, and serves as secretary of the Coalition to Protect Yurok Cultural Legacies at O-pyuweg (Big Lagoon). Platt blogs on history and memory at http://GoodToGo.typepad.com.

Nicky Rousseau teaches history at the University of the Western Cape in Cape Town, South Africa. She is a former researcher for the South African Truth and Reconciliation Commission (TRC), and was part of the team that wrote the TRC's seven-volume report. Subsequently she worked as a research consultant to South Africa's National Prosecuting Authority on post-TRC investigations, prosecutions, and missing persons. She has published a number of articles on the TRC, and more recently has returned to her TRC research with a view to rethinking questions of the national security state and counter-revolutionary warfare. Her current research interests include truth commissions, violence, histories of liberation, and human remains.

Frances Tay obtained her degree in Economics from Australian National University in 1994, her MA in Social Development at the University of Reading, and is currently pursuing her PhD in History at the University of Manchester. She has had a varied career; including senior manager of the education and training department at the British Council, general manager of an exhibition and events company, and co-founder of a research project with Lithuanian Holocaust survivors which culminated in a touring exhibition and education programme in Lithuania, the UK, Ireland, and South Africa. She lives in London and is co-owner of Woolfson & Tay bookshop in Bankside.

Tim Thompson is a Reader in Biological and Forensic Anthropology at Teesside University and a practising consultant in this field. Previously he completed his PhD in the Department of Forensic Pathology at the University of Sheffield, was Lecturer in Forensic Anthropology at the University of Dundee, and was Senior Lecturer in Crime Scene Science at Teesside University. He is a Fellow of the Chartered Society of Forensic Sciences and the Royal Anthropological Institute, and is on the editorial board for the *Journal of Forensic Sciences* and the *Journal of Forensic and Legal Medicine*. His main areas of research focus on the human body and how it changes (particularly in the modern context), and the role of forensic anthropology/ists in the world at large. He has published over 50 peer-reviewed papers in international journals and books, and is senior editor of the book *Forensic Human Identification: An Introduction* (Boca Raton, FL: CRC Press, 2007) and co-author with Rebecca Gowland of *Human Identity and Identification* (Cambridge: Cambridge University Press, 2013).

Sari Wastell is a Legal Anthropologist and Lecturer in the Anthropology Department at Goldsmiths, University of London. She has also taught at Cambridge (where she took her PhD in Social Anthropology) and Edinburgh (where she studied both Law and Anthropology and completed her first degree to MA level, completing a dissertation on Basque nationalism and memory politics). At Goldsmiths, her teaching focuses on social theory and the anthropology of rights, although her own research interests centre on international criminal law, 'transitional justice', and an anthropology of international relations, conflict management, and security studies. She is the Principal Investigator on 'Bosnian Bones, Spanish Ghosts: "Transitional Justice" and the Legal Shaping of Memory after Two Modern Conflicts', as well as 'Transitional Justice Mapping' projects, both generously funded through the European Research Council. Her forthcoming book, co-authored with Kirsten Campbell and Hannah Starman and entitled *Testifying to Trauma: The Codification of Atrocity in International Humanitarian Law*, will be published by Routledge Cavendish.

Acknowledgements

Most of the chapters in this volume proceed from presentations given at the conference 'Search and identification of corpses and human remains in post-genocide and mass violence contexts', convened at the University of Manchester on 9, 10, and 11 September 2013, organized by the international and comparative research programme 'Corpses of mass violence and genocide'.

Due to the success of the conference and the engaging discussions that followed, the editors want to warmly thank a number of individuals and research institutions for their involvement in preparing the event and the publishing of this volume. They include the School of Arts, Languages and Cultures at the University of Manchester for accommodating the conference, and its director Jeremy Gregory for giving the opening remarks; Laurence Radford (ERC project 'Corpses of mass violence and genocide', the University of Manchester) for dealing with the overall organization of the conference and for his editorial commitment to the publication; Emmanuelle Gravejat ('Corpses of mass violence and genocide', EHESS-Paris) and the team at the Institut de recherche interdisciplinaire sur les enjeux sociaux in Paris; Caroline Fournet (University of Groningen); Jon Shute (University of Manchester); and Sévane Garibian (University of Geneva) for assisting with the event's preparation.

We must also thank Luis Fondebrider (Equipo Argentino de Antropologia Forense, Argentina), Francesco Ferrandiz and Luis Rios (CCHS-CSIC, Spain), Isaac L. Baker and Brittany Card (Harvard Humanitarian Initiative, USA), Belen Rodriguez Cardoso (Banco Nacional de Datos Geneticos, Argentina), Victor Toom (Northumbria University, UK), Admir Jugo and Senem Skulj (Goldsmiths, University of London, UK), Rachel Hatcher (University of Saskatchewan, Canada), Caroline Bennett (University of Kent, UK), Sabina Subasic (University of Sarajevo, Bosnia-Herzegovina) and Ernesto Schwartz-Marin (University of Manchester) for their participation at the conference.

Finally, we are indelibly grateful to the European Research Council for their ongoing support for the research programme 'Corpses of mass violence and genocide', which, in turn, brought the conference and resulting publication to fruition.

Élisabeth Anstett and Jean-Marc Dreyfus

Introduction: why exhume? Why identify?[1]

Élisabeth Anstett and Jean-Marc Dreyfus

This book arises from the second annual conference of the 'Corpses of mass violence and genocide' research programme held in Manchester on 9–11 September 2013, forming one part of a three-phase study.[2] The first phase, which was the subject of a conference in Paris in 2012 and subsequent publication, focused on the treatment of dead bodies just after the murders themselves.[3] Studying the fate of cadavers that have been abandoned, destroyed, dismantled, hidden, traded, or desecrated in situations of mass violence has helped open new avenues of research, demonstrating, in particular, the procedural dimension of extreme violence and illuminating how the ideology of agents of death is once again translated into the very treatment of bodies.

The second phase of the programme, the preliminary findings of which are presented in this volume's contributions,[4] interrogates the treatment of corpses and human remains after the disaster, focusing specifically on their possible discovery and identification. The study of these two separate enterprises – the search for bodies and their identification – has traditionally remained in the hands of forensic science and has so far only marginally attracted the interest of history, social anthropology, or law despite the magnitude of their respective fields of application. In this context, one of the primary contributions of this volume is to connect the social and forensic sciences, for the first time, in a joint and comparative analysis of how societies engage in the process of searching for and identifying the corpses produced by mass violence, and thereby to initiate a truly interdisciplinary dialogue.

The third phase of the programme, investigating the place of human remains in the process of patrimonialization and commemoration of extreme violence, was the subject of a conference in September 2014 and of a forthcoming volume published in this series.

The contributions to the present volume thus document, in very different contexts, the specific fate of dead bodies after life and the variety of techniques and technologies used for their location and identification. These texts take as their starting point the observation, which strikes anyone who simply reads the news, that the last decade of the twentieth century and the first years of the twenty-first century witnessed a tremendous resurgence of corpses produced by the extreme violence of the twentieth century: tens and sometimes hundreds of thousands in many countries. Cases are numerous, from the forensic anthropologists' search for those 'disappeared' by the Argentine dictatorship from 1983, to the identification, now nearly systematic, of the bodies of victims of crimes committed in Bosnia and the utilization of the work of forensic pathologists by the International Criminal Tribunal for the former Yugoslavia in 1995, or even the large-scale opening – only beginning in 2000 – of the mass graves of the Spanish Civil War. In Rwanda the victims of the genocide committed against the Tutsis were exhumed and reburied, sometimes repeatedly, by the tens of thousands between 1994 and today. This case of incomparable scale, which is sometimes accompanied by the exhibition of certain human remains or of entire bodies in memorials like those of Murambi or Ntarama, contrasts sharply with the situation in Cambodia, where mass crimes were perpetrated between 1975 and 1979. No extensive attempt to recover or identify bodies of victims of the Khmer Rouge has so far been undertaken, although some bones have been gathered in local memorials.

The studies on which this volume is based deal with the fate of the bodies of civilian victims resulting from mass violence and genocide, as delimited by the twentieth and twenty-first centuries. They are by no means intended to be exhaustive, but seek to treat a number of important case studies with a comparative and exploratory goal in mind. Thus, the treatment of soldiers' remains does not fall within the scope of our research programme. Of course, the first mass exhumations of the previous century were initiated by European states after the Second World War, in an unprecedented enterprise of identifying and repatriating the bodies of combatants.[5] In addition, techniques for the management of corpses and human remains on a grand scale, for classification and record-keeping, were developed by the military before civilian agencies were forced to do so. And the Joint Prisoners of War/MIA Accounting Command, a large US Army forensics lab located on the island of Oahu in Hawaii, continues to work to identify the bodies of soldiers killed in the Pacific theatre during the Second World War. However, the search for and identification of the bodies of combatants follows a logic specific to the military world, which seemingly cannot be transposed to civil society without major theoretical and methodological difficulties.

From the outset, then, the questions addressed in this volume are organized around two distinct but intrinsically connected themes: search and identification. However, the search for bodies or human remains, and before them, of mass or individual graves, where these exist, do not automatically lead to attempts at identification. Therefore we have to carefully distinguish between the two enterprises. Thus, in the case of exhumation of the victims of the Great Purge, conducted in Russia in an extremely limited capacity after the fall of the USSR, the discovery of mass graves and bones was not accompanied by forensic procedures for the identification of bodies, much less by research on the victims' DNA. Certainly, the artefacts, clothes, and documents found in the graves offer some legible indications, but to this day, no systematic attempt has been made to determine the identity of the human remains, as we are reminded in this volume by Viacheslav Bitiutckii, lawyer and head of the NGO 'Memorial', who oversaw the exhumations in the Voronezh region.

Additionally, sometimes bodies resurface without being sought for. This was the case in the ravine of Babi Yar in Kiev, where the city's Jews had been killed and hastily buried (33,771 people, according to the German killers' official statistics) in September 1941. A nearby dam gave way in the late 1960s, and the subsequent flooding unearthed hundreds of bodies that were then reinterred without any attempt at identification.[6] Other cases may be cited, such as the graves of the Dachau concentration camp, discovered by chance during excavation work for the construction of a road in 1948. The unearthed bodies were then identified by means of the forensic medicine of the time.[7] There are even cases where there has been the discovery *and* identification of bodies without their having been the subject of a prior search, but there remain numerous cases of a search for and localization of mass graves, of exhumations and reinterments of bodies without any attempt at identification. This fact can be explained primarily by the lack of technical and financial resources, but also, as in Rwanda or the territories of the former

Soviet Union, for political reasons when the systematic identification of corpses risks destabilizing society or the political party in
power, creating problems that outweigh the benefits expected from
a reburial.

To date, the best-documented cases of a large-scale search for
human remains (with or without identification) remain those of
Rwanda, the Latin American dictatorships, Bosnia, and Spain.
However, the dimensions of these killings are extremely varied, and
the proportion of victims identified also differs considerably. Thus,
only 500 of the 900 bodies recovered have been identified to date
in Argentina (out of approximately 10,000 known to have disappeared). In Bosnia, out of the 100,000 war dead, 14,000 exhumed
victims have been identified by their DNA, with 6,877 of these from
the genocide at Srebrenica alone.[8] More than 6,500 bodies have been
exhumed in Spain since 2000, with the number of persons identified still unknown, but several hundred graves containing tens of
thousands of victims remain untouched.[9] And given that more than
250,000 bodies have been reinterred by the Kigali Memorial Centre
alone, the total number of victims of the genocide of the Tutsi as well
as that of the exhumations undertaken by Rwanda remains uncertain at present. As for the bodies and remains of the 6 million Jewish
victims of the Holocaust, only a minuscule percentage of them were
exhumed and even fewer identified.

These cases, emblematic of the twentieth century's heritage of
extreme violence, raise questions for us about the emergence of a
'forensic turn', in the words of historian Robert Jan van Pelt at the
Paris Conference in September 2012. This forensic turn can be
defined, in the first place, by the arrival of forensic pathologists and
anthropologists on the scene of mass violence and genocide as the
decisive agents of practices in the search for bodies; the political,
social, and diplomatic dimensions of which are immediately manifest. These forensic pathologists and anthropologists now see their
legitimacy buttressed by the increasing effectiveness of their work
and the use of advanced technologies such as geolocation and DNA
identification. This forensic turn is largely globalized, facilitated by
the movement of professionals throughout the world, bringing their
expertise – and their equipment – to the four corners of the globe
and sometimes participating in the training of local teams.[10] An
account of its origins might even be in the process of being offered,
centring on the figure of Dr Clyde Snow, an American pathologist present as a consultant in Bosnia since 1992, who brought his
expertise to the teams in charge of the first exhumation conducted in

Argentina in the early 1980s.[11] As a crucial figure in the emergence of this potential 'forensic turn', Clyde Snow helped found the EAAF (Equipo Argentina de Antropología Forense (Argentinian Forensic Anthropology Team)), which to this day has been working to identify the bodies of missing persons, intervening in dozens of countries around the world, and whose director, Luis Fondebrider, was a guest at our conference in Manchester.

The temporality of the search for and identification of corpses, and not just their globalized character, is thus an important element in the analysis of these phenomena. In some countries, the search for bodies began immediately after the massacres, such as in Poland in 1945, where Jewish survivors tried to give the victims of the death marches a dignified burial.[12] But in Spain, it was not until sixty years after the end of the Civil War and twenty-five years after the restoration of democracy that the first exhumation of the Republican dead could take place (while the bodies of Francoist combatants and civilians had been honoured much earlier). We must therefore keep in mind that the timing of exhumation always depends on the political (and sometimes geopolitical) context, such as the national politics of amnesty or the local politics of memory. This chronology also depends on unique and complex social contexts that allow (through the emergence of a consensus) or else prevent (when divisions persist) the search for victims' remains.

The contributors to this volume have thus attempted to answer many questions related to the conditions and terms of the rapid emergence of this 'forensic turn'. They have inquired into the agents and agencies through which bodies are recovered and/or identified, the practices and techniques used, and, finally, the motives and interests that explain the emergence of mass exhumations. Who is then responsible for exhumations? Who takes the initiative, having been accorded the right to do so legitimately, and how is this legitimacy constructed? The agents present within this domain are often many and varied, including families, non-governmental organizations, civil, religious and judicial institutions, survivors' associations, judges, and the media themselves. The combined contributions here show that the agents may be local or national, often reinforced by an intervention (technical, legal, political, or financial) emanating from elsewhere and frequently from abroad, by way of criminal courts, governmental or non-governmental organizations, or occupation or peacekeeping forces.

With regard to the techniques used for the search and identification of bodies, in the face of multiple constraints, these can range from the most rudimentary – location of mass graves by direct witnesses or survivors, and exhumations by shovel or hand – to the most sophisticated, with the use of remote sensing equipment, the establishment of wide-area archaeological surveys for corpses, and the use of lab analyses to decode DNA samples. As such, the mass exhumations and identification procedures undertaken during the twentieth century generated substantial transfers of expertise and a progressive standardization of practices. These collective moments have, in turn, initiated new funerary practices including new social or religious rituals for the treatment of the dead. In this regard, the contributors to this volume have also undertaken the description of an entire economy – both material and symbolic – of the treatment of bodies.

The ten chapters collected here show how the motives governing the implementation of these exhumations are many, varying, and complicated, how they can give rise to power plays of varying intensity, and how they call an entire society into question. These motivations may arise in connection with identity and remembrance, with familial or collective ties, with politics, but also, let us not forget, with religions. Studying these motives and interests, then, considerably illuminates a society's functioning after the catastrophe and the slow construction of a collective mourning process. These issues also address the emergence of the symbolic and legal status of corpses, a central point for all of the studies. They call for new anthropological studies of contemporary societies' relations with human remains in all their forms: whole or dismembered corpses, complete skeletons or single bones, tissues, organs, appendages, and finally, ashes. Indeed, it seems important to us to understand what is at stake in the 'exhumatory' act itself, and thereby to attempt, as far as possible, to resituate the history, geography, and sociology of these mass exhumations.

One of the first results of the research presented here thus obliges us, quite unsurprisingly, to move away from a triumphalist narrative regarding the search for and identification of bodies, always and everywhere contributing to the march towards justice and truth and to the healing of post-genocidal societies. For exhumations are not all virtuous with many carrying their share of conflicts, opening up new gaps and new questions. Our works also encourage the hypothesis of a real paradigm shift in remembrance, a shift of which the forensic turn would constitute both a consequence and a cause. It in fact appears that societies involved in mass crimes have gradually, over the last thirty years, given up on constructing an intelligible account of extreme violence from the survivors' narrative, instead giving special attention to the material evidence of the disaster; collective memories would then no longer be drawn from the testimonial paradigm but from the paradigm of material evidence.

However, insofar as the studies presented here, like those presented at the conference, aim to open up new avenues of research, it also seems important to us to bring real lucidity to some points that have heretofore remained obscure. Thus, certain landscapes, certain incidents of mass violence, and not only a few, remain largely underdocumented when we raise the question of the search for victims' bodies and there can be no doubt that we see a clear disparity in the existing studies. There is, for example, almost no research on the treatment of the corpses, human remains, or ashes of the millions of Jews murdered in the Holocaust, much less the other victims of Nazism, such as the Sinti and Roms. Similarly, we know very little about what happened to the remains of the victims of the Cambodian genocide. And nearly a hundred years after the disaster, we have so far seen no study on the fate of the corpses of the Armenian genocide. Does the very dimension of the mass murder, then, entail a singular difficulty in planning and implementing the search for and identification of human remains?

The linguistic aspect of practices of search and identification also remains largely unexplored. The terms and the manner in which human remains and corpses are designated in different contexts of violence still seem to be decisive. The Argentine and Rwandan cases show us that to name the dead is quite often to have already taken a political position. A study of the lexicon used in countries where the exhumations took place, lexicons which may differ depending on the agents (vernacular terminologies, technical or scientific nomenclatures, or classifications emanating from religion, poetry, or slang), could open up new vistas for research in this regard. The translation of these terms, by experts in both forensic medicine and law, but also by researchers who study these social facts, thus deserves to be given attention and fully analysed insofar as words seem to carry much more meaning than their speakers at first seem to attribute.

The specifically ethical issues raised by research on the fate of the victims of mass violence could also be articulated, although all the professionals involved in this research are in direct contact with human remains. For if handling such remains within cultural and research institutions is now largely framed by laws or administrative procedures in most Western countries, large-scale exhumations are still conducted that generate a set of unprecedented practices and situations that go beyond the boundaries initially conceived by legislators. Moreover, the agents on the scene often act within a personal ethical vision that is not always fully expressed, composed of a concatenation of social and religious norms and sometimes of audacious symbolic improvisations and constructions. These often syncretic and heterodox approaches deserve to be examined and compared (in their origins as well as in their effects) to the ethical frameworks governing scientific research. To these must be added those issues posed by the long intimacy with death and the dead engendered through the very process of academic research, which few of the contributors to this book have sought to document.

At the same time, the rich contributions in this volume offer much to research, first by shedding light on the logic of the agents of these searches, exhumations, and identification procedures, which typically entail competing goals. We can establish a hierarchy of agents, from the single individual whose initiative may cause a political earthquake (as was the case in Spain), to the most powerful state institutions such as, in the case of Guatemala, the army. These agents may be invested with ideologies, but also with age-old religious traditions. The religious authorities nonetheless rarely initiate searches that are seen as likely to disrupt their own legitimacy, at a time when this rather demands to be strengthened or restored. These agents also live within a material, even sensory, culture – think of the smells of burned or rotted bodies, and those of bone-cleansing products – which is unique, within which they also establish new points of reference. The combined contributions here show in this regard the importance of all of this material culture of exhumations and of the treatment of human remains: coffins, shrouds, the uniforms worn by forensic pathologists or their equipment, and also, finally, the individual or collective tombstones and monuments erected at sites of reburial. Thus, as documented by several of the texts gathered here, new social and cultural practices are constructed through the search for bodies.

The contributions collected here also help bring to light a second logic of territories and their control. The study of the treatment of corpses during the phase of massacre has demonstrated the importance of the geography of murder sites, and of the topography, forests, rivers, etc. It has also underlined the degree to which the anthropological perception of the landscape has influenced the treatment of bodies. Exhumations, too, seem determined by this physical and mental geography. The texts in this volume show that it is often the status of the territories formed by mass graves and pits that is at stake in the exhumation, as well as their control and ownership. The question generated by mass grave looting is, for example, situated within this logic, as well as the opening of graves by unaccredited agents, which is analysed in various contributions.

The third logic that emerges from this volume, of course, is that of politics. For exhumations also – primarily – form part of a process of community building or the construction of a post-genocidal state. The search for bodies, then, always takes place within constraints that remain to be negotiated and conflicts that remain to be resolved. And there are many cases – as almost all of the texts gathered here indicate – in which the stakes of diplomacy, of the quasi-diplomacy of non-governmental organizations, but also those of geopolitics, are involved. Questions of a specifically legal nature concerning the legality of exhumations and identifications ordered or protected by national and international courts also arise within this context. For this logic remains in broader terms the logic of transitional justice.

These three approaches – via the power of the agents, the territory, and state building – are interdependent in more ways than one, and several authors in this volume show that we can identify mutualities among them without thereby making it easier for them to be prioritized.

Thus, in a text which here serves as a preamble, Tony Platt describes the fate of the graves of Native Americans in California. Tacking against a narrative that describes this state as a liberal region, home to high-tech enterprises, the chapter shows that the European settlement was built on the almost total destruction of the indigenous populations during the eighteenth and nineteenth centuries. Starting from a personal reflection on the experience of mourning for his son, he first questions the motives of agents engaged in the search for Indian graves, but also those of the social scientists who study the product of this search. He explains how the denial of the Native American genocide was bolstered by the instrumentalization of Indian graves and the systematic looting of the artefacts and bones they contained. The bones were sent to museums in bulk – with Platt giving the staggering figure of between 600,000 and 1 million tombs thus opened and destroyed – but they also constituted huge collections in the anthropology departments. UC Davis remains, as such, a veritable ossuary. In pointing this out, Platt warns against a triumphalist reading of exhumations, showing that they can instead participate in the creation and imposition of a largely mythic historical narrative through institutions and the general public.

In the first section devoted to the agents of the search for and identification of bodies, Gabriel Finder shows how the Polish Jewish survivors of the Holocaust themselves tried to give a dignified burial to members of their family and community in the immediate post-war period. However, even if the number of the bodies exhumed from mass graves and buried a second time with an official ceremony – and Jewish prayers – might seem substantial, it represents only a fraction of the bodies of 3 million Polish Jewish victims. The chapter analyses the real collective impact of individual initiatives undertaken locally under the tight control of the Soviet occupation authorities and relayed at a distance by diasporic Jewish communities. Karel Berkhoff, in turn, describes how the silence of Soviet and Ukrainian authorities on the existence of one major mass grave of the victims of the Stalinist purges was jeopardized for decades by many agents: German occupation troops during the war, grave robbers, and Ukrainian and Polish nationalists, with their differing motives, were the agents whose actions prompted a chaotic but progressive effort to mark the sites of the violence, ending in the construction of an official monument. Finally, José López Mazz explains how only a radical political change in Uruguay has permitted the formation of a commission to search for the bodies of those who disappeared under the dictatorship. Since 2010, with the aid of archaeological expertise, this commission has engaged in the difficult task of exposing and circumventing the strategies of concealment employed by the military, slowly and patiently bringing to light the physical evidence of the implementation of 'Operation Carrot', which involved the illegal exhumation and systematic destruction of the remains of the dictatorship's victims.

Opening the section on the means and methods employed in the search for bodies, the Russian lawyer Viacheslav Bitiutckii, head of the local branch of the NGO 'Memorial', describes the only exhumations of the bodies of Stalinist purge victims that took place on Soviet territory in the Voronezh region south of Moscow. Describing the extremely limited resources deployed locally by a group of volunteers to pursue the task of exhumation over the course of some twenty years, he analyses the reasons for the failure to complete the process of identification, underlining what continues to be the political dimension of the exhumation and identification of victims more than seventy-five years after the crimes were committed. By contrast, the next contribution in the 'methods' section illuminates the more technological side of this research, first focusing on the development of new techniques for identification in forensic medicine, with particular attention to the scientific and ethical issues entailed by the use of DNA samples (Thompson and Fowler). Concluding this section, Wastell and Jugo show precisely how the multiplicity of practices employed during the exhumation and identification of victims in Bosnia and Herzegovina could themselves disrupt the process while helping to reconstruct Bosnian society as a whole.

In a third and final section, contributors examine the stakes arising from exhumations. Nicky Rousseau, who is herself an agent in the transition to justice in South Africa, takes advantage of her dual affiliation as a researcher and a member of the Truth and Reconciliation Commission to describe and analyse the socio-political sources of the search for bodies of ANC militants murdered by the police of the apartheid regime. She shows this by clarifying not only the issues of political positioning, but also of social class, which are set up around families who are returning the body of a loved one. For his part, historian Rémi Korman analyses the interactions and competition between the different agents' agendas towards the exhumations in Rwanda. He deconstructs the sources of state attempts to impose a funerary and memorial policy which is not always the one desired by the Church and survivors, including the routine anonymization of reinterred victims. The final text in the volume focuses on the Asian continent. Frances Tay is interested in the exhumations ordered in Malaysia by the British military courts in the course of trials for Japanese atrocities committed during the occupation of the peninsula. These exhumations have indeed reflected the policy of restoring the colonial regime, while the process of memorializing the victims – which later drew on other exhumations – revealed the importance of the Chinese minority in the construction of an independent Malaysian state. In this respect, the last section of the volume offers a perfect transition to the further studies we wish to conduct in turning attention to the fate of corpses and human remains in commemorative and patrimonial processes.

Ultimately, the ten contributions to this volume show both the diversity of situations and possible interpretations that can arise from the search for the bodies produced by mass violence and genocide. They show how the very drama of human destiny, of human beings facing their own death, was restaged in the twentieth century and is being restaged today – a drama that is even more incomprehensible in situations of mass death, of non-individualized death, when it is a matter of murder on a grand scale. Exhumations, as demonstrations of a willingness to learn, itself also a desire to see and understand, seem to represent, in this respect, one of many societal responses to the mystery of mass violent deaths.

Notes

1 Translation from the authors' French by Cadenza Academic Translations.
2 Recipient of a starting grant from the European Research Council, no. 283–617. See the website: www.corpsesofmassviolence.eu.
3 É. Anstett & J.-M. Dreyfus (eds), *Destruction and Human Remains: Disposal and Concealment in Genocide and Mass Violence* (Manchester: Manchester University Press, 2014).
4 Further studies will be published in *Human Remains and Violence: An Interdisciplinary Journal* by Manchester University Press in spring 2015.
5 See for example on this undertaking in France and Italy, B. Pau-Heyriès, 'La démobilisation des morts français et italiens de la Grande Guerre', *Revue Historique des Armées*, 250 (2008), 66–76, http://rha.revues.org/185 (accessed 19 February 2014).
6 K. Berkhoff, 'The dispersal and oblivion of the bones and ashes of Babi Yar', in Lauren Faulkner & Wendy Lower (eds), *Lessons and Legacies XII* (Evanston, IL: Northwestern University Press, forthcoming).
7 On the discovery of the mass grave at Leitenberg, see H. Marcuse, *Legacies of Dachau: The Uses and Abuses of a Concentration Camp, 1933–2001* (Cambridge: Cambridge University Press, 2001), pp. 142–50.
8 Figures provided by the ICMP on their website, 15 October 2013; see www.ic-mp.org/icmp-worldwide/southeast-europe/ (accessed 20 January 2014).
9 See the official map published by the Spanish Ministry of Justice, http://mapadefosas.mjusticia.es/exovi_externo/CargarInformacion.htm (accessed 19 February 2014).
10 On the circulation of forensic specialists, see C. Koff, *The Bone Woman: Among the Dead in Rwanda, Bosnia, Croatia and Kosovo* (London: Atlantic, 2004).
11 C. C. Snow, 'Forensic anthropology', *Annual Review of Anthropology*, 11 (1982), 97–131; C. C. Snow, L. Levine, L. Lukash, L. G. Tedeschi, C. Orrego & E. Stover, 'The investigation of the human remains of the "disappeared" in Argentina', *American Journal of Forensic Medicine and Pathology*, 5:4 (1984), 297–9.
12 G. Finder, 'Yizkor! Commemoration of the dead by Jewish displaced persons in postwar Germany', in A. Confino, P. Betts & D. Schumann (eds), *Between Mass Death and Individual Loss: The Place of the Dead in Twentieth-Century Germany* (Oxford and New York: Berghahn Books, 2008), pp. 234–57.

Bibliography

Anstett, É. & J.-M. Dreyfus (eds), *Destruction and Human Remains: Disposal and Concealment in Genocide and Mass Violence* (Manchester: Manchester University Press, 2014)

Berkhoff, K., 'The dispersal and oblivion of the bones and ashes of Babi Yar', in Lauren Faulkner & Wendy Lower (eds), *Lessons and Legacies XII* (Evanston, IL: Northwestern University Press, forthcoming)

Finder, G., 'Yizkor! Commemoration of the dead by Jewish displaced persons in postwar Germany', in A. Confino, P. Betts & D. Schumann (eds), *Between Mass Death and Individual Loss: The Place of the Dead in Twentieth-Century Germany* (Oxford and New York: Berghahn Books, 2008), pp. 234–57

Koff, C., *The Bone Woman: Among the Dead in Rwanda, Bosnia, Croatia and Kosovo* (London: Atlantic, 2004)

Marcuse, H., *Legacies of Dachau: The Uses and Abuses of a Concentration Camp, 1933–2001* (Cambridge: Cambridge University Press, 2001)

Pau-Heyriès, B., 'La démobilisation des morts français et italiens de la Grande Guerre', *Revue Historique des Armées*, 250 (2008), 66–76

Snow, C. C., 'Forensic anthropology', *Annual Review of Anthropology*, 11 (1982), 97–131

Snow, C. C., L. Levine, L. Lukash, L. G. Tedeschi, C. Orrego & E. Stover, 'The investigation of the human remains of the "disappeared" in Argentina', *American Journal of Forensic Medicine and Pathology*, 5:4 (1984), 297–9

1

Bitter legacies: a *war of extermination*, grave looting, and culture wars in the American West[1]

Tony Platt

And so they are ever returning to us, the dead.

(W. G. Sebald, 1993)

I don't think we ought to focus on the past.

(Ronald Reagan, Bitburg Cemetery, 1985)

Let not your sorrow die, though I am dead.

(Shakespeare, *Titus Andronicus*)

In 2012, the 'Corpses of mass violence and genocide' annual conference turned a critical eye on *agents of injustice* and asked, what do practices of *mass destruction* tell us about larger political, social, and cultural issues? At the 2013 conference, we asked, what do practices of *exhumation* of victims of mass destruction tell us about larger political, social, and cultural issues? What does it mean to turn a critical eye on *agents of justice*, on *ourselves*?

Introduction

I have lived in the United States, mostly in Berkeley, since I left Manchester, UK, in 1963. And for almost forty of those years I have been lucky to own a share of a vacation cabin in northwest California in a wondrous place called Big Lagoon, a coastal village surrounded by ocean, lagoon, and forest. The area is typically described in tourist guides as having a 'wilderness feeling', a pristine place 'where you can connect with Nature'.[2]

My relationship with this place was always associated with life – with renewal, restoration, and revival – until my forty-year-old son Daniel died in 2006, leaving a request for a 'Viking funeral' at Big Lagoon. After his death and spectacular send-off, my relationship with Big Lagoon changed, as did my research and pedagogical interests.[3] I know from personal experience how death can transform the meaning of a place, its historical and cultural associations. (Does anybody remember that lovely pre-1933 resort and artists' centre in Germany known as Dachau?)

I started reading up on Native American, especially the local Yurok, death ceremonies, and quickly realized that our ceremony for Daniel reflected a 'promiscuity between the living and the dead' that has a long history in funerary practices around the world.[4] I also came across a brief reference in a technical archaeological report to the allegation that in the 1930s local collectors had dug up Yurok graves in Big Lagoon (about a quarter of a mile from our cabin) and taken away their contents, body parts and all.

This was news to me. My son's farewell on my mind, I felt compelled to take action, helping to organize a Coalition to Protect Yurok Cultural Legacies at O-Pyuweg (Big Lagoon) and, later, investigating the practices and politics of archaeological exhumations. To carry out this research, I had to leave the rural quiet of Big Lagoon and travel to museums in New York, Washington, DC, and Europe, and delve into long-forgotten archives, shuttered cabinets, and basements stacked with human remains.

The focus of this chapter is the exhumation of Native American gravesites in the American West in the twentieth century. But to understand this history's bitter legacies requires a larger context and backstory, one in which archaeological-scientific abuse was one of three interrelated catastrophes that indigenous people experienced.

Catastrophe one: destruction

The Native people of what became California lived for thousands of years in decentralized, but by no means provincial 'tribelets', speaking a variety of languages, living relatively good and long lives. Then, to use Yurok imagery, it was 'the time when stars fell' and the world lost its balance.

The 'grisly statistics' tell the story of changes in California's indigenous population over a period of about 150 years. From, minimally, 300,000 in 1769, to 200,000 in 1821 under Spanish occupation (1769–1834), to 30,000 in the 1850s under American rule, to a nadir of about 15,000 in the 1900s.[5] It is a decline of well over 90 per cent, comparable to that of Tutsis under the Hutu regime, albeit over a much longer period of time.[6]

There is a tendency to divide what happened in the West into two master narratives: one emphasizes the unfortunate, unintentional result of diseases that shredded Native immune systems from the late eighteenth to mid-nineteenth centuries throughout the Americas, what Tom Bender refers to as 'the greatest human demographic disaster in the historical record'.[7] The other narrative emphasizes the role of human agency in population reduction in the second half of the nineteenth century, variously attributed to policies of 'extermination', the discovery of lucrative natural resources (gold and lumber in California), and malign neglect.

Scholars generally agree (with a few dissenters) that what happened under American rule in California meets the standards of the United Nations post-Second World War definition of 'genocide'.[8] In the early 1940s, historian John Caughey used the term 'heartless liquidation',[9] while demographer Sherburne Cook preferred 'social homicide'.[10] More recently, novelist Larry McMurtry puts it colloquially: 'During the Gold Rush, exterminationists were thick on the ground. Indians were killed as casually as rabbits.'[11]

Following the suggestion of Elissa Mailänder, 'destruction' might be a better, more general, and less legalistic term to describe what happened to the Indians of California because their demise involved everything from massacres to psychological torture and starvation, 'fast as well as stealthy and slow killings'.[12]

I think it is useful to understand Native deaths resulting from disease and malice as interrelated, just as Holocaust scholars regard the estimated 20 per cent of Jews who died in the camps from malnutrition and exhaustion as victims of genocide.[13] No doubt Spanish and American colonialisms had their own particular regimes of domination, but it is helpful to take the long view that the period from the mid-eighteenth to late nineteenth centuries is interconnected and part of the 'violent process of nation-making' occurring worldwide.[14] The loss of life under Spanish colonialism in what is now central and southern California was driven by contagious diseases, but the mission system was authoritarian and brutal, marked by 'the sight of men and women in irons, the sound of the whip, the misery of the

Indians'.[15] The susceptibility to disease was facilitated by policies that removed Indians from their land, banished their cultural traditions, disrupted familial relations, and tried to replace long-standing ways of understanding the world with Catholic dogma.[16]

The missionaries gave the neophytes a short course in Christianity before converting them en masse. But when they died en masse, they received burials fit for savages, not Christians: they are stacked ten and more deep in anonymous pits underneath the grounds and iconic buildings of one of California's leading tourist attractions, its missions. 'We don't know the exact location of their burial', says a guide at Mission Dolores in San Francisco, referring to 11,000 mostly Ohlone corpses.[17] I am reminded of a witness to the genocide of Armenians in Turkey in 1916 who reported that the dead were 'past counting'.[18]

In February 2012, I accompanied Louise J. Miranda Ramirez, tribal chairwoman of the Ohlone/Costanoan-Esselen Nation, as she conducted a blessing over the 'graves of the ancestors' in the cemetery behind the basilica at the famous Carmel Mission. As I followed her around the small symbolic cemetery, she studied the ground carefully, stooping every few minutes to pick up items from the ground. 'Look', she says, 'these are human bones dug up by gophers. I've asked them to bring in soil and cover the graves with some protection, but they don't do anything.' It was hard for me to look at the pieces of human remains. Ramirez was almost matter-of-fact. 'I do this every time I come here, every time.'[19]

Under the American regime, many thousands died as the result of an organized, politically endorsed 'war of extermination', via what California Governor Peter Burnett called 'the irregular mode of warfare'.[20] In one county alone, between 1850 and 1864, fifty-six massacres of Native people occurred.[21] Burnett recognized, albeit with 'personal regret', that such a war 'must be expected'. Certainly there was guerrilla-style resistance in the rugged northwest, but Native fighters were no match for the sudden influx of hundreds of thousands of miners and settlers, backed up by greed, a sense of entitlement, and armed militias.

Many (maybe as many as half) Native people in California also died from malnutrition, disease, and psychological despair. Between 1850 and 1950, Yurok life expectancy halved.[22] A decade of post-Gold Rush massacres, bounty hunting, indenture and debt peonage, impoverished misery, kidnapping and selling of children as servants, agricultural workers and maids, was followed by concentration in penal colonies or 'reservations', and systematic efforts at cultural annihilation by so-called 'Friends of the Indian'.[23] As Richard Pratt told a social work conference in 1892, 'All the Indian there is in the race should be dead. ... Kill the Indian in him, and save the man.'

What happened to the Native populations of California was similar to what happened in many places to other self-sufficient, pre-capitalist rural communities, but worse because destruction rather than assimilation was the prevailing mode of conquest. 'Their story', observes Albert Hurtado, 'shows clearly the human costs of bringing California into the ambit of the modern world economic system.'[24]

Agents of modernization not only destroyed and reorganized what was left of Native communities. They also dug up their graves and appropriated their dead.

Catastrophe two: exhumation and looting

Between the late eighteenth and mid-twentieth century in the United States, Native remains were taken from graves without familial or tribal permission and transported to museums, universities, laboratories, and private collections. This harvesting of corpses in the name of science, education, collecting, and sport was especially prevalent in California in the twentieth century, coinciding with the rise of professional anthropology and the expansion of public museums, and facilitated by the fact that decimated and defeated Native communities on the west coast were unable to protect their ancient village sites.

Unauthorized exhumation was not an exclusively American phenomenon. In the 1830s, British scientists brought back Tasmanian Aborigine corpses to London. Hundreds, possibly thousands of Aboriginal remains from Australia ended up in universities and collections in England and Scotland.[25] Dutch colonists sent the head of an Ahanta king in Ghana back to the Netherlands in 1838, where it was kept at Leiden University's Medical Centre until repatriation in 2009.[26] By the end of the nineteenth century, there were perhaps 300 Maori preserved heads in collections around the world.[27] Similarly, in the 1900s German scientists removed hundreds of Herero Namibian remains from southwest Africa for research in Berlin.[28] But the scope and volume of the practice in the United States was unprecedented.

Between the 1780s, when Thomas Jefferson excavated a thousand human remains near his home in Virginia, and the 1960s, when the Red Power movement successfully challenged the right of archaeologists and scientists to treat their dead as specimens, between 600,000 and 1 million Native grave sites were excavated. We will never know the exact number, but I do not think 1 million is an unreasonable estimate.[29]

The looting of graves was linked to the rise of the modern museum and scientific curiosity about human origins and human differences. Initially, exhumation was motivated by the search for rare Native artefacts, a global enterprise generated first by international military operations. George Vancouver's Pacific expedition (1790–95) had several collectors on board, including George Hewettt, whose Yurok collection eventually ended up in the British Museum. In the nineteenth and early twentieth centuries, the trade in collectibles was led by wealthy patrons of the arts who financed a frenzy of collecting. As the market for Native artefacts boomed worldwide, entrepreneurial traders, ambitious anthropology departments, local museums, amateur archaeologists, hobbyists, and 'pothunters' joined the hunt.[30]

Most artefacts were acquired through trade, but in places such as California, where Native survivors were desperate for basic necessities, anthropologists and collectors rarely paid market value. The distinguished, liberal, Berkeley anthropologist Alfred Kroeber had no compunction about trying to hustle Native men twice his age or dismissing their desire to preserve their past. 'The intrinsic value of an old house', he instructed his staff in 1909, 'is practically nothing these days, and the people are attached to them chiefly for sentimental reasons.'[31]

The artefacts removed from graves or bought cheap from impoverished tribes ended up in private collections and public display cases around the world, from Moscow to San Francisco, as museums competed to accumulate 'a kind of Noah's ark collection, two from each area, two of each type'.[32] Researchers and scientists were unable to keep up with the avalanche of materials that filled up the basements and display cases of museums.[33]

By the mid-nineteenth century, there was also a brisk trade in Native body parts, propelled by the popularity of commercial and recreational collecting, scientific curiosity, and the heritage industry.[34] Scientists in universities and museums joined the hunt in the hope that Native bodies would shed light on the origins of the species or on racial typologies of human difference. They were particularly interested in the bodies of Indians, who, they believed, had been metaphorically frozen in time since the Stone Age, and whose remains therefore were thought to hold the key to 'secrets of human origins', as well as provide physical evidence for claims about European superiority and Native degeneracy. This perspective was anchored in the scientific racism that dominated American eugenics.[35]

In widely read treatises – such as Samuel Morton's *Crania America* (1839), Ales Hrdlicka's *Directions for Collecting Information and Specimens for Physical Anthropology* (1904), and Edward Gifford's *California Anthropometry* (1926) – the measurement of brain cavities, nostrils, and degree of slope in foreheads generated all kinds of essentialist scientific quackery to justify the civilizational superiority of white Europeans and innate inferiority of Native peoples.[36] Morton, Hrdlicka, and Gifford encouraged amateur archaeologists to dig up graves and send them any remains they discovered. 'The fresher the product, the better', wrote Hrdlicka in his 1904 manual.

There has been a tendency in popular and scientific literature to blame 'local pothunters' for the desecration of sacred lands for fun and self-aggrandisement, but the responsibility for ignoring the long-time record of Native opposition to excavations, for profiting off sorrows, for suspending human needs in the name of science, and for crass insensitivity can be distributed among a wide array of respectable individuals and established institutions.

There were three primary groups involved in excavations of graves: local collectors – many of whom considered themselves self-educated archaeologists contributing to scientific knowledge – who were involved as traders and hobbyists; teachers and museum curators, who encouraged sales and donations of ceremonial artefacts to build up collections for educational purposes; and academic researchers, whose surveys and digs in Indian country were important to the development of academic anthropology.

An important distinction, however, must be made between the people who conducted the excavations and nationally celebrated patrons of culture with big pockets and large egos, men and women such as George Gustav Heye, Collis Huntington, and Phoebe Hearst, who imagined themselves to be making and not just collecting history. Heye, a New York banker, acquired the largest number of Native American artefacts collected by a single person – 800,000 items, enough to fill his own museum in 1919. Heye commissioned expeditions around the world, paid dealers to look out for rare grave goods, and bought up collections from regional collectors.[37]

While the removal of Native human remains from gravesites was done in the name of Science – to explain the origins of the species or to identify racial differences among 'civilizations' or to account for the apparent 'natural' demise of Native peoples – the overwhelming majority of exhumations violated the most basic scientific procedures (not to mention prevailing ethical and legal standards regarding burials). The provenience of Native corpses was for the most part not documented; body parts were routinely mixed together; and corpses were never identified by name. Moreover, scientists harvested far more corpses than they could ever study. Tens of thousands of Native dead were stashed in boxes, cellars, and personal collections, only to be resurrected for display in cabinets of curiosities, museums, schools, and international expositions.

In California, a skull collected on Santa Rosa Island was included in the US exhibition at the Columbian Historical Exposition in Madrid in 1892. In the 1920s and 1930s, Ralph Glidden, a self-styled archaeologist, filled and decorated the Catalina Museum of Island Indians with hundreds of crania and bones taken from Tongva and other graves.[38] By 1948, Berkeley was boasting to *Life* magazine that its Native American collection included 'more than 10,000 Indian skeletons, many of them complete'. A full-page photograph depicted a room full of human remains and a graduate student using a 'craniometer to measure an ancient Indian skull'. A colleague recalls seeing human bones displayed on the Berkeley campus in the landmark Campanile in the early 1960s. To this day, the Favell Museum in Klamath Falls, Oregon, proudly displays Native artefacts looted from graves.[39]

Acknowledgment of crimes against humanity and the repatriation of corpses and artefacts was a central demand of the American Indian movement for more than a hundred years. This struggle culminated in the passage in 1990 of a significant piece of national legislation, the Native American Graves Protection and Repatriation Act (NAGPRA), which set up a process for returning human remains and grave goods to officially recognized tribes. While the legislation fundamentally changed relations between governments, museums, universities, and tribes, after twenty-three years in force less than 5 per cent of human remains has been repatriated and NAGPRA is stuck in bureaucratic wrangling and recriminations.

The University of California is the main repository of Native remains in the Far West. Here too repatriation is stalled. The Davis campus retains more than 90 per cent of its collection.[40] 'There are more dead Indians on the Davis campus than alive', says a Native American activist working on a film about the Anthropology Department's morgue.[41] As of June 2013, Berkeley had repatriated only 315 of its 10,000 remains. Why so little progress?

First, the process is slow and expensive, as claimants must make their ponderous way through institutional committees. The legal burden is on tribes to prove provenience and provenance. Secondly, tribes unrecognized by the federal government until recently had no legal right to make a direct claim. Thirdly, some university scientists, concerned about losing samples that might reveal new findings in the future, are making it difficult for their institutions to comply with NAGPRA. Finally, and most significantly, as a result of unscientific methods of work, the majority of exhumed remains are unidentifiable as to origins or tribal affiliation.

From the perspective of Native Americans, there is also considerable ambivalence in pursuing repatriation of corpses. For many elders, the remains are now spiritually as well as physically contaminated. Yurok funeral rites, for example, ensured that the dead did not contaminate the living. Once the dead were buried, the survivors urged their spirits to find a resting place, never to return. Exhumation violates the journey from life to death. There is also a quandary about where reburial should take place, given that the original burial sites are often unknown or on land that is no longer owned or controlled by Native communities.

There are no easy solutions to this impasse, but museums and universities could begin a process of reconciliation by interrogating their past involvement in the looting of graves, issuing formal public apologies for decades of malpractice, accelerating the repatriation process, and offering land or compensation for reburials.

Meanwhile, the genocidal and archaeological past weighs heavily on the present here and now, aggravated by a cultural cover-up that promotes silence, amnesia, and fanciful narratives of History.

Catastrophe three: cultural cover-up

The catastrophes that struck Native communities in California were well known and publicized in the late nineteenth century. Reformers who advocated cultural over physical destruction spoke out against the 'sin' of the 'brutal treatment of the California tribes'.[42] 'Never before in history', wrote a popular journalist in the early 1870s, 'has a people been swept away with such terrible swiftness, or appalled into utter and unwhispering silence forever and forever.'[43] But by the early twentieth century, racist views about Native people predominated, and the brutality of colonial settlers was retrospectively justified. How did this happen?

The production of California history was a popular enterprise, regularly incorporated into grandly produced 'theatres of memory', such as world fairs and local spectacles, and into travel books, memoirs, adventure stories, textbooks, and magazines that exported the 'California Story' far beyond the state, long before Hollywood entered the picture. It was not the work of handpicked professional historians or a master political authority, but rather the creative invention of independent writers, journalists, boosters, and businessmen who, as Mailänder suggests in the case of state functionaries in Nazi Germany, incorporated ideology into their own cultural practices.[44]

The Orwellian shaping of the 'California Story' to 'make lies sound truthful and give an appearance of solidity to pure wind' reminds me of several examples from the 2012 conference.[45] How Hitler promoted cultural stereotypes of partisans in Eastern Europe as inherently barbarous. 'The struggle we are waging there', he said in August 1942, 'resembles very much the struggle in North America against the Red Indians.'[46] How the Argentine military command, from the 1950s through the 1970s, inculcated in rank-and-file soldiers 'a negative conception of otherness' that prepared them for the work of assassination and disposal of bodies during the 'dirty war'.[47] And how the techniques of genocide in Rwanda were facilitated by images of the Tutsi body as foreign and unnatural.[48]

The California experience, however, differs in one important respect from these examples. With its weak state apparatus in the 1840s and 1850s, the construction of a fully articulated cultural rationale *followed* rather than preceded the era of destruction. We do not really know in any detail how or if the perpetrators justified their actions.

The creation of a public narrative of the state's past both excused and legitimated racist and racialized images of Native Americans, making it easier for future generations to sleep untroubled and evade a reckoning with the region's tragic and sorrowful history. The logic of nineteenth- and early twentieth-century scientific racism was central to framing the near extermination of Native peoples in the imagery of natural rather than social history, subject to inevitable processes of erosion and decline, rather than as the result of human intervention and genocide.

California's anthropologists played a significant role in allowing a racist narrative to prevail. Of course they knew about the catastrophes that accompanied the Mission system and Gold Rush, but they chose public silence. 'What happened to the California Indians following 1849 – their disruption, losses, suffering, and adjustments – fall into the purview of the historian', wrote Alfred Kroeber in 1954, 'rather than the anthropologist whose prime concern is the purely aboriginal, the uncontaminatedly native.'[49] Many Native people to this day hold Kroeber accountable because as one of the country's leading anthropologists he had resources and authority to influence public opinion. Of course, no one person, even Kroeber, wielded such power, but he became the personification of amnesia.

The 'California Story' created a cultural firewall between past and present, successfully embedding a particular historical narrative in everyday life, namely that: (1) Native people were a *disappearing race*, despite the fact that in the American northwest they not only persisted during the worst of times, but continued to live and work in the region, have children, practise ceremonies, and give interviews to anthropologists. (2) Native people were *predestined to extinction* as a result of their own biological weaknesses – murder and contagious diseases were not something done to them, but something they did to themselves. (3) Native people were either *sub-human or super-human*, never fully human: *racially different and racially inferior*, or an exotic remnant of a time when the human race lived with and in Nature. (4) Native people were *childlike and in need of the firm hand of civilizing institutions*, thus the retrospective defence of the mission system (bringing to mind the post-Reconstruction defence of slavery as a means to civilize savage Africans). (5) In the aftermath of military defeat, dispossession, and forced poverty, Native people's best hope of salvation was through economic and cultural *assimilation*.[50] (6) Native groups, with few exceptions, were *passive and devoid of resistance*, and therefore complicit in their own demise (comparable to 1940s and 1950s images of Jews during the Holocaust as sheep too easily led to their slaughter), despite a long history of opposition, from guerrilla warfare in the mid-nineteenth century, to young men and women in boarding schools at the turn of the century plotting their future resistance, to political organizing against looting of graves from the early twentieth century.[51]

By the 1930s, a popular textbook could relegate the ruin of California's Native people to a footnote.[52] A typically sunny version of California history, written in 1962, described Spain's mission policies as designed to keep the Indians 'contented with food and with cloth for clothes or else they would go off to live as they pleased'.[53] And as late as 1984, an elementary school textbook transformed the bloody horrors of the 1850s into a mild case of culture conflict: 'The people who came to look for gold and to settle in California did not understand the Indians. They made fun of the way the Indians dressed and acted.'[54] (Imagine a German textbook that says, 'When the Nazis came to power in 1933, they did not understand the Jews. They made fun of the way the Jews dressed and acted.') And the current required textbook, written in 2006, does not do much better. Colonialism is reduced to an educational self-help project – 'in the 1500s, European countries wanted to learn about new places'[55] – while the thorny problem of genocide is simply skipped. The textbook leaps from the Spanish teaching lazy Indians how to 'work hard' in the eighteenth century to pictures of happy tribal self-government today.

The upbeat version of the 'California Story' as a place of entrepreneurial ingenuity and cutting-edge modernity numbs us to the state's bloody history. This practice of 'scrupulous forgetting', to use German historian Jörg Wollenberg's phrase, is echoed in California's sanitized public history that erases its tragic past, turning profound injustices into a narrative of progress. In this respect, California echoes Turkey's official amnesia about the genocide of Armenians[56] and post-Second World War Yugoslavia's silence about massacres in Croatia.[57]

Searching California for public remembrances of its tragic past is as frustrating as searching Lisbon for public recognition of the central role of the slave trade in Portugal's glorious past.

In San Francisco, a large wall text on 'Treatment of Indians', prominently displayed in the Mission Dolores museum, interprets the near-demise of Native peoples under Spanish colonialism as a matter of natural inevitability. 'Unable to solve complex medical, social and environmental problems, the Indian population was drastically reduced, especially through disease. … Whether Spanish, English, Russian, or even if no settlers had preceded the Americans, the result would have been the same.'[58]

Elsewhere, in California, there are no plaques or markers along the state's 'Redwood Highway' inviting travellers and locals to consider the thousands of Native peoples who lost their lives and then their dead. No memorials that ask us to reconcile a place of extraordinary beauty with the horrors of history. Nothing to disturb the public image of northwest California as an 'outdoor paradise' and 'eco-tourist's heaven'.

California continues to be shaped, culturally and socially, by bitter legacies and divisions. Doing justice to the past means speaking the unspeakable, making human-made tragedies a matter of public recognition, creating histories that speak to all the diverse populations of the region, and recognizing that the United States is not exceptional but one among many nations, that we too – just like a Germany, a Rwanda, a Cambodia – need to come to terms with our sorrowful past.

Never too late

It's never too late to honor the dead.

(Toni Morrison, 2008)

Experts working on specialized projects relating to crimes against humanity – historians, forensic scientists, social scientists, lawyers, medical researchers, anthropologists, and archaeologists – face several challenges, in addition to doing the job competently and thoroughly. To acquire a deep knowledge of the mass destruction that motivates this work so that, however technically specialized the focus, one stays morally and ethically rooted in the quest for social justice. To develop collaborative, cooperative, consultative, and often slow and time-consuming relationships with the descendants of the dead who after all are the main beneficiaries of such work. To not only humanize the victimized, reified dead but also consider whether they have any rights that outlive their deaths. To be alert to the social-political uses and abuses of scientific knowledge, its eugenic past and present, and its misappropriation by popular culture. And to be prepared to articulate and defend this work in the public sphere, to be citizen-scholars aware of wider responsibilities beyond academia.

In the United States, exemplary work is done at the African Burial Ground National Monument in New York. Here, after years of grass-roots organizing, a collaborative project between community groups, government agencies, historians, and scientists generated a respectful, moving, and educational memorial to the thousands of Africans who were interred in the 'Negros Buriel Ground' in the seventeenth and eighteenth centuries in a few acres of marshy, god-forsaken land outside the city's palisades. The remains were discovered in 1991 when ground was excavated for a federal building in what is now prime real estate in Lower Manhattan. Today, you can learn about the daily lives of Africans and the importance of slavery to New York's economic development in large part as a result of the analysis of human remains by Howard University scientists. There is hope, then, for partnerships between Native people and anthropologists, and the possibility that science can enhance the humanity of history. But the lesson of the New York monument is that it takes struggle, determination, organizing, and the persistence of a long-distance runner to do justice to the past.

It is not the search for knowledge, the use of technical expertise, or the application of scientific techniques that should worry us.

Rather, we need to be sensitive to unequal relations of power between investigator and subject; to ensure that we pay as much attention to the social responsibilities and contexts of our work as we do to our disciplinary skills; and to make sure that the products of our work are used in politically responsible ways.

Notes

1 This chapter was originally presented at 'Search and Identification of Corpses and Human Remains in Post-Genocide and Mass Violence Contexts', 2nd Annual and International Conference of the Research Programme, 'Corpses of Mass Violence and Genocide' (European Research Council), 9–11 September 2013, University of Manchester, UK.

2 Unless otherwise noted, documentation can be found in T. Platt, *Grave Matters: Excavating California's Buried Past* (Berkeley, CA: Heyday, 2011).

3 Since 2006 I have taught a course called 'Obituary', written a book titled *Grave Matters*, and published pieces named 'Dead end', 'The living and the Dead', 'Memento mori', 'To die for', 'Death's double standard', and 'Life after death'. And now here I am participating in a conference about corpses.

4 P. Ariès, *Western Attitudes towards Death from the Middle Ages to the Present* (Baltimore: Johns Hopkins University Press, 1974), p. 25.

5 A. L. Hurtado, *Indian Survival on the California Frontier* (New Haven: Yale University Press, 1988), p. 1.

6 R. Korman, 'The Tutsi body in the 1994 genocide: ideology, physical destruction, and memory', in É. Anstett & J.-M. Dreyfus (eds), *Destruction and Human Remains: Disposal and Concealment in Genocide and Mass Violence* (Manchester: Manchester University Press, 2014), pp. 226–42.

7 T. Bender, *A Nation among Nations: America's Place in World History* (New York: Hill and Wang, 2006), p. 21.

8 See for example B. Kiernan, *Blood and Soil: A World History of Genocide and Extermination from Sparta to Darfur* (New Haven: Yale University Press, 2007); and J. Rawls, *Indians of California: The Changing Image* (Norman: University of Oklahoma Press, 1984).

9 J. W. Caughey, *California* (New York: Prentice-Hall, 1940), p. 391.

10 S. F. Cook, *The Conflict between the California Indian and White Civilization* (Berkeley: University of California Press, 1943).

11 L. McMurtry, *Oh What A Slaughter: Massacres in the American West, 1846–1890* (New York: Simon & Schuster, 2005), p. 56.

12 E. Mailänder, 'A specialist: the daily work of Erich Muhsfeldt, chief of the crematorium at Majdanek concentration and extermination camp (1942–1944)', in Anstett & Dreyfus (eds), *Destruction and Human Remains*, pp. 46–68.

13 According to van Pelt, 1 million Jews died from starvation and disease. See R. J. van Pelt, '*Sinnreich erdacht*: machines of mass incineration in fact, fiction, and forensics', in Anstett & Dreyfus (eds), *Destruction and Human Remains*, pp. 117–45. In some camps, such as Majdanek in Poland, two-thirds died this way. See Mailänder, 'A specialist'.

14 Bender, *A Nation among Nations*, p. 162.

15 M. Margolin, *Introduction to Life in a California Mission: The Journals of Jean François de la Pérouse* (Berkeley, CA: Heyday, 1989), p. 48.

16 This interpretation is ignored in public history and public education, where a generally benevolent and simplistic narrative prevails. A battle of ideas is taking place as the Catholic Church seeks to canonize Junipero Serra (architect of the mission system) in celebration of his 300th birthday.

17 T. Platt, 'The result would have been the same', http://GoodToGo.type-pad.com, January 2012.

18 R. H. Kévorkian, 'Earth, fire, water: how to make the Armenian corpses disappear', in Anstett & Dreyfus (eds), *Destruction and Human Remains*, pp. 89–116.

19 T. Platt, 'I am here for our history', http://GoodToGo.typepad.com, 1 March 2012.

20 Governor P. H. Burnett, Governor's Annual Message to the Legislature, 7 January 1851, *Journals of the Senate and Assembly of the State of California* (San Francisco: G. K. Fitch and V. E. Geiger, 1852), p. 15.

21 R. Raphael & F. House, *Two Peoples, One Place* (Eureka, CA: Humboldt County Historical Society, 2007), pp. 172–8.

22 M. Ferreira, 'Sweet tears and bitter pills: the politics of heath among Yuroks of northern California' (unpublished PhD dissertation, University of California, 1996), p. 20.

23 The selling of Indian children by their dispossessed and impoverished families reminds me of the Armenian parents who sold their children before their deaths during the 1915–16 Turkish genocide. See Kévorkian, 'Earth, fire, water'.

24 A. L. Hurtado, *Indian Survival on the California Frontier* (New Haven: Yale University Press, 1988), p. 218.

25 J. Hinde, 'Invaluable resource or stolen property?', *Times Higher Education Supplement*, 21 September 2007.

26 'Dutch return head of Ghana king', BBC News, 23 July 2009, http://news.bbc.co.uk/1/hi/world/africa/8165497.stm (accessed 7 July 2014).

27 M. Werry, 'Moving objects (on the performance of the dead)', paper presented at conference of International Federation of Theatre Research, Barcelona, 21–26 July 2013.

28 M. Nunuhe, 'Cabinet approves return of skulls', *New Era*, Namibia, 25 March 2011.

29 My research found that one notorious collector in one county in California, by his own account, was responsible for excavating six hundred graves.

30 D. Cole, *Captured Heritage: The Scramble for Northwest Artifacts* (Norman: University of Oklahoma Press, 1995).

31 A. L. Kroeber, 'Specimens', in A. L. Kroeber Papers, 1869–1972, Bancroft Library, University of California, Berkeley, 1909.

32 L. Davis, 'Review of "Time's Flotsam"', *Journal of California and Great Basin Anthropology*, 17:1 (1995), 140.

33 Cole, *Captured Heritage*, pp. 286–7.

34 A. Fabian, *The Skull Collectors: Race, Science and America's Unburied Dead* (Chicago: University of Chicago Press, 2010).

35 A. Stern, *Eugenic Nation: Faults and Frontiers of Better Breeding in Modern America* (Berkeley: University of California Press, 2005); T. Platt, *Bloodlines: Recovering Hitler's Nuremberg Laws, from Patton's Trophy to Public Memorial* (Denver: Paradigm Publishers, 2006).

36 S.G. Morton, *Crania America* (Philadelphia: J. Dobson, 1839); A. Hrdlicka, *Directions for Collecting Information and Specimens for Physical Anthropology* (Washington, DC: US Government Printing Office, 1904); E. Gifford, *California Anthropometry* (Salinas, CA: Coyote Press, 1926).

37 M. J. Lenz, 'George Gustav Heye', in D. B. Spruce (ed.), *Spirit of a Native Place: Building the National Museum of the American Indian* (Washington, DC: National Geographic Society and National Museum of the American Indian, 2004), pp. 86–115.

38 Two hundred remains collected by Glidden are currently housed at the University of California, Los Angeles.

39 T. Platt, 'UC and Native Americans: unsettled remains', *Los Angeles Times*, 18 June 2013.

40 Personal communication from Brook Colley, UCD 'Uneasy Remains' project, 9 June 2013.

41 Platt, 'UC and Native Americans'.

42 B. A. Davis, *Edward S. Curtis: The Life and Times of a Shadow Catcher* (San Francisco: Chronicle Books, 1985), p. 70.

43 S. Powers, *Tribes of California* (Berkeley: University of California Press, 1976), p. 404.

44 Mailänder, 'A specialist'.

45 G. Orwell, 'Politics and the English language', *Horizon*, April 1946.

46 H. Trevor-Roper (ed.), *Hitler's Table Talk, 1941–1944* (New York: Enigma Books, 2000), p. 621.

47 M. Ranalletti, 'When death is not the end: towards a typology of the treatment of corpses of "disappeared detainees" in Argentina from 1975 to 1983', in Anstett & Dreyfus (eds), *Destruction and Human Remains*, pp. 146–79.

48 Korman, 'The Tutsi body'.

49 A. L. Kroeber, 'Two papers on the Aboriginal ethnography of California', Reports of the University of California Archaeological Survey 56 (1 March 1962), p. 58.

50 This campaign was led by female social workers and field matrons, who paradoxically found their own personal and professional fulfilment outside *their* homes by removing children from Native families, by training young Native women to become servants of the urban gentry, and by entering the homes of Native families and attempting to regulate the most intimate spaces of Native families and bodies: how they cared for and raised their children; the organization of their dwellings, their

sexuality, their marriage practices, their gender relation, and the ways in which they adorned their bodies and styled their hair. See C. Cahill, *Federal Fathers and Mothers: A Social History of the United States Indian Service, 1869–1933* (Chapel Hill: University of North Carolina Press, 2011); M. D. Jacobs, *White Mother to a Dark Race: Settler Colonialism, Maternalism, and the Removal of Indigenous Children in the American West and Australia, 1880–1940* (Lincoln: University of Nebraska Press, 2009); S. Bernardin & M. Graulich, *Trading Gazes: Euro-American Women Photographers and Native Americans, 1880–1940* (Newark, NJ: Rutgers University Press, 2003).

51 For an example of early twentieth-century legal resistance, see T. Platt, 'The Yokayo vs. the University of California: an untold story of repatriation', *News of Native California*, 26:2 (Winter 2012–2013), 9–14.

52 A. A. Gray, *History of California from 1542* (Boston: D. C. Heath, 1934), p. 338.

53 M. T. Nelson, *California, Land of Promise* (Caldwell, ID: Caxton Printers, 1962), p. 96.

54 D. C. Anema, *California Yesterday and Today* (Morristown, NJ: Silver Burdett, 1984), p. 167.

55 W. E. White, *Our California* (Glenview, IL: Pearson Education, 2006), p. 37.

56 Kévorkian, 'Earth, fire, water'.

57 M. Bergholz, 'As if nothing ever happened: massacres, missing corpses, and silence in a Bosnian community', in Anstett & Dreyfus (eds), *Destruction and Human Remains*, pp. 15–45.

58 Platt, 'The result would have been the same'.

Bibliography

Anema, D. C., *California Yesterday and Today* (Morristown, NJ: Silver Burdett, 1984)

Anstett, É. & J.-M. Dreyfus, 'The tales destruction tells: disposal, concealment, and destruction of corpses in genocide and mass violence', in É. Anstett & J.-M. Dreyfus (eds), *Destruction and Human Remains: Disposal and Concealment in Genocide and Mass Violence* (Manchester: Manchester University Press, 2014), pp. 1–12

Ariès, P., *Western Attitudes towards Death from the Middle Ages to the Present* (Baltimore: Johns Hopkins University Press, 1974)

Bender, T., *A Nation among Nations: America's Place in World History* (New York: Hill and Wang, 2006)

Bergholz, M., 'As if nothing ever happened: massacres, missing corpses, and silence in a Bosnian community', in É. Anstett & J.-M. Dreyfus (eds), *Destruction and Human Remains: Disposal and Concealment in Genocide and Mass Violence* (Manchester: Manchester University Press, 2014), pp. 15–45

Bernardin, S. & M. Graulich, *Trading Gazes: Euro-American Women Photographers and Native Americans, 1880–1940* (Newark, NJ: Rutgers University Press, 2003)

Burnett, Governor P. H., 'Governor's Annual Message to the Legislature, January 7 1851', *Journals of the Senate and Assembly of the State of California* (San Francisco: G. K. Fitch and V. E. Geiger, 1852)

Cahill, C., *Federal Fathers and Mothers: A Social History of the United States Indian Service, 1869–1933* (Chapel Hill: University of North Carolina Press, 2011)

Caughey, J. W., *California* (New York: Prentice-Hall, 1940)

Cole, D., *Captured Heritage: The Scramble for Northwest Artifacts* (Norman: University of Oklahoma Press, 1995)

Cook, S. F., *The Conflict between the California Indian and White Civilization* (Berkeley: University of California Press, 1943)

Davis, B. A., *Edward S. Curtis: The Life and Times of a Shadow Catcher* (San Francisco: Chronicle Books, 1985)

Davis, L., 'Review of "Time's Flotsam"', *Journal of California and Great Basin Anthropology*, 17:1 (1995), 140–2

Fabian, A., *The Skull Collectors: Race, Science and America's Unburied Dead* (Chicago: University of Chicago Press, 2010)

Ferreira, M., 'Sweet tears and bitter pills: the politics of heath among Yuroks of northern California' (unpublished PhD dissertation, University of California, 1996)

Gifford, E., *California Anthropometry* (Salinas, CA: Coyote Press, 1926)

Gray, A. A., *History of California from 1542* (Boston: D. C. Heath, 1934)

Hinde, J., 'Invaluable resource or stolen property?', *Times Higher Education Supplement*, 21 September 2007

Hrdlicka, A., *Directions for Collecting Information and Specimens for Physical Anthropology* (Washington, DC: US Government Printing Office, 1904)

Hurtado, A. L., *Indian Survival on the California Frontier* (New Haven: Yale University Press, 1988)

Jacobs, M. D., *White Mother to a Dark Race: Settler Colonialism, Maternalism, and the Removal of Indigenous Children in the American West and Australia, 1880–1940* (Lincoln: University of Nebraska Press, 2009)

Kévorkian, R. H. 'Earth, fire, water: how to make the Armenian corpses disappear', in É. Anstett & J.-M. Dreyfus (eds), *Destruction and Human Remains: Disposal and Concealment in Genocide and Mass Violence* (Manchester: Manchester University Press, 2014), pp. 89–116

Kiernan, B., *Blood and Soil: A World History of Genocide and Extermination from Sparta to Darfur* (New Haven: Yale University Press, 2007)

Korman, R., 'The Tutsi body in the 1994 genocide: ideology, physical destruction, and memory', in É. Anstett & J.-M. Dreyfus (eds), *Destruction and Human Remains: Disposal and Concealment in Genocide and Mass Violence* (Manchester: Manchester University Press, 2014), pp. 226–42

Lenz, M. J., 'George Gustav Heye', in D. B. Spruce (ed.), *Spirit of a Native Place: Building the National Museum of the American Indian* (Washington, DC:

National Geographic Society and National Museum of the American Indian, 2004), pp. 86–115

Mailänder, E., 'A specialist: the daily work of Erich Muhsfeldt, chief of the crematorium at Majdanek concentration and extermination camp (1942–1944)', in É. Anstett & J.-M. Dreyfus (eds), *Destruction and Human Remains: Disposal and Concealment in Genocide and Mass Violence* (Manchester: Manchester University Press, 2014), pp. 46–68

Margolin, M., *Introduction to Life in a California Mission: The Journals of Jean François de la Pérouse* (Berkeley, CA: Heyday, 1989)

McMurtry, L., *Oh What A Slaughter: Massacres in the American West, 1846–1890* (New York: Simon & Schuster, 2005)

Morton, S. G., *Crania America* (Philadelphia: J. Dobson, 1839)

Nelson, M. T., *California, Land of Promise* (Caldwell, ID: Caxton Printers, 1962)

Nunuhe, M., 'Cabinet approves return of skulls', *New Era*, Namibia, 25 March 2011

Orwell, G., 'Politics and the English language', *Horizon*, April 1946

Platt, T., *Bloodlines: Recovering Hitler's Nuremberg Laws, from Patton's Trophy to Public Memorial* (Denver: Paradigm Publishers, 2006)

Platt, T., *Grave Matters: Excavating California's Buried Past* (Berkeley, CA: Heyday, 2011)

Platt, T., 'The result would have been the same', http://GoodToGo.typepad.com, 1 January 2012

Platt, T., 'I am here for our history', http://GoodToGo.typepad.com, 1 March 2012

Platt, T., 'UC and Native Americans: unsettled remains', *Los Angeles Times*, 18 June 2013

Platt, T., 'The Yokayo vs. the University of California: an untold story of repatriation', *News of Native California*, 26:2 (Winter 2012–2013), 9–14

Powers, S., *Tribes of California* (Berkeley: University of California Press, 1976)

Pratt, R., 'The advantages of mingling Indians with Whites', *Proceedings of the National Conference of Charities and Correction* (Denver, CO, 1892)

Ranalletti, M., 'When death is not the end: towards a typology of the treatment of corpses of "disappeared detainees" in Argentina from 1975 to 1983', in É. Anstett & J.-M. Dreyfus (eds), *Destruction and Human Remains: Disposal and Concealment in Genocide and Mass Violence* (Manchester: Manchester University Press, 2014), pp. 146–79

Raphael, R. & F. House, *Two Peoples, One Place* (Eureka, CA: Humboldt County Historical Society, 2007)

Rawls, J., *Indians of California: The Changing Image* (Norman: University of Oklahoma Press, 1984)

Stern, A., *Eugenic Nation: Faults and Frontiers of Better Breeding in Modern America* (Berkeley: University of California Press, 2005)

Trevor-Roper, H. (ed.), *Hitler's Table Talk, 1941–1944* (New York: Enigma Books, 2000)

Van Pelt, R. J., '*Sinnreich erdacht*: machines of mass incineration in fact, fiction, and forensics', in É. Anstett & J.-M. Dreyfus (eds), *Destruction and Human Remains Disposal and Concealment in Genocide and Mass Violence* (Manchester: Manchester University Press, 2014), pp. 117–45

Werry, M., 'Moving objects (on the performance of the dead)', paper presented at conference of International Federation of Theatre Research, Barcelona, 21–26 July 2013

White, W. E. *Our California* (Glenview, IL: Pearson Education, 2006)

2

Final chapter: portraying the exhumation and reburial of Polish Jewish Holocaust victims in the pages of yizkor books

Gabriel N. Finder

The Jewish population of pre-war Poland numbered about 3.5 million. But only a remnant of this largest Jewish population in Europe survived the Holocaust. The total number of Polish Jewish survivors probably never exceeded 350,000 to 400,000. This rate of mortality – in Poland, around 90 per cent – was higher only in the Baltic states. The majority of Poland's Jewish population died on Polish soil. The Germans and their accomplices killed Poland's Jews mainly in death camps and concentration camps, but a sizable proportion of the victims perished in ghettos, in hiding, in open fields, in forests, by the side of roads, and in small labour camps unequipped to cope with a cascade of dead bodies. And since the rate of killing in death camps and concentration camps eventually exceeded their capacity to incinerate their victims, by the end of the Second World War these camps, too, were overrun by corpses. By the same token, hundreds of Jewish cemeteries lay in ruins, desecrated, their human remains exposed, manhandled, dismembered, and strewn helter-skelter. In other words, under the Nazi occupation of Poland from 1939 to 1945, the Germans and their accomplices turned Poland into a boundless graveyard of their Jewish victims, with the corpses of Jews buried unceremoniously in mass graves, partially buried, or simply left unburied. This is what Polish Jewish survivors encountered when they returned to or emerged from hiding in their home towns in the immediate aftermath of the Holocaust.

Domicile in Poland proved unsustainable for the vast majority of these returning Jews, whose numbers reached some 220,000 by June 1946. Although the resumption of normal life for Jewish victims of the Holocaust was difficult everywhere, the difficulty was exacerbated in immediate post-war Poland by a variety of factors: Polish antisemitism and anti-Jewish violence, private and state-sanctioned confiscation of Jewish property, and the desire by most Jews to steer clear of communism. Moreover, most returnees, already traumatized, could not bear to remain on Polish soil since, in the words of Simcha Mincberg, a survivor who returned to his home town of Wierzbnik, only to find a handful of survivors like himself and resolved to leave Poland – words repeated by countless survivors ad infinitum – the country 'had become now in my mind a cemetery for Polish Jewry'.[1] Mincberg left Poland for Israel in August 1949. Their lives under constant threat, unable to locate their relatives and friends, let alone recover any property, and drawn to the prospect of resettlement in various Western countries and the nascent State of Israel, most returning Jews saw no reason to stay in their home towns and every reason to leave Poland forever. By 1950, when emigration from Poland became virtually impossible, the Jewish population had been reduced to roughly 60,000.

However, regardless of whether Polish Jewish survivors of the Holocaust stayed in Poland or left it, they took pains to afford the Jewish dead a proper burial, exhuming their corpses and then reburying them with dignity in accordance with Jewish ritual in, if possible, a Jewish cemetery, which itself generally required extensive restoration. Even Jews who harboured no intentions of remaining in post-war Poland returned to their home towns with this sole purpose in mind. Some returning Jews took snapshots of the exhumation and reburial of their relatives and friends, thereby etching the final resting place of their loved ones in their personal memories and for posterity.[2] Others recorded the disinterment and reinterment of fellow Jews for posterity in communal memorial books or 'yizkor books'.

Written mainly in Yiddish and Hebrew, yizkor books (*yizker bikher* in Yiddish; *sifrei zikaron* in Hebrew) were the product of grass-roots efforts by surviving members of hundreds of destroyed Jewish communities. Meant to commemorate these communities, yizkor books were published in small runs, primarily in the 1950s, 1960s, and 1970s, by *landsmanshaftn*, mutual-aid societies of Jews located mainly in Israel and North America but also in South America, Australia, and various countries in Western Europe who came from the same town or region in Eastern Europe. Six hundred yizkor books have been published. Ninety per cent pertain to Jewish communities within the borders of interwar Poland, most of the rest concern Jewish communities in Lithuania, Latvia, and the Soviet Union.[3]

Their funerary function is central to yizkor books. As literary scholar James E. Young puts it, 'For a murdered people without graves, without even corpses to inter, these memorial books often came to serve as symbolic tombstones.'[4] That said, a large number of yizkor books recount attempts by returning survivors to recover and rebury the corpses of their relatives, friends, and neighbours, that is to say, they recount survivors' attempts to place *actual* gravestones on the site of their loved ones' and acquaintances' final resting place. Indeed, one theme in particular from the exhumation and reburial of Polish Jewish victims of the Holocaust throughout Poland in the immediate aftermath of the Holocaust runs like a thread through scores of yizkor books: the single-minded effort of one man to give the Jewish dead a dignified burial in accordance with Jewish tradition. Such was the case in a large number of mid-size and small towns, in which one returning survivor seized the initiative to exhume and rebury the Jewish dead with honour in a Jewish cemetery, almost always restored after its desecration, and indefatigably pursued this objective. This fact is reflected in myriad yizkor books.

My first example of the depiction in a yizkor book of the exhumation and reburial of Polish Jewish victims of the Holocaust by Jews returning to Poland comes from the yizkor book of Żelechów, published by the Żelechów *landsmanshaft* in Chicago in 1953. Żelechów lies in east-central Poland, 85 kilometres from Warsaw. About 5,500 Jews, two-thirds of the town's population, lived there on the eve of the Second World War. The German army entered Żelechów on 14 September 1939, and on the following day the Nazis set fire to the synagogue. During 1940–41 more than 2,000 Jews, mostly from surrounding smaller towns and villages, were resettled in Żelechów. In the fall of 1940 an open ghetto was established there. On 30 September 1942, the ghetto was liquidated and all its inhabitants were deported to Treblinka and gassed there. Only a few hundred Jews managed to flee prior to the liquidation of the ghetto. No Jewish community was reconstituted in Żelechów after the war. Organizations of former Jewish residents were active in Israel, the United States, Brazil, and Argentina.[5]

The concluding section of the Żelechów yizkor book includes an account by Shmuel Laksman, a religious survivor from Żelechów who single-handedly initiated the exhumation and reburial of Jewish Holocaust victims in his region. Resettled in Israel, Laksman describes in the yizkor book the threat posed to the few Jews who returned temporarily to Żelechów by their Polish neighbours, who were displeased to see them. Undeterred and tireless, Laksman solicited the assistance of fellow Jews and local civilian and military authorities, including Red Army officers, to undertake his self-appointed task. His first effort in this regard was modest and deeply personal. With the aid of a friend who had returned to Żelechów with the Polish division of the Red Army, he travelled to a neighbouring village to exhume the bodies of his three children, whom he then buried in the Jewish cemetery in Żelechów. The funeral of Laksman's children was attended by practically all of the Jews who were then residing in Żelechów and it elicited deep emotions. In Laksman's words, 'The wish to bury their families in a Jewish cemetery was awakened in everyone watching the funeral.'[6] After the funeral, a brother and sister beseeched Laksman to travel with them to a small town in the vicinity with the aim of exhuming their sister and reburying her in the Jewish cemetery in Żelechów. Laksman then conducted the exhumation of another daughter of his who had been killed by Poles. After her funeral, Laksman resolved to find the Poles who murdered his children. They were the same Poles who had handed over eighteen Jewish men to the police, who then shot them. However, Polish anti-Jewish violence forced him to abandon his plans for revenge and, like many of his fellow Jews, leave Żelechów. In his case, he moved to the Polish city of Łódź, which in the immediate aftermath of the Holocaust evolved into the centre of post-war Jewish life in Poland.[7]

Undaunted, Laksman continued his work from Łódź. He helped formed a committee there composed of surviving Jews from Żelechów and Garwolin, a neighbouring town, to exhume and rebury Jewish victims of the Holocaust in the administrative district of Garwolin, which included the two towns. Appointed to attend to the welfare of the few remaining Jews in Żelechów and Garwolin by the Central Committee of Polish Jews, which from its office in Warsaw represented the interests of Polish Jews in the immediate post-war period, Laksman revisited Żelechów, this time accompanied by an armed guard, and was informed by city officials that the corpses of two Jewish families murdered by the Germans lay in surrounding fields. He resolved to give them a proper burial in the Jewish cemetery. Since the Central Committee of Polish Jews lacked sufficient funds to subsidize the exhumation and reburial of Holocaust victims, Laksman turned successfully to the American *landsmanshaft* of Żelechów for financial support. With its support in hand, in May 1947 he then successfully petitioned Polish regional authorities to conduct the exhumation of the seventeen bodies – the members of two Jewish families, the Popowskis and the Zadoks, from Żelechów, whose hiding places in the countryside the Germans had discovered, and three unidentified women – and had them buried in the Jewish cemetery in Żelechów in the presence of three additional Jews originally from Żelechów, Polish officials, and Russian officers.[8]

Not yet finished, in 1948 Laksman oversaw several exhumations and reburials of the Jewish dead. He persuaded the Central Committee of Polish Jews, with the approval of Polish authorities, to conduct the exhumation and reburial of a large group of Jewish partisans, among them Jews from Żelechów, including two brothers, Max and Sergei, who fell in battle with German forces in October 1942. He then led the exhumation and reburial of two related Jewish families, the Godlens and the Lichtensteins. At the behest of relatives, Laksman then supervised the disinterment and reinterment of thirty-six Jews from the town of Parysów, including the Marski, Landan, Hermanowicz, and Herc families. Finally, he uncovered three mass graves and had their forty victims exhumed and reburied. He reburied all of the corpses discovered in 1948 in the Jewish cemetery in the town of Garwolin.[9]

Laksman left Poland for good in March 1949, his ultimate destination Israel. His account in the Żelechów yizkor book includes no final tally of the number of corpses whose disinterment and reinterment he led, but on the basis of his own account, he was responsible for the exhumation and reburial of at least 100 Jewish corpses between 1944 and 1948.

Three features in Laksman's account are especially noteworthy. First, his was a one-man effort. He recruited help, but without his initiative and sheer resolve, no Jewish corpses in Żelechów and its environs would have been exhumed and reburied. Another distinctive feature of Laksman's account is his use of names. By invoking the names of those whom he exhumed and then reburied, Laksman restored to these Jewish victims their humanity, which is precisely what the Nazi regime sought to deny them. Also of interest is Laksman's portrayal of ethnic Poles. He recounts early in his account his desire 'to do everything to take revenge' (*alts tsu ton kdey nekome tsu nemen*) on Poles who collaborated in the murder of his children and other Jews from Żelechów. He abandoned this project, though, because, in his own words, 'However, later I had to withdraw from

עקסהומאַציע לויה אויפן זשעלעכאָווער בית עלמין

פֿון משפחה פּאַפּאָווסקי (מומער אין 2 סעכטער), משפחה צדוק (צדוק בעקער,, 11 פֿערזאָן) אין 3 אומבאָקאַנטע.

משפחה און אויך זיין שוואגער, דוד ליכטענשטיין מיט זיין משפחה.

אזוי זוי עס איז געווען שפעטּו, האָב איך שוין גישט באַװױון צו פֿירן די עקסהומירטע קיין זשעלעכאָווי, זיי זענען געקומען צו קבורה אין גאָרוואָליו, עם האָבן זיך צו מיר דעמאָלט געווּאָנדן די בּרידער העריץ און נאָר יידן פֿון פּאָ־ ריסאָזיו, איך זאָל דאָדס דורכפירן אַן עהסהומאציעס און

די לעצטע עקסהומאַציעס

פֿון שמואל לאַקסמאַנס זכרונות

שפּעטעּר, נאָר מיינע גריוסע אינטערוויועצן אין וואַרשע, אַט דער צענטראַל-קאָמיטעט צוזאַמען מיט דער יידישער הילה באַשלאָסן דורכצופירן עקסהומאַציעס פֿון די געוועזענע

Figure 2.1 Shmuel Laksman overseeing the reburial of the Popowski and the Zadok families from Żelechów and three unidentified women in the Jewish cemetery in Żelechów, May 1947.

my plan because the antisemitic Poles continued to spill Jewish blood.'[10] Many Jewish survivors like Laksman had no choice but to flee the home towns to which they had returned to larger Polish cities in search of security in the face of intensive anti-Jewish violence, especially from the end of the Nazi occupation of Poland through the second half of 1946. But, by the same token, Laksman's account also demonstrates a large measure of gratitude for the numerous Polish officials who helped him fulfil his duty to bury his fellow Jews with dignity. The general image of Poles in yizkor books is negative, but without the assistance of Poles, Laksman's mission would have been unfeasible. Perhaps there is a glimmer of hope, Laksman seems to imply, for cooperation between Jews and Poles in tending to the memory of the Holocaust. In this regard, though, Laksman's voice is singular.

Moreover, Laksman's narrative does not appear in isolation; it is accompanied – and supported – by a photograph (Figure 2.1). The photograph is from 29 May 1947. It is from the exhumation and impending reburial of the Popowksi and Zadok families and three unidentified women. It shows Laksman, standing behind three caskets, presumably one for the skeletal remains of each family and the women. Laksman is surrounded by two or three other Jewish men, a couple of Polish officials, Russian and Polish officers, a couple of soldiers, one brandishing a rifle, and Polish labourers who probably exhumed the bodies and are about to rebury them. They all stare sternly and directly into the camera. The solemnity of the occasion, for all those in attendance, Jews and non-Jews alike, is palpable. But the dignity and resolve of the figure in the middle – Laksman himself – evident from his gaze and his taut posture, is the outstanding feature visible in this photograph. Indeed, each account discussed in this chapter contains photographs of exhumation and reburial, and the faces of all the survivors in them resemble Laksman's in their dignity and resolve.

My next example comes from the yizkor book of Skierniewice. Skierniewice lies halfway between Warsaw and Łódź in central Poland. At the outbreak of the Second World War there were about 4,300 Jews in Skierniewice, who constituted roughly one third of the town's population. The German army entered the town on 8 September 1939. Persecution of the Jews began immediately. In 1940 over 2,000 Jews from Łódź and the towns in its vicinity were forced to settle in Skierniewice, whose Jewish population expanded to about 6,500. In December 1940 a ghetto was established, but after two months all the Jews were ordered to leave and resettle in the Warsaw ghetto. By the beginning of April 1941 there were no Jews left in Skierniewice. They shared the fate of Warsaw Jewry and were deported to Treblinka.[11] But prior to their expulsion from the town, dozens of Jews were killed at the hands of the Nazis.

The surviving Jews of Skierniewice, organized in *landsmanshaftn* in Tel Aviv and New York, published a yizkor book in 1955. Resettled in Australia, Chaim Frenkel describes his return to Skierniewice after his demobilization from the Red Army and his efforts to exhume and rebury Holocaust victims in his essay in the Skierniewice yizkor book. The avuncular Frenkel, fresh from his army service, cuts the figure of a self-assured Jewish man on a mission.

Frenkel became aware of the presence of impromptu graves of Jews who had been shot in the fields and forests surrounding Skierniewice. Although Frenkel soon obtained his visa for Australia, he was determined not to depart before exhuming some of the victims and reburying their bodies in the restored Jewish cemetery. Receiving permission from the Polish authorities to dig in the fields for bodies, Frenkel set himself to what he terms 'this sacred endeavor' (*di heylike zakh*).[12] Frenkel and another Jew, Moshe Buki, laboured for two weeks in the fields, locating forty-seven bodies, which were brought to rest in a collective grave – Frenkel calls it a 'fraternal grave' (*bruder-keyver*), probably borrowed from the Russian equivalent (*bratskaya mogila*), which he would have picked up during his service in the Red Army – in the restored Jewish cemetery.[13] They added a memorial headstone, which was unveiled on 7 August 1947 in a public ceremony, preceded by a procession in the town in which several Jewish organizations from throughout Poland took part, waving banners. Several Jewish dignitaries from Warsaw and Łódź attended the ceremony, which was led by Rabbi David Kahane, the chief rabbi of the Polish armed forces, in the presence of the Polish mayor of Skierniewice, who received the honour of unveiling the monument. The unveiling seems to have made a deep impression on those who attended it. Frenkel makes mention of the reaction of Rabbi Kahane and Michał Mirski, the editor of *Dos naje lebn*, the popular Yiddish-language newspaper published by the Central Committee of Polish Jews. 'After the ceremony', Frenkel writes, 'Rabbi Kahane and the editor Mirski told me that they had no words to express everything that they experienced here. What they saw here today they have never seen in any other town in Poland!'[14] Several photographs of the event that appear in the Skierniewice yizkor book attest to the solemnity of the occasion.[15] In one a group of some thirty solemn-looking survivors surround the grave and the monument (Figure 2.2).

Frenkel and his wife left shortly thereafter for Australia. Frenkel ends his account in the Skierniewice yizkor book with the following words: 'I did everything that a proud Jew can do for Jewish honor and for our conscience, and we left Skierniewice with a heavy heart.'[16] Frenkel's invocation of Jewish honour is indicative of his sense of obligation in returning to Skierniewice to recover and rebury the Jewish dead with dignity.

A third example comes from the yizkor book of Wierzbnik, which was published in 1973 Tel Aviv by *landslayt* – Yiddish for people originally from the same town or region in Eastern Europe – living in both Israel and North America. Wierzbnik is located in central Poland, about 150 kilometres south of Warsaw. Its pre-war Jewish population numbered about 3,000. When the Germans entered Wierzbnik, they set fire to the synagogue, passed one edict after another severely restricting the life of the Jewish community, looted Jewish property, and generally treated Jews brutally, with sporadic killings. The Germans established an open ghetto in Wierzbnik in April 1941, which included Jews who fled to the town from other places or who were forcibly resettled there. Together with Ukrainian auxiliaries, the Germans

ביים ענטהילן דעם דענקמאל אויפן ברודער-קבר

Figure 2.2 Survivors from Skierniewice surround the collective grave of the town's Jewish victims and the monument erected in their memory during its unveiling in August 1947.

liquidated the ghetto on 27 October 1942, deporting some 4,000 Jews to their death in Treblinka, murdering sixty to eighty Jews on the spot, and sending 1,600 Jews to three factory slave-labour camps in nearby Starachowice. At the end of July 1944, the Germans liquidated the Starachowice camps, deporting roughly 1,200 to 1,400 Starachowice Jews to Auschwitz-Birkenau. About sixty Jews were killed trying to escape; many were killed on the periphery of the main camp during a breakout attempt on the eve of the deportation. Others were killed when the Germans discovered them hiding in bunkers below the barracks. Some 600 to 700 Jews who were deported from Starachowice to Birkenau survived to see the end of the war.[17] No Jewish community was re-established in Wierzbnik after the war.

Simcha Mincberg, mentioned above, was one of a handful of survivors who returned to Wierzbnik after liberation in 1945. He had been the head of Wierzbnik's Jewish Council before the German liquidation of the ghetto. He made his way to Starachowice and discovered the bodies of those killed in and under the barracks during its liquidation and those killed on the edge of the camp during their failed escape attempt. Uppermost on his mind was to exhume and rebury them, a task for which he recruited an additional survivor. 'As a first and sacred obligation [*ershter un heyliker khov*] we

נאָך דער באפרייאונג האָט מען אייפגעשטעלט א דענקמאָל
שמחה מינצבערג האלט א רעפעראט

Figure 2.3 Speech by Simcha Mincberg to mark the reburial of victims from Wierzbnik and unveiling of the monument dedicated to their memory, 1945.

took pains to afford a Jewish burial to the tens of victims who were shot on the day of the liquidation; and those who were buried near the camp.'[18] This was not an easy matter for obvious reasons, but also because intermingled with the remains of Jews were the corpses of Poles. After considerable effort Mincberg received permission from the local authorities to construct two collective graves, one for Jews, the other for Poles. His friend Leybish Herblum, the head of a Jewish burial society (*chevra kadisha*) established by a few of the survivors in the town, would continue even afterwards to search for the remains of Jewish victims in the vicinity and rebury them in the collective grave, a task deemed by Mincberg to be a 'sacred duty' (*heylike flikht*). For their part, the Poles did likewise.

Mincberg and Herblum then went to a Polish stone carver, who constructed a monument for them to be placed adjacent to the Jewish collective grave. On the day of the unveiling, Mincberg gave a speech (Figure 2.3). In the Wierzbnik yizkor book Mincberg describes this solemn occasion in a mournful tone:

> The entire Polish population gathered at the site and from among us, unfortunately – a handful of Jews from the surviving remnant [*sheyris-hapleyte*]. I then ascended the rostrum and held my sad eulogy, which

was moving, heartrending, and full of sorrow, bitterness, and tears. In point of fact, this was the end of the Jewish community in Wierzbnik.[19]

'The end' is my translation of Mincberg's apt use of the Yiddish term *stimas hagolel*, derived from Hebrew, which literally means 'covering the grave'.

A fourth example comes from the yizkor book of Otwock, which was published in 1968 by *landsmanshaftn* in Israel, France, the United States, and Canada. Otwock is located near Warsaw. On the outbreak of the Second World War there were 14,200 Jews in Otwock. In October 1939, one month after the occupation of the town, the Nazis burned all the synagogues there. A closed ghetto was established in January 1941. A year later, 150 young men were deported to the newly opened Treblinka death camp, where they were among its first victims. In April 1942, 400 Jews were deported to the nearby forced-labour camp in Karczew. The great deportation to Treblinka began in August 1942. About 7,000 Jews were deported and exterminated in Treblinka, while 3,000 others, who offered limited resistance and hid themselves, were found, and most were killed on the spot. Another 700 Jews who succeeded in fleeing into the surrounding forests were killed by German armed groups searching the woods. The forced-labour camp in Karczew was liquidated on 1 December 1942. After the war about 400 Jews settled in the town, but eventually all of them left Poland.[20]

One of the returning survivors was Mordechai-Menachem (Mendl) Braf, who returned to Otwock in 1945 after fighting in the Polish division of the Red Army. Braf came from a large and distinguished family, of whom only he survived. Braf went to Karczew after the war in search of the mass grave in which his family was buried. Unsuccessful in his first attempt to locate the mass grave, he returned a second time and while he was searching, a man approached him who knew his father and showed him the location of the mass grave. After Braf and his brother-in-law applied to no avail to the local Polish authorities to exhume the corpses, Braf, an officer in the Polish army, petitioned Polish military officials and received permission to dig. Braf then ordered three coffins from a Polish carpentry shop.

One morning Braf, his brother-in-law, Shimon Friedman, himself a survivor of Treblinka, and two Polish labourers returned to the site of the mass grave and started digging. What they discovered stunned them. Braf writes:

> Over the course of several hours we extract and collect it all – corpses, bones, muscles, scraps of clothing – and wrap them in sheets that we

had brought with us. My sister [Fredl-Masha] was completely intact, although her skull had been cracked by [the impact of] bullets, but her body, her beautiful blond hair – everything [appeared] as if she had been buried yesterday! I recognized half of my father's body since I knew what he had been wearing. [Freydl-Masha's] six children were entirely intact.

How to describe what came over us on that day, from where we drew the spiritual strength to cope with all of this?[21]

Braf and Friedman exhumed the bodies and human remains and placed them in the coffins (Figure 2.4). Then Braf, Friedman, and the two Polish labourers transported the coffins, which also included several indentified victims, to what remained of the Jewish cemetery on a wagon. They all dug a large collective grave. But Braf himself dug two separate graves for his father and sister and lowered them into their final resting place. Their mission complete at sunset, Braf and Friedman bade the Polish labourers leave them alone so that they could unite in their grief one last time with their loved ones.

The last example comes from the Kutno yizkor book, published by *landsmanshaftn* in Israel and the Jewish Diaspora in 1968. Kutno is a town in central Poland, located in the Łódź province. In 1939 Kutno had 6,700 Jewish inhabitants out of a total population of 27,000. After the Germans took Kutno they burned down the synagogue. In June 1940 the Jews were transferred to a ghetto on the site of a destroyed sugar refinery. Close to 7,000 people were crowded into this small area. Conditions deteriorated in the latter half of 1941 when the ghetto was sealed because of renewed epidemics. By the end of March 1942 the entire Jewish population was rounded up and sent to the Chełmno death camp.[22]

Efraim Weichselfish returned to Kutno after liberation in January 1945 while still serving in the Polish army. On his first day in his home town he looked for Jews but did not find any. On the second day he decided to visit the Jewish cemetery. His commander provided Weichselfish, himself an officer, with a pistol, two armed military guards, and one policeman. The cemetery was badly desecrated. In the absence of bodies to bury, Weichselfish resolved to bring ashes from Chełmno, where the Germans had gassed Kutno's Jews, to Kutno for reburial. Weichselfish met other Jews from Kutno in Łódź and Warsaw and shared with them his idea to transport ashes from Chełmno and rebury them in Kutno, with a monument to mark the site. They formed a committee and received the permission of local authorities. The committee delegated two survivors from Kutno to travel to Chełmno, where they placed ashes from the crematorium in a black box.

Figure 2.4 Mordechai Braf of Otwock kneels beside the coffin of his sister Freydl-Masha in 1945 after he had exhumed her body from the mass grave in which nineteen members of his family had been buried helter-skelter after the Germans shot them. Mordechai Braf's own caption reads: 'After prolonged digging a frightful picture revealed itself before our eyes. For what seemed like an eternity we stood in shock. The corpses of my sister Freydl-Masha (Frania), the wife of Shimon Friedman, who was present at the site, and their six children were completely intact – three years after they were murdered! It was as if they hadn't yet made peace with their fate.'

The ashes were laid to rest in a solemn ceremony attended by leaders from the Central Committee of Polish Jews, the chief rabbi of the Polish military, David Kahane, and local officials. Speeches described the destruction of and remembered Kutno's Jewish community. A solemn procession escorted the casket containing the

א. וויינסלפיש וו. פאסערשטיין, עדני הצבא הפולני. בין נושאי המטה עם אפר הקדושים, הרב כהנא (סימין) עורך תפילת "אל מלא רחמים".
א. וויינסלפיש און ו. פאסערשטיין, אפיצירן פון דער פוילישער ארמיי, טראָגן די מיטה מיטן אפן פון די קדושים, רעכטס — הויפט־ראַבינער פון דער פוילישער ארמיי. פאלקאװניק כהנא, ריכט אָפ די תפילה "אל מלא רחמים".

Figure 2.5 Ephraim Weichselfish (centre) and Y. Fasserstein (left) bear the coffin holding the ashes taken from Chełmno during the ceremony, presided over by Rabbi David Kahane (above right), to rebury them in Kutno, 1945.

ashes through the streets of Kovno to the synagogue; the pall-bearers were Weichselfish and another Polish Jewish officer (Figure 2.5). There Rabbi Kahane eulogized the victims and *kaddish*, the Jewish prayer for the dead, was intoned. The procession then continued to the Jewish cemetery. After the casket was lowered into the grave, the monument was unveiled (Figure 2.6). During the unveiling, Rabbi Kahane spoke one last time. According to Weichselfish, the ceremony was extremely emotional. The handful of survivors who attended the ceremony were overcome by grief. 'From eight thousand Kutno Jews there remains but a mound [of ashes].'[23] So ends Weichselfish his description of the ceremony. All of the survivors in attendance probably shared this sentiment.[24]

Among these five men – Laksman, Frenkel, Mincberg, Braf, and Weichselfish – only Laksman was an observant Jew. One can infer from Braf's description of his family that he came from a traditional home. In any event, even assimilated Jews in Poland were conversant to varying degrees with Jewish customs, which was in all likelihood true in the cases of Frenkel, Mincberg, and Weichselfish. There are several prescriptive and customary practices in Judaism pertaining to burial. Jewish law ordinarily forbids exhumation (except for reburial in Israel) and the transfer of corpses and human remains from one

Figure 2.6 Survivors from Kutno surround the monument unveiled in 1945, during the reburial of ashes from Chełmno, in memory of the town's Jewish victims; Ephraim Weichselfish is visible in uniform to the far left.

grave to another. Rabbinical authorities do recognize certain exceptions to the rule prohibiting exhumation and reburial. These exceptions include the reburial of a person to a grave close to his family and relatives and to a safer site should the grave be threatened by desecration.[25] Landsberg, Frenkel, Mincberg, Braf, and Weichselfish, like countless other Jews who replicated their efforts elsewhere in Poland, must have been cognizant more or less of these regulations. But they do not seem to have mattered very much to them. None of them apparently ever inquired of a rabbi about the propriety of disinterment and reinterment in Jewish law. Rather, they were guided by their instincts. Indeed, their actions were for the most part separated from the theological roots of Judaism. Exhumation and reburial were hardly constrained by formal religious regulations because they simply seemed like the appropriate response to the unceremonious or partial burial of Jewish bodies and human remains in mass graves, let alone the sheer exposure of many corpses and body parts to the elements. However, since religious ritual did accompany reburial in most instances, even the non-observant men from among the five clearly acceded to Jewish communal norms, indeed embraced them, not because these norms were religious per se but because they underlined the Jewish identity of the act.

In the event, the instincts of all five men were in harmony with rabbinical rulings issued during and after the Holocaust. An authoritative contemporary source was Rabbi Ephraim Oshry, a rabbi and expert in Jewish law who survived the Holocaust in hiding in the ghetto in Kovno (Kaunas), Lithuania. Throughout the Nazi occupation and in the immediate aftermath of the Holocaust, Rabbi Oshry responded to questions posed to him by Jews who wished to follow Jewish law even under the most extreme conditions. A comprehensive collection of his responsa from the Holocaust and the post-war period was published over the course of several years after the war. As rabbi of the surviving remnant of the Kovno Jewish community after the Russians' liberation of the city in August 1944, he led the search for Jewish bodies and human remains, which he and his helpers discovered scattered throughout Kovno. He supervised the reburial of approximately 3,000 corpses and bones and limbs. He had clearly recognizable bodies buried individually, but because it could not be determined which bones and limbs belonged to particular individuals, he buried them together in a collective grave. He also had the bones of Jews executed and buried hastily in a non-Jewish cemetery removed to a Jewish cemetery for burial. Clearly, the ubiquitous presence of mass graves and the scattering of human remains demanded a departure from regular Jewish law and practice. For one thing, Jewish law, he ruled, permitted unclaimed corpses to be transferred to a permanent burial ground lest they become prey to natural scavengers. (He must have also had human scavengers in mind. They certainly proliferated in Poland after the war, vandalizing graves of Holocaust victims in search of cash and valuables and desecrating their corpses, extracting gold teeth or valuables secreted in the victims' bodies if they discovered them.)[26] For another, Jewish law, Oshry pronounced, required that dead Jews be buried to prevent disgrace and shame to the unburied body. But there was a deeper level to his ruling permitting the exhumation and reburial of Jewish corpses even when Jewish tradition normally prohibits disinterment and requires an unclaimed, unburied corpse to be buried where it is found: a demand for divine justice and an appeal to memory. Citing earlier rabbinical edicts, Oshry explains why he ruled that Jews killed in a non-Jewish cemetery should be transferred to a Jewish cemetery:

'Bury those who are murdered [by gentiles] separately because there is a constant Divine command for justice which is not satisfied until the murderer's blood is shed, as it is written, "He who sheds the blood of a human being, his blood must be shed.'" I also required that a permanent memorial be placed upon the common grave of the bones so that future generations would remember what the murderers had destroyed and how much holy Jewish blood they shed. Earth! Do not cover their blood! It cries out to [God] from you and demands that [God] avenge it.[27]

Although Laksman, Frenkel, Mincberg, Braf, and Weichselfish do not seem to have been aware of any rabbinical ruling, let alone Oshry's – Oshry was, after all, a rabbi in Lithuania, not Poland – permitting the exhumation and reburial of Jewish corpses, by their actions they seem to have anticipated or intuited it.

Katherine Verdery has explored 'the political lives of dead bodies' in postcommunist Eastern Europe; personal grief aside, the reburial of the opponents of communist policies has become tantamount throughout the region to a political argument for spatial realignment, social reconfiguration, and accountability and punishment among other things.[28] For Laksman, Frenkel, and the other Jews who virtually single-handedly buried their fellow Jews after the Holocaust, dead Jewish bodies possessed no political capital. They harboured no dreams of a reconstituted Jewish community in Poland and planned themselves to leave the country in the foreseeable future. For its part, the Polish state, formally communist by 1947, was uninterested in the reburial and exhumation of dead Jews since living Jews were, from the state's perspective, irrelevant to state-building in future while Jewish cemeteries in mid-size and small towns generally lay on the geographical and mental periphery of towns, out of sight. To be sure, in reburying the Jewish dead the survivors wanted to prove to local Poles that Jews had returned despite widespread Polish approval for and occasional Polish complicity in the Nazis' campaign to destroy Polish Jewry. But they could not have realistically hoped that the freshly dug graves of the Jewish dead in desolate Jewish cemeteries, marked by modest monuments, would serve as admonitions to Poles or ultimately stave off the erasure of Jewish memory in Poland. Indeed, two days after the ceremony in Kutno, vandals destroyed the monument placed atop the grave where the ashes of the town's victims were buried. And even if the wilful obliteration of the memory of the Jewish presence in Poland over centuries would eventually subside, whom could the survivors expect to tend to the gravesites of reburied Jews once they themselves left Poland for good?

In contrast, when Jews in displaced persons camps in the American and British zones of post-war occupied Germany exhumed and reburied Jews who had died on German soil, inherent in their affording the victims a proper burial was a political argument for a Jewish state in Palestine; a Jewish state was what the world owed the Jews for their suffering, embodied by the Jewish dead. Moreover, very often Germans, including former Nazis in American or British custody, were forced to dig the graves in which their victims were buried under the eyes of the displaced persons – a token of revenge for the survivors.[29]

To be sure, revenge was not far from the minds of Laksman, Frenkel and the others; one can find the word 'revenge' (in Yiddish, *nekome*; in Hebrew *nekamah*) in the accounts by Laksman and Weichselfish. For his part, Weichselfish made the decision to bring the ashes from Chełmno to Kutno for burial after a visit to the sugar refinery where the Jews of Kutno were concentrated before the Germans sent them to their deaths. In the now deserted and desolate building, he pictures the pain and suffering of Kutno's Jews on the eve of their deportation to the death camp:

> It seemed to me as if the naked walls of [the sugar refinery] were crying out to me only one word, which was carried by the wind throughout Poland, and possibly throughout the entire world: revenge! And I swore at that moment to bring some ashes from Chełmno and bury them in the Kutno [Jewish] cemetery. The ashes of the martyrs (*kedoyshim*) should be given a Jewish burial.[30]

But even if Jewish survivors returning to Poland desired revenge, their primary motivation in exhuming and reburying the bodies of their loved ones and neighbours was decidedly not political – the exhumation and reburial of Polish Jews lacked any political argument or advantage – but, rather, deeply personal. They were first and foremost dead bodies with a claim to be buried in dignity.

It should be added that bereavement in Judaism entails several prescriptive and customary practices that precede and even follow burial. Burial should take place as soon as possible after death. It is the task of volunteers belonging to the *chevra kadisha* to prepare a body for proper Jewish burial. They wash it, ritually purify it, and wrap it in a shroud, all the while keeping guard over it until burial. There is frequently a funeral procession to accompany the corpse to its final resting place. *Kaddish*, the prayer for the dead, is recited. There is often a eulogy. Then there are well-defined stages of mourning after burial. A tombstone is unveiled after a prescribed period of time – in Europe twelve months. Relatives annually mark the death of their loved one.[31] Very few of these rituals were – or could be – observed by Laksman, Frenkel, and the others.

It is tempting to see in these men the modern equivalent of Antigone, the eponymous heroine of Sophocles' tragic play. In Sophocles' hands Antigone's heroism is motivated by her sisterly love for Polynices; aware of what will be her punishment, she disobeys authority to afford her brother an honourable burial. Like Antigone, Laksman, Frenkel, Mincberg, Braf, and Weichselfish acted out of respect for the honour of their loved ones and neighbours. But in their own eyes, they are not heroes. Indeed, the self-representation of these men in the yizkor books – after all, they describe their own deeds – is understated, perhaps because they must have been painfully aware that theirs was a partial success, that the bodies they found, the ashes they gathered, were but a drop in the bucket, as the bodies of most victims of the Holocaust were never found. If they nevertheless took such pains it was because exhumation and reburial were not merely for the sake of the dead – in Frenkel's words, 'this sacred endeavor' (di heylike zakh)[32] – but also for their own sake, for sake of the living – what Laksman terms his 'human obligation' (mentschlikher khov).[33] In the words of Robert Pogue-Harrison, a literary scholar who has written eloquently on the importance of the dead to the living, 'To be human means above all to bury.'[34] How much more so is this assertion true in respect of the survivors like Laksman and the others, who had struggled mightily to maintain their humanity in the face of the Germans' colossal attempt to dehumanize Jews. Anthropologists Jack Kugelmaas and Jonathan Boyarin agree. 'The problem of exhumation and proper burial', they write, 'was not merely an obligation to the dead; it had implications for the living. How were the survivors to re-establish any connection with the memory of the martyrs? How were they to locate and communicate with the dead, to obtain the ancient comfort of mourning?'[35]

Perhaps for this very reason, however, perhaps because the survivors who returned to Poland, by the very act of exhuming and reburying the relatives and neighbours of their landslayt, their townspeople, afforded them, the living, a degree of solace and enabled them to reconnect with the dead without the feeling of guilt associated with leaving their loved ones and acquaintances lying somewhere unburied, in the eyes of their landlayt, those whose grass-roots efforts made it possible to publish yizkor books in the first place, Laksman, Frenkel, Mincberg, Braf, Weichselfish, and countless other returnees like them were heroes. Thus the deep expression of appreciation and praise for Laksman's efforts by the editorial board of the Żelechów yizkor book, which appears in its pages alongside his account.[36] Likewise, preceding Frenkel's account the reader encounters an encomium penned by Chaim Leyb Fuchs, a survivor of Skierniewice, to Frenkel, whom he dubs 'the heroic captain'.[37] Heroic or not, the returning survivors ran a high risk when they exhumed and reburied the dead, for the volatility of antisemitic violence in post-war Poland placed their personal safety in constant jeopardy.[38] Perhaps for this reason, women do not seem to have initiated exhumation and reburial. Although the dissolution of Jewish families during the Holocaust led to a drastic reshaping of traditional gender roles in many cases, with women assuming more responsibility for the welfare, if not survival, of family members, exhumation and reburial required searching for, recovering, and burying bodies in the open in a highly charged, antisemitic, and non-permissive post-war Polish environment – a task deemed by men and women alike too perilous for women, especially after the war, when Jewish men and women were often eager to reassume traditional gender roles.[39] Moreover, to search for, disinter, move, and rebury Jewish corpses and remains in a Jewish cemetery in accordance with Jewish ritual required physical and mental stamina, which many survivors, extremely weak after their ordeal, simply lacked.[40]

The depiction of the exhumation and reburial of Jewish corpses in yizkor books entails, of course, not only the event itself but also memory: first, the preservation of the memory of the victims in the minds and hearts of those who were there and took part in it and the preservation of their memory in the minds of those who were not there, either fellow townspeople or offspring. The portrayal of exhumation and reburial in yizkor books, rooted in the memory of their authors, has, however, a deeply ironic aspect. The point of this entire effort to exhume the corpses and then rebury the victims of the Holocaust with dignity was to enshrine the memory of their names for time immemorial, to prevent the erasure of memory. Yet, after Laksman and the others left Poland, the victims' graves were left, with few exceptions, untended while their names largely faded into oblivion.

By the same token, even the hundreds of exhumations and reburials undertaken by returning survivors could not contain the dead; there were just too many dead Jews to be exhumed and reburied. This is also part of the narrative of the yizkor books, the hidden narrative that, in the final analysis, destabilizes the accounts by Laksman, Frenkel, Mincberg, Braf, and Weichselfish. For all of their success in exhuming and reburying Holocaust victims, a painstaking process that was meant to bring a measure of peace to the living, to some families and members of the community, in the final analysis there is in their accounts a sense of failure.

Notes

1   S. Mincberg, 'Noch der befrayung', in M. Schutzman (ed.), *Sefer virz-bnik-starakhovitz* (Tel Aviv: Mif'al ha-va'ad ha-tzibori shel yotz'ey virz-bnik-starakhovitz ba-'aretz uve-tefutzot, 1974), pp. 345–8, here 347.

2   See G. N. Finder & J. R. Cohen, 'Memento mori: photographs from the grave', *Polin: Studies in Polish Jewry*, 20 (2008), 55–73.

3   A. Kopciowski, *Księgi pamięci gmin żydowskich: Bibliograifa; Jewish Memorial Books: A Bibliography* (Lublin: Wydawnictwo Uniwersytetu Marii Cuire-Skłodowskiej, 2008), p. 19.

4   J. E. Young, *The Texture of Memory: Holocaust Memorials and Meaning* (New Haven and London: Yale University Press, 1993), p. 7.

5   Y. Slutsky & S. Krakowski, 'Zelechow', in M. Berenbaum & F. Skolnik (eds), *Encyclopaedia Judaica*, 2nd edn, vol. 21 (Detroit: Macmillan Reference USA, 2007), p. 500.

6   S. Laksman, 'In mayn geburt-shtot nokh der milkhome', in A. W. Jasny (ed.), *Yizker-bukh fun der zhelikhover yidisher kehile; Sefer yizkor li-kehilat zhelihov* (Chicago: Tsentrale zhelikhover landsmanshaft in Shikago, 1953), pp. 315–17, here 315.

7   See S. Redlich, *Life in Transit: Jews in Postwar Lodz, 1945–1950* (Boston: Academic Studies Press, 2010).

8   Laksman, 'In mayn geburt-shtot nokh der milkhome', p. 317; 'Ekshumatsiye un levaye fun 17 hitler-korbones in zhelikhov', *Dos naje lebn*, 13 July 1943, reprinted in Jasny (ed.), *Yizker-bukh fun der zhelikhover yidisher kehile*, pp. 320–1.

9   S. Laksman, 'Di letste eksumatsiyes', in Jasny (ed.), *Yizker-bukh fun der zhelikhover yidisher kehile*, p. 322; see also the documents on pp. 323–6.

10 Laksman, 'In mayn geburt-shtot nokh der milkhome', p. 315.

11 A. Cygielman & S. Krakowski, 'Skierniewice', in Berenbaum & Skolnik (eds), *Encyclopaedia Judaica*, vol. 18, pp. 658–9.

12 C. Frenkel, 'In undzer kharuver heym-shtot', in I. Perlow (ed.), *Seyfer skernyevits: Lezeykher der fartilikter kehile kdushe* (Tel Aviv: Irgun yoytsey skernyevits beyisroel mit der hilf fun skernyevitser landsmanshaft in nju-york, 1955), pp. 652–65, here 661.

13 *Ibid.*, p. 662.

14 *Ibid.*, p. 663.

15 The photographs appear on pp. 662–4. Frenkel mentions that the event was filmed. Rare footage of the unveiling is available at the YIVO Institute in New York.

16 Frenkel, 'In undzer kharuver heym-shtot', p. 665.

17 See C. R. Browning, *Remembering Survival: Inside a Nazi Slave-Labor Camp* (New York and London: W. W. Norton, 2010).

18 Mincberg, 'Nokh der befrayung', p. 345.

19 *Ibid.*, p. 347.

20 S. Krakowski, 'Otwock', in Berenbaum & Skolnik (eds), *Encyclopaedia Judaica*, vol. 15, p. 546.

21 M.-M. (Mendl) Braf, ''iti 'eykh 'etbol be-dam', in S. Kanc (ed.), *Sefer zikaron 'otwotzk kartshev; Yizker-bukh tsu fareybikn dem ondenk fun*

di kheyruv-gevorene yidishe kehilos otvotsk karschev (Tel Aviv: ''Irgun yotz'ey 'otvotzk be-yisra'el' bay der mithilf fun di otvotsker un kartshever landsmanshaftn in frankraykh, amerike un kanade, 1968), cols 971–6, here 974.

22   S. L. Kirshenboim & D. Dombrowska, 'Kutno', in Berenbaum & Skolnik (eds), *Encyclopaedia Judaica*, vol. 12, pp. 398–9.

23   E. Weichselfish, 'Kutne in Yanuar 1945', in D. Shtokfish (ed.), *Sefer kutnah ve-hasevivah* (Tel Aviv: 'Irgun yotz'ey kutnah ve-hasevivah be-yisra'el uve-hutz la-'aretz, 1968), pp. 402–5, here 405.

24   It was not uncommon for survivors to collect, transfer, and bury the ashes of Holocaust victims. See J.-M. Dreyfus, 'Ashes and human remains during and after the Holocaust', unpublished conference paper delivered at Lessons and Legacies XII, Northwestern University, Evanston, Illinois, November 2012.

25   M. Lamm, *The Jewish Way in Death and Mourning* (New York: Jonathan David Publishers, 1969), pp. 71–2.

26   See J. T. Gross & I. G. Gross, *Golden Harvest: Events at the Periphery of the Holocaust* (New York: Oxford University Press, 2012).

27   E. Oshry, *Responsa from the Holocaust* (New York: The Judaica Press, 2001), pp. 157–8; on Oshry, see A. Goldberg, 'Oshry, Ephraim', in G. D. Hundert (ed.), *The Yivo Encyclopedia of Jews in Eastern Europe*, vol. 2 (New Haven and London: Yale University Press, 2008), pp. 1298–9.

28   K. Verdery, *The Political Lives of Dead Bodies: Reburial and Postsocialist Change* (New York: Columbia University Press, 1999).

29   See M. M. Feinstein, *Holocaust Survivors in Postwar Germany, 1945–1957* (New York: Cambridge University Press, 2010), pp. 85–105.

30   Weichselfish, 'Kutne in Yanuar 1945', p. 403.

31   See Lamm, *The Jewish Way in Death and Mourning*.

32   Frenkel, 'In undzer kharuver heym-shtot', p. 661.

33   Laksman, 'In mayn geburt-shtot nokh der milkhome', p. 315.

34   R. P. Harrison, *The Domination of the Dead* (Chicago and London: University of Chicago Press, 2003), p. xi.

35   J. Kugelmass & J. Boyarin (eds), *From a Ruined Garden: The Memorial Books of Polish Jewry*, 2nd edn (Bloomington: Indiana University Press, 1998), p. 31.

36   'Tsu keyver-yisroel', in Jasny (ed.), *Yizker-bukh fun der zhelikhover yidisher kehile*, p. 320.

37   C. L. Fuks, 'Der heldisher kapitan', in Perlow (ed.), *Seyfer skernyevits*, pp. 650–1.

38   See J. T. Gross, *Fear: Anti-Semitism in Poland after Auschwitz. An Essay in Historical Interpretation* (New York: Random House, 2006). Compare their effort with that of survivors in displaced-persons camps in American-occupied post-war Germany. Like returning survivors in Poland, Jewish displaced persons, who came mainly from Poland and elsewhere in Eastern Europe, deemed it their solemn responsibility to afford a proper burial to Jewish victims of Nazism who, in this case, had died on German soil, either in concentration camps or on death marches, but were largely strangers to the survivors. Forming committees for this

purpose, displaced persons buried or exhumed and reburied the Jewish dead under the protection, albeit frequently begrudging protection, of the American military, with the financial support of the American Joint Distribution Committee (JDC), which also intervened with American commanders for permission to exhume and transfer Jewish corpses, and with the assistance of American rabbis serving in the capacity of military chaplains. In contrast, the returnees to small towns in Poland were essentially one-man operations. See G. N. Finder, 'Yizkor! Commemoration of the dead by Jewish displaced persons in postwar Germany', in A. Confino, P. Betts & D. Schumann (eds), *Between Mass Death and Individual Loss: The Place of the Dead in Twentieth-Century Germany* (New York and Oxford: Berghahn Books, 2008), pp. 232–57, here 236–40.

39 On the reshaping of traditional gender roles during the Holocaust and the significant degree to which they were readopted by Jewish displaced persons after war, see Feinstein, *Holocaust Survivors in Postwar Germany*, pp. 107–58; and A. Grossmann, *Jews, Germans, and Allies: Close Encounters in Occupied Germany* (Princeton and Oxford: Princeton University Press, 2007), pp. 184–235.

40 In this vein, see Oshry, *Responsa from the Holocaust*, p. 155.

Bibliography

Braf, M.-M. (Mendl), "iti 'eykh 'etbol be-dam', in S. Kanc (ed.), *Sefer zikaron 'otwotzk kartshev; Yizker-bukh tsu fareybikn dem ondenk fun di kheyruv-gevorene yidishe kehilos otvotsk karschev* (Tel Aviv: "Irgun yotz'ey 'otvotzk be-yisra'el' bay der mithilf fun di otvotsker un kartshever landsmanshaftn in frankraykh, amerike un kanade, 1968), cols 971–6

Browning, C. R., *Remembering Survival: Inside a Nazi Slave-Labor Camp* (New York and London: W. W. Norton, 2010)

Cygielman, A. & S. Krakowski, 'Skierniewice', in M. Berenbaum & F. Skolnik (eds), *Encyclopaedia Judaica*, 2nd edn, vol. 18 (Detroit: Macmillan Reference USA, 2007), pp. 658–9

'Ekshumatsiye un levaye fun 17 hitler-korbones in zhelikhov', *Dos naje lebn*, 13 July 1943, reprinted in A. W. Jasny (ed.), *Yizker-bukh fun der zhelikhover yidisher kehile; Sefer yizkor li-kehilat zhelihov* (Chicago: Tsentrale zhelikhover landsmanshaft in Shikago, 1953), pp. 320–1

Feinstein, M. M., *Holocaust Survivors in Postwar Germany, 1945–1957* (New York: Cambridge University Press, 2010)

Finder, G. N., 'Yizkor! Commemoration of the dead by Jewish displaced persons in postwar Germany', in A. Confino, P. Betts & D. Schumann (eds), *Between Mass Death and Individual Loss: The Place of the Dead in Twentieth-Century Germany* (New York and Oxford: Berghahn Books, 2008), pp. 232–57

Finder, G. N. & J. R. Cohen, 'Memento mori: photographs from the grave', *Polin: Studies in Polish Jewry*, 20 (2008), 55–73

Frenkel, C., 'In undzer kharuver heym-shtot', in I. Perlow (ed.), *Seyfer skernyevits: Lezeykher der fartilikter kehile kdushe* (Tel Aviv: Irgun yoytsey skernyevits beyisroel mit der hilf fun skernyevitser landsmanshaft in nju-york, 1955), pp. 652–5

Fuks, C. L., 'Der heldisher kapitan', in I. Perlow (ed.), *Seyfer skernyevits: Lezeykher der fartilikter kehile kdushe* (Tel Aviv: Irgun yoytsey skernyevits beyisroel mit der hilf fun skernyevitser landsmanshaft in nju-york, 1955), pp. 650–1

Goldberg, A., 'Oshry, Ephraim', in G. D. Hundert (ed.), *The Yivo Encyclopedia of Jews in Eastern Europe*, vol. 2 (New Haven and London: Yale University Press, 2008), pp. 1298–9

Gross, J. T., *Fear: Anti-Semitism in Poland after Auschwitz: An Essay in Historical Interpretation* (New York: Random House, 2006)

Gross, J. T. & I. G. Gross, *Golden Harvest: Events at the Periphery of the Holocaust* (New York: Oxford University Press, 2012)

Grossmann, A., *Jews, Germans, and Allies: Close Encounters in Occupied Germany* (Princeton and Oxford: Princeton University Press, 2007)

Harrison, R. P., *The Domination of the Dead* (Chicago and London: University of Chicago Press, 2003)

Kirshenboim, S. L. & D. Dombrowska, 'Kutno', in M. Berenbaum & F. Skolnik (eds), *Encyclopaedia Judaica*, 2nd edn, vol. 12 (Detroit: Macmillan Reference USA, 2007), pp. 398–9

Kopciowski, A., *Księgi pamięci gmin żydowskich: Bibliograifa; Jewish Memorial Books: A Bibliography* (Lublin: Wydawnictwo Uniwersytetu Marii Cuire-Skłodowskiej, 2008)

Krakowski, S., 'Otwock', in M. Berenbaum & F. Skolnik (eds), *Encyclopaedia Judaica*, 2nd edn, vol. 15 (Detroit: Macmillan Reference USA, 2007), p. 546

Kugelmass, J. & J. Boyarin (eds), *From a Ruined Garden: The Memorial Books of Polish Jewry*, 2nd edn (Bloomington: Indiana University Press, 1998)

Laksman, S., 'In mayn geburt-shtot nokh der milkhome', in A. W. Jasny (ed.), *Yizker-bukh fun der zhelikhover yidisher kehile; Sefer yizkor li-kehilat zhelihov* (Chicago: Tsentrale zhelikhover landsmanshaft in Shikago, 1953), pp. 315–17

Laksman, S., 'Di letste eksumatsiyes', in A. W. Jasny (ed.), *Yizker-bukh fun der zhelikhover yidisher kehile; Sefer yizkor li-kehilat zhelihov* (Chicago: Tsentrale zhelikhover landsmanshaft in Shikago, 1953), p. 322

Lamm, M., *The Jewish Way in Death and Mourning* (New York: Jonathan David Publishers, 1969)

Mincberg, S., 'Noch der befrayung', in M. Schutzman (ed.), *Sefer virzbnik-starakhovitz* (Tel Aviv: Mif'al ha-va'ad ha-tzibori shel yotz'ey virzbnik-starakhovitz ba-'aretz uve-tefutzot, 1974), pp. 345–8

Oshry, E., *Responsa from the Holocaust* (New York: The Judaica Press, 2001)

Redlich, S., *Life in Transit: Jews in Postwar Lodz, 1945–1950* (Boston: Academic Studies Press, 2010)

Slutsky, Y. & S. Krakowski, 'Zelechow', in M. Berenbaum & F. Skolnik (eds), *Encyclopaedia Judaica*, 2nd edn, vol. 21 (Detroit: Macmillan Reference USA, 2007), p. 500

Verdery, K., *The Political Lives of Dead Bodies: Reburial and Postsocialist Change* (New York: Columbia University Press, 1999)

Weichselfish, E., 'Kutne in Yanuar 1945', in D. Shtokfish (ed.), *Sefer kutnah ve-hasevivah* (Tel Aviv: 'Irgun yotz'ey kutnah ve-hasevivah be-yisra'el uve-hutz la-'aretz, 1968), pp. 402–5

Young, J. E., *The Texture of Memory: Holocaust Memorials and Meaning* (New Haven and London: Yale University Press, 1993)

3

Bykivnia: how grave robbers, activists, and foreigners ended official silence about Stalin's mass graves near Kiev

Karel C. Berkhoff

The story of Bykivnia is one of boundless mass murder by Stalin's People's Commissariat of Internal Affairs, or NKVD, against Soviet and Polish citizens, but also the depressing tale of how, for seven post-war decades, Soviet and post-Soviet authorities attempted to relegate the killing site to oblivion, how boys and men mangled and looted the skulls and bones for years, and how even after the official veil of silence and deceit was lifted, the state took decisions about the gravesite in haste and secrecy, without anything resembling public debate.

Both the Soviet authorities and the leaders of independent Ukraine attempted to block investigation of the thousands of corpses of victims of Stalin's pre-war and wartime terror in a forest east of Kiev, near the village of Bykivnia, which now falls under Kiev's jurisdiction. None of the numerous German, Soviet, and post-Soviet excavations that took place intended to uncover the whole truth; in fact, the Soviet diggings *erased* much of the evidence. But this cover-up failed, thanks to pressure from within – activists and, gruesomely, grave looters, who mistreated the human remains – and from abroad, mainly from Poland. Ukraine's rulers have acknowledged that the graves of Bykivnia hold Soviet citizens and Polish citizens and soldiers, all of whom were murdered by the NKVD. Yet not they, but grave looters, activists, and foreign investigators broke the state-imposed silence about Stalin's mass graves near Kiev.

A site for 'special needs'

The Soviet political police shot over 800 people from Kiev, which became the capital of the Ukrainian Soviet republic in 1934, and the surrounding area between 1930 and 1936. They died as alleged counterrevolutionaries. But unprecedented mass murder, the Great Terror, arrived under Soviet Ukraine's People's Commissars of Internal Affairs Izraïl Leplevskii (appointed in June 1937) and Aleksandr Uspenskii (appointed in January 1938). Both acted under specific directives from Moscow, but the ethnic Russian Uspenskii seemingly believed that almost all Ukrainians were nationalists and that all ethnic Germans and Poles were spies and saboteurs. As a result, from 5 August 1937 to 27 November 1938, at least 12,823 persons were shot in Kiev, almost all on the decision of extrajudicial *troikas*, groups of three officials.[1] The figure included 1,199 of the NKVD's own officers.[2] Thousands more death verdicts were imposed up to 19 September 1941, the day when the German army occupied Kiev. The victims included, for instance, 1,745 alleged German spies and close to 2,000 Polish citizens, mostly military men imprisoned in 1939.[3]

The total number of people shot in Kiev in the Stalinist terror up to mid-1941 is still unclear. Ukraine's former NKVD archives are largely held by a successor organization, the Security Service of Ukraine. It has stated that it can document the execution in Kiev and subsequent burial in Bykivnia of 14,191 named people.[4] Although various independent researchers make much higher estimates of the total death toll – 115,000, for instance – and these are now repeated by officials, they cannot be taken at face value, as they are based on questionable suppositions, namely the total *available* burial space and estimates of the time and car rides spent on shooting people and transporting bodies.[5]

The main killing locations were a prison at Rosa Luxemburg Street (today's Lypky Street), where the NKVD of the Kiev oblast (region) had its headquarters and shot people in the cellar; a prison in the Lukianivka district, where prisoners were brought up in an elevator; the republican NKVD's headquarters on Instytutska Street, known as the October Palace (rebuilt after the Second World War and now housing an International Centre of Culture and Arts); and a police prison at Korolenko Street (now Volodymyr Street). Whatever the location, the shootings were always carried out between 10 p.m. and 2 a.m.

Although there are stories of unannounced shootings in corridors and on stairways, according to Andrii Amons, a retired military prosecutor who probably read more NKVD files in Kiev than anyone else, formal procedures were usually followed. The arrestee was brought into a room by the local commander and an assistant. There a prosecutor asked, for example, 'Are you Ivanov Ivan Petrovich?', and after the victim's 'yes' he would continue with, 'By resolution of the troika [or dvoika, or military tribunal] you have been sentenced to capital punishment.' The victim's arms were at once tied behind the back, and in that very same room, he or she was forced to kneel and face the wall, restrained if he or she resisted, and murdered by one or two shots in the back of the head. The prosecutor and a physician verified if death had occurred. At the height of the Great Terror, about a hundred persons were shot in this way almost every day.[6] Relatives who inquired with the NKVD about the disappeared were told that they had been exiled without the right to correspondence. After Stalin died, the lie was changed: the convicts had supposedly succumbed to disease in captivity in the 1940s.

It was official ever since the 1920s that the corpses of such victims had to be buried in the clothes worn at the time of death 'without any ritual, so as not to leave traces of the grave.'[7] Up to the mid-1930s, in Kiev the shot people were placed in pits at the edge of the Lukianivka Cemetery and possibly also at two other sites.[8] But when space ran out, the NKVD began transporting the corpses to pits east of the city, across the Dnieper, near the hamlet of Bykivnia.[9] On 20 March 1937, the presidium of the Kiev city soviet decided on the 'allotment and demarcation of land for special needs'. KGB veterans confirmed five decades later that these 'special needs' (Ukrainian: *spetspotreby*) referred to the burial of shot people.[10] Working at night, 800 metres off the road from Kiev to Brovary, the NKVD erected what locals dubbed the Green Fence – a 2.5-metre-high wooden fence, without any openings other than the gate, painted green and topped with barbed wire. It enclosed about 200 by 260 metres, or about 4 hectares. Armed guards in civilian clothing watched outside; in June 1941, they donned their NKVD uniforms.[11]

Like the arrests, interrogations, and shootings, the transports and burials to the site took place at night. A veteran NKVD lorry driver recalled in 1989 that at Rosa Luxemburg Street, special pincers were used to hoist the corpses by the legs and neck, after which canvas was used to cover the gruesome cargo. To keep blood from flowing through the cracks, there was also canvas on the bottoms of the lorries.[12] A man who worked as a signalman at the October Palace recalled this scene as well, which he used to witness from a window (in the summer, there was early morning light at loading time). It haunted him for the rest of his life.[13]

Two or three NKVD cars accompanied the convoy. It made a right turn into the forest and drove through the gate toward empty pits. (Who dug them is unclear.) Before the war, Dmytro Makarenko used to drive a three-coach tram, number 23. Frequently at 2 a.m., on his last trip, two to five canvas-covered lorries crossed the track from left to right. This was half a kilometre from the fence. He also had a passenger who probably guarded there and used to demand that the tram halt at 'Pioneer Camp', a stop that officially had been abolished.[14] NKVD men cleaned the vehicles and the canvas in a nearby pond.[15]

But the secrecy could not be total: locals who at first suspected that weapons were stored behind the mysterious fence did notice. In the mornings, herdsmen would find objects that had fallen off the trucks. Moreover, as a local woman recalled in 1988, 'on the road leading toward the gate of that fence we saw bloody spots. Many saw those bloodstains, but were afraid to talk about them.'[16]

In the autumn of 1939, or early in 1940, Polish prisoners arrived at the nearby train station in Darnytsia. They came from the Starobilsk camp in eastern Ukraine as part of the large number of Polish civilians and military arrested by the NKVD in 1939.[17] Whether they were shot in Kiev or Bykivnia, their corpses were buried at Bykivnia. Definitely shot at Bykivnia, from June 1941, were Red Army members and civilians who probably came from western Ukraine.[18]

The role of the German occupiers, 1941–42

The Germans occupied the region in September 1941. Local witnesses agree that they neither shot nor buried anyone in the Bykivnia region.[19] Instead, they came to investigate the graves. As early as 21 September, a German who had arrived on a motorcycle with a sidecar asked, 'Where are the corpses?' and ordered locals whom he designated to carry out a modest exhumation. As the daughter in the Dembovsky family recalled in the late 1980s, the Germans

> pointed out a freshly loosened part of the ground and told us to dig there. I dug to the depth of the spade end and could not go further, for there was something. I cleaned the earth from the place and suddenly saw the corpse of a woman with a dead child in her arms. The corpses had not yet decomposed. Below them were other corpses.

Pictures were taken.[20] The German News Agency wrote an item, and various newspapers brought out the news, such as the *Berliner*

Börsen-Zeitung and Kiev's *Ukraïnske Slovo*, on 30 September and 8 October, respectively.[21]

Other German-supervised exhumations followed. When one of the diggers, Petro Kukovenko, told his father about it, the latter went to see for himself. He returned with the identity papers found on one corpse – and, apparently, gave them to a Jewish man who was staying with them.[22] In April or May 1942, Germans wearing uniforms ordered Vira Nikitina and Vasyl Makarenko to come with them and to bring two spades. 'They'll bury you there!', someone cried out. The soil seemed rock-solid, so they used a crowbar to break the layer of lime or alabaster. The corpse they found was that of a man in blue trousers with light-blue stripes, officer's boots, a tunic, a belt, and a belt buckle. A German took a picture and ordered them to fill up the hole. In a second pit they found a woman in brown shoes, a blue dress, and pre-war stockings. More pictures were taken, and they covered this body as well.[23]

According to Mrs A. S. Dembovska, others began arriving as well, on their own initiative. 'Many Kievans', she recalled, according to a record from 1989, 'started coming here to excavate the burials and to look for their relatives. A woman who stayed overnight at our place recognized the corpse of her son or husband.' Dembovska seems alone in acknowledging that even at that time, a certain gold rush began: people from Bykivnia and nearby 'made excavations, whereby they found gold wares, personal items, and also things, clothes, and shoes that one could actually still use as intended. All of this was bartered for produce, and some enriched themselves from this. This was in 1941–1943.'[24] A memorial was not placed, even though the auxiliary city administration prepared one, apparently because the German authorities disallowed it.[25]

The Soviet authorities who arrived when the Germans left took a manifold approach to Bykivnia. The village elder (mayor) was arrested and he confessed that he had discovered the corpses of 'enemies of Soviet rule executed by the NKVD' (as the record put it) and had made arrangements for a memorial. Symon Dembovsky, who had been mentioned in the Nazi-sponsored press, was beaten into confessing that he had *invented* the pre-war executions, and was sentenced to ten years. He was released in 1954.[26] The authorities ordered or allowed locals to appropriate the fence for rebuilding homes, which the retreating Germans had burned to the ground, and levelled the terrain and planted acacias.[27] The Extraordinary State Commission for investigation of Nazi crimes (ChGK) was not involved; as yet, there was no Soviet claim that the Germans had buried people there.

Marauders, the KGB, and government commissions, 1961–87

Nothing happened until the 'Thaw' – the lessening of censorship under Soviet leader Nikita Khrushchev. At a commemoration in Kiev of Ukrainian intellectuals and artists shot in Soviet Karelia, a tearful woman approached one of the organizers, the theatre director Les Taniuk. Frosyna Mykytivna's message stunned him: there were mass graves in the forest near Bykivnia, holding a very large number of corpses – 'half of Kiev'. She introduced Taniuk to Petro Kukovenko, one of the diggers of 1941, who on 26 August 1962, showed him the site and told his story. Also present were Taniuk's companions Alla Horska and Vasyl Symonenko. Taniuk wrote about it in his diary:

> We walked along the perimeter of the absent green fence. A huge territory. … This morning it was damp, foggy, and drizzling a bit. The earth gave way under our feet, and it was an awful sensation to walk on human remains. Vasyl took me by the elbow: 'Look …'. On a small cleared space five lads were playing football. A sixth one, unusually overweight, who found running difficult, stood at the goal. 'Boys will be boys', I said. 'They're playing a game.' 'But look *what* they're playing with …'. I went closer. The lads were playing football with a skull, shot through from the back, at the top. I reached for that skull. It seemed to me that of a child. For it was still very small. The children were playing football with the skull of a child, filled with hay. Skulls – bigger ones – also lay at the goal. The earth had washed away, and time had polished them. We looked around. The area was scattered with skulls.

Right there, Symonenko composed a verse that he later included in a poem that became famous in Ukraine: 'We trample underfoot our enemies and friends./O poor Yoricks, all in the same style!/In the graveyard of executed illusions/There is no room for graves.'[28]

The three sent a memorandum about Bykivnia to the city soviet. The Kiev Club of Creative Youth to which they belonged was immediately dispersed, and some of its members were arrested or fired from their jobs. Taniuk felt compelled to move to Odessa, where the KGB confiscated many documents from him, and then to Moscow. He returned from this exile only in 1986. Symonenko was viciously beaten in the street and died from his wounds. Horska became engaged in 'dissident' work and in 1970 was murdered, officially by her father-in-law.[29]

It is easy to find assertions that after the war, grave robbery at Bykivnia took decades to start.[30] But that seems unlikely if looting had already begun during the war. Diggers came and found pre-war Polish coins and banknotes and buttons with the Polish eagle, but their real quest was for gold.[31] The marauders severed skulls from trunks. In conversation with the writer Marco Carynnyk in 1991, Kukovenko recalled not only that these skulls and bones 'began to lie around in the whole area' but also that 'children brought them to school. … Everyone saw them. I went there. I saw what was going on. They'd dig up graves, the foresters would fill them in, and then they'd dig them up again.'[32]

On 13 April 1971, militiamen arrested three boys who had removed gold teeth and crowns from skulls that they dug up. It turned out that in total, sixteen boys from Darnytsia had removed over a hundred skulls from at least nineteen pits. By then, the graves-ite already had over a hundred such holes. Two days later, for the first time since the 1930s, the organization that had perpetrated the crime, now renamed the KGB, began digging, with the assistance of a forensic expert and a local public prosecutor. They all worked under the false premises formulated by Ukrainian KGB chief Vitalii Fedorchuk: the prisoners came from a camp, not a prison, and had been shot during the Great Patriotic War, as the Soviet–German war was called.[33]

Accordingly, Minister of Internal Affairs Ivan Holovchenko chaired a special Government Commission for the Investigation of the Crimes Committed by the Hitlerites in the Region of the Dnieper Forest Area of the City of Kiev. The commission gave itself just four to five days to investigate and bury the human remains. The speed was meant to preclude "conversations" before the 9 May commem-oration of the Second World War.[34] For eight days, Soviet Ukraine's chief forensic-medical expert, O. Hryshchenko, investigated. He counted 3,805 corpses in 207 pits and followed instructions in con-cluding that they were buried no more than thirty years ago. The skulls and bones were thrown into thirty or more large wooden trunks and lowered into a deep pit.[35]

Petro Shelest, the leader of the Communist Party of Ukraine from 1963 to 1972, paid a visit and wrote in his diary that he found the 'dis-covered' (as he put it) graves a horrible sight. He even added, dishon-estly, it seems: 'Who these people are, why they were executed, and who executed them is not yet known, but I guess it's possible to find traces of this crime.'[36] In its very first publication about the Bykivnia graves, on 24 April the Soviet Ukrainian press reported the burial.[37]

A research team of the regional KGB studied archives and ques-tioned NKVD veterans.[38] It also destroyed evidence, including traces

Figure 3.1 KGB officers look on as a forensic expert examines human bones extracted from the Bykivnia mass graves. April 1971.

of the Polish identity of many of the victims. A man called Feodosii Riaboshtan worked at a furnace at the Ninth Forest Factory on the Left Bank. One night two uniformed men visited him and ordered him to burn the contents of six or seven bags that had a stench of corpses. Riaboshtan saw they were old passports, birth certificates, and similar documents, and refused – until he was promised a bottle of liquor. He died in unusual circumstances shortly thereafter.[39]

In the years that followed the authorities brought in heavy machinery to level the surface. 'The skeletons, bones, skulls – everything was crushed and spread across the territory', Andrii Amons has noted. 'They brought in a 1.5-meter layer of earth and covered it.' The authorities also seem to have ordered foresters to plough the area around the graves so as to hamper access to the terrain.[40]

Yet the reburials, levelling, and ploughing did not bar grave looters. They kept coming well into the 1980s. In 1989, a Ukrainian journalist who referred to unnamed witnesses reported that a very large area near Bykivnia was disturbed up to 2 metres deep, using home-made ladders. Scattered about lay bottles of vodka and eau-de-Cologne and 'hundreds, thousands of skulls'. One of the looters was arrested when he tried to sell a jar with gold teeth at a bus stop for three bottles of vodka. An experienced digger, he told his captors, could fill up a jar in one night.[41]

But there were also secret commemorations. In the late 1960s, if not earlier, unknown people placed wooden crosses with icons on them in the area.[42] Mykola and Halyna Lohvanov lived in Bykivnia. They and their relatives and friends visited the graves on Easter or Victory Day.[43] Such visits resembled the custom of *pomynky*: wakes on the first night after a person's death, on the tenth day, and a year later. Mykola Lysenko, an agricultural econo-mist from Kiev, visited the Lohvanovs, who were his in-laws, in May 1986.

> We went there to offer them our congratulations, he's a veteran of the Second World War, to give them our best wishes on Victory Day. When we came there, they were preparing baskets, packages, in order to go somewhere. 'Where are you going?' I said. 'On this day', they said, 'and on Easter we always go to the pits to commemorate the dead, those who were shot before the war by the NKVD satraps.' Well, we joined the pro-cession and went. It isn't very far, maybe a kilometre or a kilometre and a half at the most. When we got there, a horrible picture opened before our eyes. An area of several hectares was dug up and covered with human bones. Remnants of clothing, shoes, children's toys, and then skulls and bones, and it was all lying around dug up and scattered. Well, you know, the women began wailing because it's horrible when people show such disrespect … for their own people. We had a meal there.

Lysenko vowed to tell the world about the terrible crime and began taking pictures and questioning about fifteen fearful local wit-nesses. He also took some skulls with bullet holes with him. After a year, he asked for help from the Writers' Union's party bureau. Ivan Drach and Serhii Plachynda from that bureau took pictures them-selves, and, in late 1987, Drach and the secretary of the Writers' Union Communist Party committee, Oleksa Musiienko, asked Kostiantyn Masyk, the first secretary of the party committee for the city of Kiev, to take measures for the creation of a single mass grave and the placement of a sign 'To the Victims of the Stalinist Terror from the Ukrainian People'. Masyk rushed to Bykivnia to see for himself. That same month, December 1987, the KGB studied the terrain and found pits (a recent one was 1.5 by 2.5 metres), cavities, 2-metre-high earthen walls, and 'parts of human skeletons – skulls, bones of arms and legs, and also partly decayed remains of shoes and other clothing items'. It proposed that the militia guard the site – but not so much to preclude looting as to prevent 'use of the mentioned circumstances for hostile purposes' – and that the KGB's internal troops 'put [it] in order'. Police troops did surround the site and placed 'No Entry' signs.[44]

Within a week, the republic's Prime Minister Volodymyr Shcherbytsky agreed to 'measures to uncover the possible inciters and to interrupt the provocative conjectures intending to link the events during the fascist occupation with so-called "victims of Stalinist terror"'.[45] KGB officers told witnesses that their story must be that they had never seen or known *anything*. In turn, these witnesses tearfully reproached Lysenko that they would be arrested.[46] That same month, a criminal investigator called V. Hubriienko studied the area for five days. He concluded that there were human remains in an area about 200 by 260 metres, totalling about 4 hectares. He counted 2,158 skeletons, mostly in the central part, at a depth of 0.2 to 4 metres.[47]

On 24 December, the government established the second Bykivnia commission, headed by Minister of Internal Affairs Ivan Hladush and including twelve others such as Iurii Kondufor, the republic's most powerful historian. Its mandate was 'researching the remains of Soviet citizens destroyed by the German-fascist invaders during the Great Patriotic War discovered in the 19th quarter of the Darnytsia Forest Area of the city of Kiev'.[48] Already the day after, it witnessed a reburial, 5 metres below the surface and right next to the reburials from 1971. This time it involved thirty-four wooden containers with human remains, and eight boxes with items such as Polish officers' boots and metal badges inscribed 'KOU NKVD USSR', Kiev Regional Department of the NKVD of the Ukrainian Soviet Socialist Republic. Ending its work as early as 30 December, the Hladush commission dated the burials to 'approximately forty-five years' ago, or '1941–1943'.[49]

The government ordered the Kiev city administration to manage the gravesite and improve the road toward it, and it ordered the construction company Kievproekt to make a design for the future memorial site. Almost as an afterthought, it also ordered a criminal investigation of the 'outrages' against the human remains.[50]

Activism and further confrontation since the late 1980s

Less than five months later, on 6 May 1988, the very first official memorial was inaugurated: a granite cube with an inscription reading 'ETERNAL MEMORY. Here are buried 6,329 Soviet warriors, partisans, underground activists, peaceful citizens tortured to death by the fascist occupiers in 1941–1943'. The deed was done by low-ranking officials, such as the deputy secretary of the city party committee, V. I. Mykhailovsky. Present in silence were city party committee secretary Masyk (who later became one of independent Ukraine's deputy prime ministers) and the head of the city soviet, V. A. Zhursky. Local people were absent, for no one had invited them and no announcement had been made. Kiev's evening newspaper reported the event the day after.[51]

The Ukrainian 'Memorial' society, recently founded to expose the crimes of Stalin's regime, organized its own commemorative meeting at Bykivnia on 15 July 1988, which was filmed by the KGB.[52] The society was gravely concerned about a proposal put forward by Zhursky and adopted by the city council to build a train station in the forest.[53] Now aid to its cause came from an unexpected source – Moscow. Bypassing Soviet Ukraine's ultra-conservative authorities, Taniuk brought the correspondent of Moscow's *Literaturnaia gazeta* (*Literary Newspaper*) to Bykivnia. Sergei Kiselev's report appeared on 30 November 1988, and had the effect of a bombshell. Soviet censorship had never before cleared an assertion that the Bykivnia graves held victims of Stalin's regime.

Ukraine's authorities dared not dismiss the report by the prestigious periodical out of hand.[54] Typically for Mikhail Gorbachev's time of glasnost (openness or transparency), the publicity was followed by rapid action by state and civil actors. Articles by foreign correspondents who visited Bykivnia added to the pressure. On 5 December, half a century after the Great Terror, Criminal Case 50–0092 was opened to investigate the killings.[55]

A meeting by Memorial and other activists at the House of Cinema on 6 December demanded an end to the construction of a railway station; a truthful memorial; dismissal of Hladush from the government commission; and a board of advisors with people recommended by civil organizations. The meeting also demanded that the relevant archives be opened and the KGB instructed to inform about all anonymous burial sites from the Stalin-era terror.[56] Two days later, the Ukrainian government reconvened ('renewed') the Hladush commission, with a revised composition, for the purpose of 'additional study of the circumstances and documents' and to come up with proposals.[57]

The Hladush commission and the criminal investigators approached the witnesses at Bykivnia, but at first they refused to speak – people in militia uniforms had been threatening them. Whether these were KGB officers is unclear; the agency claimed to be cooperating in the investigation by questioning pre-war 'colleagues' and visiting the central KGB archives in Moscow.[58] Ultimately, the

Prosecutor's Office questioned over 250 witnesses. It also carried out some kind of re-enactment, created video recordings, solicited expert opinions, and scrutinized dozens of earlier criminal files and other records.[59]

The government commission convened once a week at Hladush's office, and then once every three weeks. The journalist Kiselev could attend and heard many commission members profess a lack of qualifications to question the forensic experts' earlier conclusions about the timing of the murders. But the final meeting did acknowledge that *Literaturnaia gazeta* had written the truth, and ruled that the incorrect words be erased from the memorial stone. Just before the closing, Kiselev called out, 'What about an exhumation?!' A representative of the Communist Party in the commission smiled and declared it unnecessary, even *immoral*: 'We should not disturb the bones of those who perished – it's not Christian. All the more so because there was already an exhumation in December 1987. What's left to prove if we now know the main thing – who exterminated those people. No necrophilia, please!' Although Hladush did favour a new exhumation, his commission disbanded without deciding on the matter.[60]

All the same, a third Soviet exhumation did begin in April 1989. Unlike the archeological exhumation at Kurapaty, for instance, a similar site in neighbouring Belarus, this exhumation was thoroughly forensic, and was conducted by soldiers of the Internal Troops and a youth search club. At first Kiselev was the only journalist present. Later a correspondent of RATAU, Soviet Ukraine's press agency, joined him. For the first few days, only mangled corpses (in non-anatomical positions) were found. The diggers reburied the remains of 6,783 people – slightly more than the number on the memorial. A journalist's report gives a sense of the atmosphere:

> A soldier calls out from the pit, 'Found a skull with a bullet hole.' We come nearer. Company Sergeant Major Iu. Sh. does not hide his thoughts: 'I'm not saying that Stalin did many good things, but he did take the country out of its postwar collapse.' Private S. Sh.: 'I cannot say anything about Stalin. I don't have a personal opinion of him.'[61]

This excavation found near the memorial, at a depth of 5 metres, the chests from 1988 with Polish officers' boots and other Polish items. As in 1971 and 1988, the diggings were strictly limited in time: the company hired for the diggings had been ordered to finish by Victory Day, 9 May.[62] The haste was solely because of the lack of commitment by the authorities.

Because of that same unwillingness, as the press quickly noted, the criminal investigation ended prematurely. It had to be closed supposedly because of the lapse of time and the death of those responsible, as Prosecutor Viktor Kulyk put it on 31 May.[63] He also ruled that relatives requesting extracted items might receive them, except for gold and other valuables (which he sent to the Ministry of Internal Affairs) and extracted human remains, which he sent to the Republican Bureau of Criminal Forensics. That these sixteen skulls (and some other remains) were not reburied became known, and in January 1990, seven Ukrainian intellectuals, including the leaders of the Memorial society (officially recognized the day before), demanded that the extracted remains be reburied at a symbolic site, near the October Palace. They and other activists relented only after a solemn reburial at Bykivnia on 13 February. Kulyk had underestimated the 'social-political side' of the matter, the Communist Party warned him.[64]

In mid-1989, the Hladush commission had recommended continued research by the Prosecutor's Office, publicity about its work, and a competition for a new memorial.[65] The Ministry of Culture called this competition, but it ended inconclusively, and in May 1990, Memorial unilaterally erected a large oak cross, a memorial stone, and an artistic barbed wire fence. It also lined the forest road with five signs and placed a 6-metre-long panel at the forest entrance, with the words 'Graves of Repressed People'.[66]

Ukraine became independent in 1991, but its post-Soviet authorities were also reluctant to face Bykivnia. For instance, when city mayor Leonid Kosakivsky opened the 'Memorial Complex Bykivnia Graves' in the presence of a number of bussed-in Kievans on 30 April 1994, he did so without publicity. The roadside now had a statue of a mourning man.[67] Even though the area eventually changed in status, becoming a 'state preserve' on 22 May 2001, and a 'national preserve' five years later, the site itself did not change. The very first visit by a Ukrainian president, Viktor Yushchenko, took place only in 2004.

The fourth Katyn cemetery

The Soviet authorities had reluctantly and belatedly acknowledged that the Bykivnia graves held victims of Stalin's regime, but ignored the Polish citizens among them. Prosecutors such as Kulyk refused to meet journalists who wished to discuss this matter and the stories they had heard about the burning of documents in 1971.[68] Poland was informed not by officials, but by Ukrainian activists. In 1989, Memorial and other civic organizations told the Polish consulate about Poles at Bykivnia.[69]

In April 1990, the official Soviet media admitted for the first time that not Germans, but NKVD officers had murdered Polish prisoners at Katyn, the better-known burial site near Smolensk in Russia. Polish POW graves were also found at Kharkiv's Piatykhatky grounds, and the city administration there recognized them in 1991 with a memorial.[70] The Polish Public Prosecutor's Office in Warsaw received Lysenko in 1990, and Poland's Prosecutor Jacek Wilczur visited Bykivnia.[71] The very first Polish religious rite took place there in May, and that same year Stanislav Shalatsky, a Pole from Ukraine, handed Pope John Paul II in Rome a capsule with Bykivnia earth.[72]

But the authorities of independent Ukraine continued to claim that Bykivnia held only the remains of Soviet citizens. Ievhen Marchuk, chief of the Security Service of Ukraine, successor to the KGB, denied that his organization had any information about Polish POWs killed in Ukraine. Finally, on 5 May 1994, Marchuk's deputy Andrii Khomych showed Poland's deputy prosecutor general Stefan Śnieżko a 1940 list of 3,435 Polish POW names, which both men deemed previously unknown victims of the 'Katyn crime'.[73] Two years later, the Military Prosecutor's Office in Kiev finally gave Poland a list of Polish items found in 1971.[74]

But Poland remained barred from Bykivnia itself until 2001. On 25 June that year, Pope John Paul II included it in his tour of Ukraine, and a State Inter-Departmental Commission on Commemoration of Victims of War and Political Repression was founded. Led by Vitalii Kazakevich, it quickly came to an understanding with the Polish Council for the Protection of Struggle and Martyrdom Sites, led by Andrzej Przewoźnik.[75] This enabled five excavations to take place, in 2001, 2006, 2007, 2011, and 2012, all conducted by Poles headed by Andrzej Kola, a professor of archaeology who produced records only in the Polish language.[76] Polish television showed the activities, and a Polish photographer won an award for his work there.[77] A discovery on 25 August 2007 confirmed the burial at Bykivnia of Poles from the so-called 'Ukrainian Katyn List': the army ID sign of a senior sergeant and border guard.[78] Ultimately, the Polish investigators concluded that forty-one pits held Polish victims from 1937 and 1938, but fifty-four other pits held 1,488 Polish victims from 1940.

The latter victims were solemnly reburied on 27 October 2007, apparently along with corpses of victims of the pre-war terror. (The BBC and Reuters reported the burial of 'some 2,000' and '1,998 bodies, 474 of which were Poles'.) Four years later, on 30 June 2011, the remains of 492 persons from fifteen other 'Polish' pits were exhumed and reburied. It seems that the investigators deemed the latter also victims from murders that took place in 1940, for Przewoźnik's successor Andrzej Kunert concluded in 2012 that from a total of 69 'Polish' pits, the remains of 'at least 1980 persons' were found.[79]

But some Memorial activists (such as Roman Krutsyk – not Lysenko) publicly denounced the Polish diggings, as interference in Ukraine's internal affairs – and as illegal. Their envious frustration was easy to understand, as most victims of the pre-war terror were never excavated this thoroughly. They may also have been suspicious because Amons, who assisted the Poles, was born in Warsaw of Polish parents. But they were right about the illegality: In September 2009, a Ukrainian court imposed fines on 'Memorials of Ukraine', an entity serving the State Inter-Departmental Commission, for illegal excavations at Bykivnia. Because Deputy Prime Minister Dmytro Tabachnyk had succeeded Kazakevich as commission chairman, no one expected the verdict to be implemented, which indeed it was not.[80]

On 25 September 2010, Prime Minister Mykola Azarov told Polish President Bronisław Komorowski that a Polish cemetery would be allowed at Bykivnia. In preparation, another reburial took place there in 2011. On 4 November that year, President Viktor Yanukovych ruled that the central part of the new memorial to the 'victims of totalitarianism' be finished before 1 August 2012; and on 28 November 2011, he managed to gather Komorowski and his three Ukrainian predecessors, Leonid Kravchuk, Leonid Kuchma, and Viktor Yushchenko, for the placement of the memorial's corner stone.[81]

A small part of the terrain, holding the almost 2,000 Polish citizens, became a Polish Military Cemetery on 21 September 2012. It was inaugurated by the presidents of Ukraine and Poland, Yanukovych and Komorowski.[82] Thus emerged what Poland – but not Ukraine – calls 'the Fourth Katyn Cemetery', after Piatykhatky, Katyn, and Mednoe (all unveiled in the summer and autumn of 2000).[83] The term 'military cemetery' overlooks the fact that, like the other Katyn cemeteries, Polish civilians were among the dead of 1940. As always with Bykivnia, the matter had been stalled and then rushed. As Polish media reported in June 2013, the Polish inscriptions on the memorial are clandestine, for the Ukrainian state never signed a document allowing them. In fact, seemingly not a single document with permission for the Polish cemetery was prepared.[84]

But this opening does appear to mark the end of excavation, illegal or not. According to Andrii Kondratsky, head of the Kievan Society of Political Prisoners and Victims of Repression and a historian, grave looting had still taken place in the late 1990s.[85] Even as late as March 2004, Dmytro Malakov, of the Museum of the History of Kiev, warned me not to visit Bykivnia on my own because of the marauders there.

Conclusion

Similar large post-Soviet sites with victims of Stalin's Great Terror exist near Minsk (Kurapaty), Moscow (Butovo and Kommunarka), St Petersburg (Levashovo and Koirangakangas), Voronezh (Dubovka), and they also exist in cities such as Vinnytsia and Dnipropetrovsk. There, as at Bykivnia, no one seems to want to establish individual identities from remains, for instance through DNA analysis. In Kiev, too, the authorities successfully warded off judicial prosecution of NKVD veterans, despite many demands for them. For Bykivnia, it is clear that none of the many excavations have been probing enough, or even legal. They were undertaken by grave robbers, or, in the 2000s, by semi-secret government bodies that lacked the proper paperwork – that is, formal permission – from the state.

Activists and foreigners ended official silence about Stalin's mass graves at Bykivnia, but it took years for this pressure to put a full stop to the grave looting. Most Ukrainian citizens, meanwhile, have preferred to keep silent, out of fear, indifference, or both.

Notes

I am grateful to Jean-Marc Dreyfus and Élisabeth Anstett for inviting me to a conference where I could present these findings for the first time, and to Tymon Kretschmer and Mieczysław Góra for providing the image and allowing its publication here. Special thanks are due to Marco Carynnyk for sharing bibliographical references and the transcripts of his own interviews about Bykivnia and for commenting on an earlier version of this study.

1 A. I. Amons (ed.), *Bykivnians'ki zhertvy abo Iak pratsiuvala 'Vyshcha dviika' na Kyïvshchyni* (Kiev: Mizhnarodna akademiia upravlinnia personalom, 2007), p. 73. It is disheartening that Amons granted publishing rights to an institution that had published many antisemitic books and articles.

2 O. H. Bazhan (eds), *Pam"iat' Bykivni: Dokumenty ta materialy* (Kiev: Ridnyi krai, 2000), pp. 59–60; H. Kuromiya, *The Voices of the Dead: Stalin's Great Terror in the 1930s* (New Haven and London: Yale University Press, 2007), pp. 15–16.

3 On German spies, see Bazhan, *Pam"iat' Bykivni*, p. 60.

4 Pres-tsentr SB Ukraïny, 'Sluzhba bezpeky Ukraïny vstanovyla ta opryliudniuie imena 14191 zhertvy Bykivni', 14 May 2009, at http://sbu. gov.ua/sbu/control/uk/publish/article?art_id=86716&cat_id=39574 (accessed 22 August 2013).

5 On the procedure, see M. Lysenko, *Bykivnia: Zlochyn bez kaiattia* (Brovary: Krynytsia, 1996), p. 35.

6 Andrii Amons, interviewed in '"Stinky mizh ukraïns'kymy i pol's'kymy mohylamy mohly siahaty vs'oho 30–40 santymetriv"', *Ukraïns'kyi tyzhden'*, 24 September 2012, at http://tyzhden.ua/History/60703 (accessed 8 September 2013). On the Lukianivka Prison and on Luxemburg Street, see Bazhan, *Pam"iat' Bykivni*, pp. 56–7, 62–3.

7 V. M. Nikol's'kyi, 'Do pytannia shchodo rozshuku mists' pokhovannia zhertv politychnykh represii', in T. F. Hryhor"ieva (ed.), *VIII Vseukraïns'ka naukova konferentsiia 'Istorychne kraieznavstvo i kul'tura' (Naukovi dopovidi ta povidomlennia). Chastyna II* (Kiev and Kharkiv: Ridnyi krai, 1997), p. 158.

8 Bazhan, *Pam"iat' Bykivni*, pp. 57–8, 75.

9 M. Lysenko has said that such burials had occurred there as early as 1929, but has not offered the testimonies where this story is supposed to appear. M. Lysenko, interview in Brovary by M. Carynnyk, 12 October 1995; Lysenko, *Bykivnia*, p. 23; An NKVD man who defected to the United States in 1946 has told an unlikely story about the pre-war years: 'In three specific KGB headquarters, I saw machines that were used in lieu of burial – grinding equipment. In Kiev, the KGB had a special room approximately three-fourths of a mile from the Dnieper River. A sewer line extended from the room to the river – a specially constructed pipe of extra-wide circumference, allowing a body to be flushed into the river. Predatory fish would swiftly destroy the evidence. In the city of Kharkov [Kharkiv], there was a similar setup.' A. Contract, *The Back Room: My Life with Khrushchev and Stalin* (New York: Vantage Press, 1991), p. 30.

10 Bazhan, *Pam"iat' Bykivni*, pp. 25, 59–60.

11 Petro Kukovenko, interview outside his house in Bykivnia by M. Carynnyk, 5 October 1991; Vira Nikitina, interview at her house in Bykivnia by M. Carynnyk, 6 October 1991; Lysenko, *Bykivnia*, p. 24; Bazhan, *Pam"iat' Bykivni*, pp. 40, 49, 65.

12 M. Sh. Musorgskii, quoted in Bazhan, *Pam"iat' Bykivni*, pp. 62–3.

13 L. T. Husak, quoted in V. Savtsov, 'Bykivnia', *Radians'ka Ukraïna*, 19 April 1989, 3, partly translated in M. Carynnyk, 'The killing fields of Kiev', *Commentary*, October 1990, p. 21; Bazhan, *Pam"iat' Bykivni*, pp. 50–1.

14 Dmytro Andriiovych Makarenko, interview at his house in Bykivnia by M. Carynnyk, 5 October 1991; Bazhan, *Pam"iat' Bykivni*, pp. 63–4.

15 Lysenko, *Bykivnia*, p. 41; H. A. Shamrai, quoted in Savtsov, 'Bykivnia', partly translated in Carynnyk, 'The killing fields of Kiev', pp. 21–2.

16 M. O. Nyzenko, quoted in Bazhan, *Pam"iat' Bykivni*, pp. 49–50. On objects, see Lysenko, *Bykivnia*, p. 24.

17 Lysenko, *Bykivnia*, p. 36; S. Kiselev, 'Tragicheskaia pravda o Bykovne do sikh por zasekrechena', internet periodical *Obozrevatel'* (Kiev), 21 May 2006, at http://kiyany.obozrevatel.com/news/2006/5/21/16509.htm (accessed 8 September 2013).

18 Bazhan, *Pam"iat' Bykivni*, pp. 66, 76; Valentyn Matiiash, interview at his house in Bykivnia by M. Carynnyk, 9 October 1991; Halyna Lohvanova, interview by M. Carynnyk outside her house in Bykivnia, 5 October 1991, and in the Bykivnia forest, 9 October 1991.

19 Bazhan, *Pam"iat' Bykivni*, pp. 48, 63; Lysenko, *Bykivnia*, p. 25; interview with Makarenko; interview with Matiiash.

20 Bazhan, *Pam"iat' Bykivni*, pp. 47–8 (A. S. Dembovska); interview with Lohvanova (on the question).

21 'Ontzettende vondsten in Kiev', *Nieuwe Apeldoornsche Courant* (Apeldoorn, Netherlands), 29 September 1941, 1; A. P. Kollmus, 'GPU-Morde auch in Kiew. Hunderte der zu Tode Gequälten verschart', *Berliner Börsen-Zeitung. Tageszeitung für Politik und Wirtschaft, für Wehrfragen, Kultur und Unterhaltung*, 30 September 1941, p. 3; 'Shliakhom morduvan'. I v Kyievi lylasia nevynna krov', *Ukraïns'ke Slovo*, 8 October 1941, p. 2; 'U vil'nomu Kyievi', *Krakivs'ki visti*, 14 October 1941, p. 4; 'Kyïv zhyve novym zhyttiam. Vid nashoho spetsial'noho korespondenta', *Volyn'* (Rivne), 26 October 1941, p. 3; 'S"iohodnishnii Kyïv', *Krakivs'ki visti*, 27 November 1941, p. 4, reprinting most of P[etro] Oliinyk, 'Z ridnykh zemel'. S"ohodnishnii Kyïv', *Ukraïns'kyi vistnyk* (Berlin), no. 34, 2 November 1941.

22 Interview with Kukovenko; see also Bazhan, *Pam"iat' Bykivni*, p. 49.

23 Interview with Nikitina.

24 Bazhan, *Pam"iat' Bykivni*, p. 48.

25 L. Forostivs'kyi, 'Slidamy mychenytstva Ukraïny: "Khutir Bykovnia" ta "Babyn Iar" u Kyievi', *Svoboda*, 179, 4 August (1950), 2–3; also in L. Forostivs'kyi, *Kyïv pid vorozhymy okupatsiiamy* (Buenos Aires: Vydavnytsvo Mykola Denysiuka, 1952), pp. 75–8.

26 Bazhan, *Pam"iat' Bykivni*, pp. 48–9, 51–2.

27 *Ibid.*, pp. 66, 71; Lysenko, *Bykivnia*, p. 26; L. Taniuk, *Tvory v 60-y tomakh*, vol. 6, *Shchodennyky 1962 r.* (Kiev: Al'terpres, 2006), p. 541.

28 Taniuk, *Tvory*, vol. 6, 538–42. The translation of the poem is from Carynnyk, 'The killing fields of Kiev', p. 20.

29 Les' Taniuk, interview at Bykivnia by M. Carynnyk, 3 November 1991.

30 Andrii Amons, interviewed in 'Klucz do prawdy leży w Moskwie', *Gazeta Wyborcza*, 12 August 2006, p. 13, also at www.katyn.ru/index.php?go=Pages&in=view&id=386 (accessed 8 September 2013) ('the late 1960s'); Bazhan, *Pam"iat' Bykivni*, p. 67 ('from the middle of the 1970s'); Petro Kukovenko, interview outside his house in Bykivnia by M. Carynnyk, 5 October 1991 ('in 1971'); interview with Lohvanova.

31 Amons in 'Klucz do prawdy leży w Moskwie'.

32 Interview with Kukovenko; interview with Lohvanova.

33 Bazhan, *Pam''iat' Bykivni*, pp. 27–8.

34 *Ibid.*, pp. 29–30.

35 *Ibid.*, pp. 31–4. Four photographs from the excavation and reburial, 'Galeria – fotografie archiwalne', at http://bykownia.eu/galeria/materiay-archiwalne.html (accessed 1 October 2013).

36 Bazhan, *Pam''iat' Bykivni*, pp. 29–30. Shelest's diary says that he saw reburial in large wooden trunks on 16 April, which cannot be squared with the official and later dates for the forensic investigation: 20–27 April.

37 'Soobshchenie RATAU', *Pravda Ukrainy*, 24 April 1971, 4.

38 Bazhan, *Pam''iat' Bykivni*, pp. 30–1.

39 Oleksandr Andriiovych Kalosha, quoted in I. Radchenko, 'Pravda zavzhdy odna', *Molod' Ukraïny*, 10 December 1989, p. 2; Amons in '"Stinky mizh"'; that locals talked about this burning in the late 1980s is mentioned in V. Savtsov, 'Lis shumyt' taiemnytseiu', *Radians'ka Ukraïna*, 23 April 1989, p. 4.

40 Amons '"Stinky mizh"'; on ploughing, see Lysenko, *Bykivnia*, p. 18.

41 Savtsov, 'Bykivnia'; on the arrested looter, see Kiselev, 'Tragicheskaia pravda'.

42 M. Rozhenko, 'Vstupni zauvazhennia', in M. Rozhenko & E. Bohats'ka (eds), *Sosny Bykivni svidchat': Zlochyn proty liudstva. Knyha persha* (Kiev: Ukraïns'kyi Tsentr dukhovnoï kul'tury, 1999), p. 6.

43 Lysenko, *Bykivnia*, pp. 17–18; interview with Lohvanova.

44 Interview with Lysenko; Lysenko, *Bykivnia*, pp. 19, 27–8; Bazhan, *Pam''iat' Bykivni*, pp. 36–7, 38.

45 Bazhan, *Pam''iat' Bykivni*, pp. 39–40.

46 Interview with Lysenko.

47 Bazhan, *Pam''iat' Bykivni*, pp. 40–1.

48 *Ibid.*, pp. 42–3.

49 Kiselev, 'Tragicheskaia pravda'; Bazhan, *Pam''iat' Bykivni*, pp. 43–5.

50 Bazhan, *Pam''iat' Bykivni*, pp. 44–5.

51 S. Bilokin, 'Shcho hovoryla pam''iat' zemli, koly buly zakryti arkhivy (Bykivnia i Vinnytsia v istoriohrafiï teroru)', in A. I. Amons, *Bykivnians'ki zhertvy* (Kiev: Mizhrehional'na Akademiia Upravlinnia Personalom, 2007), pp. 42–3, earlier version at www.s-bilokin.name/Terror/Bykivnja/USSR.html (accessed 6 November 2013); S. Kysel'ov (S. Kiselev), 'Arkhipelah Bykivnia', *Suchasnist'*, 10 (1990), 58.

52 Lysenko, *Bykivnia*, p. 29.

53 Kysel'ov, 'Arkhipelah Bykivnia', pp. 59–60; interview with Matiiash; L. M. Protsenko, 'Pokhovannia represovanykh u Kyievi', in A. A. Kondrats'kyi & M. M. Rozhenko, *Materialy vseukraïns'koï konferentsiï sumnoï pam''iati velykoho teroru 1937 roku 'Zlochyn bez kary' 3–4 lystopada 1997 roku* (Kiev: Stylos, 1998), p. 152. Protsenko adds, without reference to a source, that a metro stop was also planned on the graves of the repressed.

54 Kiselev, 'Tragicheskaia pravda'; Lysenko, *Bykivnia*, pp. 29–30. The article was Sergei Kiselev, 'Taina Bykovnianskogo lesa', *Literaturnaia gazeta*,

30 November 1988, p. 2. Its Ukrainian equivalent was 'Taiemnytsia Darnyts'koï trahediï', *Vechirnii Kyïv*, 1 December 1988.

55 Bazhan, *Pam"iat' Bykivni*, p. 72. An example of the foreign press reports is B. Keller, 'Behind Stalin's green fence: who filled the mass graves?', *New York Times*, 6 March 1989, pp. 1, 8.

56 Bazhan, *Pam"iat' Bykivni*, pp. 45–6; Lysenko, *Bykivnia*, p. 30.

57 Bazhan, *Pam"iat' Bykivni*, pp. 46–7.

58 *Ibid.*, pp. 57–8; Lysenko, *Bykivnia*, p. 30.

59 Bazhan, *Pam"iat' Bykivni*, pp. 64–5. These rich materials are still largely unavailable for research.

60 Kiselev, 'Tragicheskaia pravda'. This memoir errs in calling the chairman Vasylyshyn and in asserting that the commission produced no official report. Compare 'Povidomlennia Uriadovoï komisiï, stvorenoï rishenniam Rady Ministriv URSR vid 24 hrudnia 1987 roku', *Radians'ka Ukraïna*, 16 April 1989.

61 Kiselev, 'Tragicheskaia pravda'; Bazhan, *Pam"iat' Bykivni*, p. 77. For the quotation, see Savtsov, 'Lis shumyt' taiemnytseiu'.

62 Kiselev, 'Tragicheskaia pravda'; Savtsov, 'Lis shumyt' taiemnytseiu'.

63 Bazhan, *Pam"iat' Bykivni*, pp. 72–9.

64 *Ibid.*, pp. 83–4, 85–6.

65 *Ibid.*, pp. 79–83.

66 M. H. Lysenko, 'Mohyly Bykivni chekaiut' …', in *Z arkhiviv VUChK-HPU-NKVD-KHB*, nos. 1–2 (4–5) (Kiev: Instytut istoriï Ukraïny NAN Ukraïny et al., 1997), p. 434.

67 Lysenko, *Bykivnia*, p. 47.

68 Radchenko, 'Pravda zavzhdy odna'.

69 Lysenko, *Bykivnia*, p. 37.

70 A. Etkind, R. Finnin, U. Blacker, J. Fedor, S. Lewis, M. Mälksoo & M. Mroz, *Remembering Katyn* (Cambridge: Polity, 2012), p. 70.

71 Lysenko, *Bykivnia*, p. 37.

72 A. A. Kondrats'kyi, 'Pol's'kyi slid u Bykivni', in Kondrats'kyi & Rozhenko, *Materialy vseukraïns'koï konferentsiï*, p. 112.

73 A. Kunert, A. Siwek & Z. Walkowski, *Polski Cmentarz Wojenny w Kijowie-Bykowni (Czwarty Cmentarz Katyński)* (Warsaw: Rada Ochrony Pamięci Walk i Męczeństwa, 2012), p. 11; on Marchuk see Kiselev, 'Tragicheskaia pravda'.

74 Kunert *et al.*, *Polski Cmentarz*, p. 14.

75 *Ibid.*, p. 15.

76 See *ibid.*, pp. 15, 16–17. On language, see I. Muzychenko, 'Zasudyly za Bykivniu. Rozsliduvannia pidtverdylo nezakonnist' zinitsiiovanykh Dmytrom Tabachnykom rozkopok pokhovan' zhertv komunistychnykh represiï', *Ukraïna Moloda*, 19 September 2009, at www.umoloda.kiev.ua/regions/0/163/0/52542/ (accessed 26 September 2013).

77 A. Ferens (director), *Gdzie rosną poziomki?*, Agencja Filmowa for Program 1 of TVP S.A., 2006, at http://vod.tvp.pl/dokumenty/historia/gdzie-rosna-poziomki/wideo/gdzie-rosna-poziomki/4286747 and at www.youtube.com/watch?v=I5jooz_j51Y (accessed 6 November 2013). On the award-winning photograph, see Press Club Polska,

http://pressclub.pl/?page_id=1534 (accessed 1 November 2013); M. Rigamonti, 'The opening: Bykovnia. Archeology of crime', at www.rigamonti.pl/exhibitions/125,bykovnia–archaeology-of-crime/ (accessed 1 November 2013).

78 Kunert *et al.*, *Polski Cmentarz*, pp. 15–16.

79 *Ibid.*, p. 15; 'Ukraine reburies Stalin's victims', BBC News, 27 October 2007, at http://news.bbc.co.uk/2/hi/europe/7065913.stm (accessed 11 November 2013); Reuters, 'Victims of Stalin's rule reburied near Kiev', *Moscow Times*, 29 October 2007, p. 13.

80 Open letter by S. M. Kyrylenko, deputy chair of the Kiev chapter of Memorial, 15 August 2007, at 'Bykivnia – stane Tsvyntarom orliat u vidnosynakh Ukraïna-Pol'shcha?', Vseukraïns'ke Tovarystvo 'Memorial' im. V. Stusa, at http://memorial.kiev.ua/novyny/271-bykivnja-stane-cvyntarom-orljat-u-vidnosynah-ukrajina-polshcha.html (accessed 1 November 2013); Roman Krutsyk, '"Katyns'kyi" memorial u Bykivni??', 4 March 2011, at http://memorial.kiev.ua/statti/955-katynskyj-memorial-u-bykivni.html (accessed 4 November 2013); Muzychenko, 'Zasudyly za Bykivniu'.

81 Kunert *et al.*, *Polski Cmentarz*, p. 16; Ukrinform, 'Ukrainian presidents lay corner stone of memorial in Bykovnia tombs reserve', 26 November 2011, at www.ukrinform.ua/eng/news/ukrainian_presidents_lay_corner_stone_of_memorial_in_bykovnia_tombs_reserve_237055 (accessed 14 November 2013).

82 See, for instance, the presidents' official websites (accessed 6 November 2013): 'Otwarcie Cmentarza Wojennego w Bykowni', 21 September 2012, Oficjalna strona Prezydenta Rzeczypospolitej Polskiej, at www.prezydent.pl/aktualnosci/wizyty-zagraniczne/art,188,otwarcie-cmentarza-wojennego-w-bykowni.html; 'Vustup Prezydenta pid chas vidkryttia Memorialu zhertv totalitaryzmu na terytoriï Natsional'noho zapovidnyka 'Bykivnians'ki mohyly', Prezydent Ukraïny Viktor Ianukovych, 21 September 2012, at www.president.gov.ua/news/25472.html (accessed 4 February 2014).

83 Etkind *et al.*, *Remembering Katyn*, p. 115.

84 Wojciech Mucha and Piotr Ferenc-Chudy, 'Szczątki ofiar NKWD zalane betonem. Skandal bezradna Rada Andrzeja Kunerta', *Gazeta Polska Codziennie*, 13 June 2013, at http://gpcodziennie.pl/20574-szczatki-ofiar-nkwd-zalane-betonem.html#.UdSK_W01OSo (accessed 6 November 2013).

85 Kondrats'kyi, 'Pol's'kyi slid u Bykivni', p. 107.

Bibliography

Amons, A. I., interviewed in 'Kluczdoprawdyleżyw Moskwie', *Gazeta Wyborcza*, 12 August 2006, at www.katyn.ru/index.php?go=Pages&in=view&id=386 (accessed 8 September 2013)

Amons, A. I., interviewed in '"Stinky mizh ukraïns'kymy i pol's'kymy mohylamy mohly siahaty vs'oho 30–40 santymetriv"', *Ukraïns'kyi tyzhden*',

24 September 2012, at http://tyzhden.ua/History/60703 (accessed 8 September 2013)

Amons, A. I. (ed.), *Bykivnians'ki zhertvy abo Iak pratsiuvala 'Vyshcha dviika' na Kyïvshchyni* (Kiev: Mizhrehional'na akademiia upravlinnia personalom, 2007)

Bazhan O. H. (ed.), *Pam"iat' Bykivni: Dokumenty ta materialy* (Kiev: Ridnyi krai, 2000)

Bilokin, S., 'Shcho hovoryla pam"iat' zemli, koly buly zakryti arkhivy (Bykivnia i Vinnytsia v istoriohrafiï teroru)', in A. I. Amons (ed.), *Bykivnians'ki zhertvy abo Iak pratsiuvala 'Vyshcha dviika' na Kyïvshchyni* (Kiev: Mizhrehional'na Akademiia Upravlinnia Personalom, 2007), pp. 13–63, earlier version at www.s-bilokin.name/Terror/Bykivnja/USSR. html (accessed 6 November 2013)

Carynnyk, M., 'The killing fields of Kiev', *Commentary*, October 1990, 19–25

Carynnyk, M., Transcripts of his interviews about Bykivnia, Toronto, Ontario, Canada

Contract, A., *The Back Room: My Life with Khrushchev and Stalin* (New York: Vantage Press, 1991)

Etkind, A., R. Finnin, U. Blacker, J. Fedor, S. Lewis, M. Mälksoo & M. Mroz, *Remembering Katyn* (Cambridge: Polity, 2012)

Ferens, A. (director) *Gdzie rosną poziomki?*, Agencja Filmowa for Program 1 of TVP S.A., 2006, at http://vod.tvp.pl/dokumenty/historia/gdzie-rosna-poziomki/wideo/gdzie-rosna-poziomki/4286747 and at www.youtube.com/watch?v=I5jooz_j51Y (accessed 6 November 2013)

Forostivs'kyi, L., *Kyïv pid vorozhymy okupatsiiamy* (Buenos Aires: Vydavnytstvo Mykoly Denysiuka, 1952)

Forostivs'kyi, L., 'Slidamy mychenytstva Ukraïny: "Khutir Bykovnia" ta "Babyn Iar" u Kyievi', *Svoboda*, 179, August 4 (1950), 2–3

'Galeria – fotografie archiwalne', at http://bykownia.eu/galeria/materiay-archiwalne.html (accessed 1 October 2013)

Keller, B., 'Behind Stalin's green fence: who filled the mass graves?', *New York Times*, 6 March 1989, 1, 8

Kiselev, S., 'Taina Bykovnianskogo lesa', *Literaturnaia gazeta*, 30 November 1988

Kiselev, S., 'Tragicheskaia pravda o Bykovne do sikh por zasekrechena', internet periodical *Obozrevatel'* (Kiev), 21 May 2006, at http://kiyany.obozrevatel.com/news/2006/5/21/16509.htm (accessed 8 September 2013)

Kollmus, P. A., 'GPU-Morde auch in Kiew: hunderte der zu Tode Gequälten verscharrt', *Berliner Börsen-Zeitung. Tageszeitung für Politik und Wirtschaft, für Wehrfragen, Kultur und Unterhaltung*, 30 September 1941, 3

Kondrats'kyi, A. A. & M. M. Rozhenko (eds), *Materialy vseukraïns'koï konferentsiï sumnoï pam"iati velykoho teroru 1937 roku 'Zlochyn bez kary' 3–4 lystopada 1997 roku* (Kiev: Stylos, 1998)

Krutsyk, R., '"Katyns'kyi" memorial u Bykivni??', 4 March 2011, at http://memorial.kiev.ua/statti/955-katynskyj-memorial-u-bykivni.html (accessed 4 November 2013)

Kunert, A., A. Siwek & Z. Walkowski, *Polski Cmentarz Wojenny w Kijowie-Bykowni (Czwarty Cmentarz Katyński)* (Warsaw: Rada Ochrony Pamięci Walk i Męczeństwa, 2012)

Kuromiya, H., *The Voices of the Dead: Stalin's Great Terror in the 1930s* (New Haven and London: Yale University Press, 2007)

'Kyïv zhyve novym zhyttiam, 'Vid nashoho spetsial'noho korespondenta', *Volyn'* (Rivne), 26 October 1941, 3

Kyrylenko, S. M., Open letter, 15 August 2007, at 'Bykivnia – stane Tsvyntarom orliat u vidnosynakh Ukraïna-Pol'shcha?', Vseukraïns'ke Tovarystvo 'Memorial' im. V. Stusa, at http://memorial.kiev.ua/novyny/271-bykivnja-stane-cvyntarom-orljat-u-vidnosynah-ukrajina-polshcha.html (accessed 1 November 2013)

Kysel'ov, S. (S. Kiselev), 'Arkhipelah Bykivnia', *Suchasnist'*, 10 (1990), 58–62

Lysenko, M., *Bykivnia: Zlochyn bez kaiattia* (Brovary: Krynytsia, 1996)

Lysenko, M. H. 'Mohyly Bykivni chekaiut' …', in *Z arkhiviv VUChK-HPU-NKVD-KHB*, nos. 1–2 (4–5) (Kiev, 1997), 432–6

Mucha, W. & P. Ferenc-Chudy, 'Szczątki ofiar NKWD zalane betonem. Skandal bezradna Rada Andrzeja Kunerta', *Gazeta Polska Codziennie*, 13 June 2013, at http://gpcodziennie.pl/20574-szczatki-ofiar-nkwd-zalane-betonem.html#.UdSK_W01OSo (accessed 6 November 2013)

Muzychenko, I., 'Zasudyly za Bykivniu. Rozsliduvannia pidtverdylo neza-konnist' zinitsiiovanykh Dmytrom Tabachnykom rozkopok pokhovan' zhertv komunistychnykh represii', *Ukraïna Moloda*, 19 September 2009, at www.umoloda.kiev.ua/regions/0/163/0/52542/ (accessed 26 September 2013)

Nikol's'kyi, V. M., 'Do pytannia shchodo rozshuku mists' pokhovannia zhertv politychnykh represii', in T. F. Hryhor'ieva (ed.), *VIII Vseukraïns'ka nau-kova konferentsiia 'Istorychne kraieznavstvo i kul'tura' (Naukovi dopovidi ta povidomlennia). Chastyna II* (Kiev and Kharkiv: Ridnyi krai, 1997), pp. 155–9

'Ontzettende vondsten in Kiev', *Nieuwe Apeldoornsche Courant* (Apeldoorn, Netherlands), 29 September 1941, 1

'Otwarcie Cmentarza Wojennego w Bykowni', 21 September 2012, at Oficjalna strona Prezydenta Rzeczypospolitej Polskiej, at www.prezydent.pl/aktualnosci/wizyty-zagraniczne/art,188,otwarcie-cmentarza-wojen-nego-w-bykowni.html (accessed 6 November 2013)

'Povidomlennia Uriadovoï komisiï, stvorenoï rishenniam Rady Ministriv URSR vid 24 hrudnia 1987 roku', *Radians'ka Ukraïna*, 16 April 1989

Press Club Polska, at http://pressclub.pl/?page_id=1534 (accessed 1 November 2013)

Pres-tsentr SB Ukraïny. 'Sluzhba bezpeky Ukraïny vstanovyla ta opryliud-niuie imena 14191 zhertvy Bykivni', 14 May 2009, at http://sbu.gov.ua/sbu/control/uk/publish/article?art_id=86716&cat_id=39574 (accessed 22 August 2013)

Radchenko, I., 'Pravda zavzhdy odna', *Molod' Ukraïny*, 10 December 1989, 2

Reuters, 'Victims of Stalin's rule reburied near Kiev', *Moscow Times*, 29 October 2007, 13

Rigamonti, M., 'The opening: Bykovnia. Archeology of crime', at www.riga-monti.pl/exhibitions/125,the-opening-bykovnia--archeology-of-crime/ (accessed 1 November 2013)

Rozhenko, M., 'Vstupni zauvazhennia', in M. Rozhenko & E. Bohats'ka (eds), *Sosny Bykivni svidchat': Zlochyn proty liudstva: Knyha persha* (Kiev: Ukraïns'kyi Tsentr dukhovnoï kul'tury, 1999), pp. 6–11

Savtsov, V., 'Bykivnia', *Radians'ka Ukraïna*, 19 April 1989, 3

Savtsov, V., 'Lis shumyt' taiemnytseiu', *Radians'ka Ukraïna*, 23 April 1989, 4

'Shliakhom morduvan'. I v Kyievi lylasia nevynna krov', *Ukraïns'ke Slovo* (Kiev), 8 October 1941, 2

'S"iohodnishnii Kyïv', *Krakivs'ki visti*, 27 November 1941, 4

'Soobshchenie RATAU', 24 April 1971, 4, *Pravda Ukrainy*

Taniuk, L., *Tvory v 60-y tomakh*, vol. 6, *Shchodennyky 1962 r.* (Kiev: Al'terpres, 2006)

'U vil'nomu Kyievi', *Krakivs'ki visti*, 14 October 1941, 4

'Ukraine reburies Stalin's victims', BBC News, 27 October 2007, at http://news.bbc.co.uk/2/hi/europe/7065913.stm (accessed 11 November 2013)

Ukrinform, 'Ukrainian presidents lay corner stone of memorial in Bykovnia tombs reserve', 26 November 2011, at www.ukrinform.ua/eng/news/ukrainian_presidents_lay_corner_stone_of_memorial_in_bykovnia_tombs_reserve_237055 (accessed 14 November 2013)

'Vustup Prezydenta pid chas vidkryttia Memorialu zhertv totalitaryzmu na terytoriï Natsional'noho zapovidnyka 'Bykivnians'ki mohyly', at Prezydent Ukraïny Viktor Ianukovych, 21 September 2012, at www.president.gov.ua/news/25472.html (accessed 6 November 2013)

4

The concealment of bodies during the military dictatorship in Uruguay (1973–84)[1]

José López Mazz

The political violence that occurred in Latin America during the second half of the twentieth century was deeply rooted in historic and prehistoric cultural traditions. To study it in a scientific way accordingly requires both the development of a specific set of cultural and historical methodologies and a leading role to be played by archaeological techniques and forensic anthropology.

Our focus is in part on apprehending and understanding violent practices occurring within social and political systems. Furthermore, we are also concerned with developing strategies and (field and laboratory) instruments that allow us to identify the different contexts and settings of this violence. This is a vital task for certain recent historical periods, such as the Southern Cone dictatorships, where there existed the desire to hide and mask political violence and the *disappearing* of opponents, as well as systematic practices designed to achieve this end.

Although the dictatorship lasted from 1973 until 1984, violent political practices paved the way for it from the mid-1960s. During that period there was an increase in conflicts over land ownership (sugar-cane workers) and over low salaries and civil rights (labour laws). The first instances of disappeared and murdered political detainees occurred in the early 1970s. Shortly afterwards the armed conflict with Tupamaro guerrillas and the coup itself accentuated the level of violence, which was part of a well-defined political strategy and the overall system of social control.[2]

This study focuses on the complicated problems involved in the identification of corpses, concealed in different ways across different scenarios during this violent period. In this context overcoming the challenges of the identification process became important for understanding the practices employed by the police and military in their treatment of the bodies of their political victims, during a period that would come to be referred to as one of 'state terror'. It presents the repertoire of procedures used by the repressors in 'disappearing' the bodies of political victims. It furthermore presents the strategic principles and technical activities deployed by the Grupo de Investigación en Antropología Forense (Forensic Anthropology Research Group; GIAF) of Uruguay's public university (UdelaR) in its search for and discovery of, and the examination and identification of, the bodies of disappeared detainees.

Of particular interest here is a discussion of the scientific procedures and the protocol used to ensure family members, judges, and citizens gain greater access to searches that bring a good chance of a discovery being made, a reliable identification, and a proper examination of the causes of death. Adopting scientific methods was consistently found to be the most appropriate way to address the many practical problems of the investigation. This was particularly the case when it came to dealing with misinformation that was often passed on to researchers to mislead their search activities.

The goal was to support the justice system in its cases and investigations by clearly addressing the issues involved and assessing the evidence in each case. We moreover wanted to help with rescuing and developing a social memory, as well as help to find material foundations for hypotheses relating to what is a little-understood period of Uruguay's recent history. It was necessary to design the research around specific case-by-case, problem-by-problem approaches that were capable of producing empirical examples to go with each hypothesis and existing testimony. Until 2005 all accounts and explanations of the fate of disappeared detainees remained speculative and were beyond the scope of any strategy to verify them.

The roots of political violence in the River Plate region

To understand the atrocities of the Uruguayan dictatorship (1973–84) one must take into account its different antecedents, which contributed to the political violence that took place in the River Plate region in the second half of the twentieth century and further developed its particular characteristics. Violent social practices in this region have an ancient cultural significance, and they brought their own rhythm to the area's long-term historical processes.

Acts of genocide, mass graves, clandestine grave sites, and the destruction of bodies form part of a strategy that we know from archaeological and ethnographic research has existed in this region since the first millennium BC.[3] A full repertoire of violent pre-Columbian practices that included scalping, displaying severed heads (as trophies), cannibalism, and the dismemberment of bodies has been recorded in research from the field of prehistory[4] and from ethnographic studies of the eighteenth through to the twentieth century.[5]

Significant levels of violence and social conflict emerged among the pre- and proto-historic peoples living in the lowlands of eastern Uruguay, western Argentina, and southern Brazil in tandem with new economic structures that were linked to population growth, a move towards a sedentary lifestyle, and more territorial behaviour.[6]

Furthermore, peoples from Amazonia (the Arawak and Guarani) began arriving in the region from the first millennium BC, creating conflict with and resistance from local populations (the Timbus, the Charrúa, and the Minuane). When the first Spaniards and Portuguese arrived in the region in the sixteenth century they noted a conflict between the peoples inhabiting the coast and those who not long before had been forced inland.[7]

In 1686 the Indian Lorenzo Tiembla Tierra (Lorenzo Earth-Shaker), who led a revolt against the Spaniards of the village of Santo Domingo de Soriano, was tried and executed in a way intended to serve as an example to others.[8] His body was dismembered and his head, arms, legs, and torso were displayed at the different routes that led to the city of Buenos Aires.[9] During the war with Paraguay in the second half of the nineteenth century thousands of African slaves were sent to front-line battalions. The Balkanization of the Spanish colonies that gave rise to the new nation-states of Argentina, Uruguay, and Paraguay was also a period of very violent civil wars, with ears and heads cut off, throats slit, as well as torture and mass executions.[10]

The main socio-historical contradiction of not just the Spanish and Portuguese colonies of the seventeenth, eighteenth, and nineteenth centuries but also of the nineteenth-century independence processes was identified by creole intellectuals of this region of South America as a dialectic crisis 'between savagery and barbarism'.[11] Indigenous, African and, creole (gaucho) forms of resistance were criminalized as illegitimate behaviour that was above all a product of the primitiveness of indigenous and African life.

For centuries there was a profound social crisis involving economic and political tensions that were strongly linked to the 'colonial order'. The colonial order was also characterized by daily political and social violence against Indians and African slaves. It was controlled by colonial institutions and the Catholic Church. Authoritarian and deterrent practices provoked a strong reaction from creoles who sought independence. The civilizing role of Christian religion and morality and the heavy hand of the conquerors were the key tools for making the savages of South America 'submit' to the Faith.[12]

Both interpersonal and collective violent practices are part of contemporary South America's oral tradition and collective imagination. The arrival of immigrants and the birth of the first labour unions in the early twentieth century led to new conflicts and the police disappearing some anarchists.[13]

Another more recent but critically important antecedent for understanding violence in this region was the foreign policy of the United States in Latin America, which considered the region to be its 'backyard'. During the twentieth century the United States developed a geopolitical approach based on an interest in the strategic value of certain places (Panama) and, above all, of a wide range of natural resources. During the Cold War and following the Cuban Revolution this process was accompanied by a military presence on the ground, and often the training of army officers and local police forces.

Larger numbers of American security consultants arrived during this era, in particular to help the government with confronting guerrilla forces. This cooperation resulted in the Uruguayan police developing specialisms and technical expertise in interrogating political prisoners.[14] It was also responsible for the emergence of a Death Squad that was supported by the CIA, as well as the beginnings of disappeared detainees, some years before the 1973 coup.[15] The Uruguayan police's usual, 'manual' application of torture was replaced by procedures involving the application of electrical instruments such as the famous 'prod', which were intended to deliver better results and inflict fewer marks, both on the bodies of political detainees and on public opinion.[16] The contemporary chapter of mass political violence begins with the events of 1968 and definitively comes to the fore in 1973, with coups in the region (Brazil in 1964, Argentina in 1964 and 1975, Chile in 1973, and Uruguay in 1973) consolidating army hegemony over the forces of repression. This change also created a new territorial scope for 'state terrorism', an extension of the population at which it was directed, and the setting up of a new logistical structure for it. All this would lead to an increase in the number of people who were tortured and killed. Soldiers trained by the United States in its military's School of the Americas, located in Panama, would learn counter-revolution and counter-information techniques.[17] They would also develop personal ties with other soldiers from neighbouring countries (Argentina, Brazil, Paraguay, and Chile), thus making it easier to implement regional coordination of repression. These supranational repressive mechanisms, which included a range of criminal activities that reached across the entire Southern Cone, would become known as Operation Condor.

Mass murder's pressing problem: the fate of the bodies

Over the course of the period of political repression and dictatorship, the treatment of victims' bodies followed different procedures. It must firstly be said that many of the disappeared political detainees were subject to harsh and systematic torture following their arrival in clandestine prisons. Systematic torture had begun some years earlier, resulting in guerrillas attacking and killing police officers and soldiers belonging to the Death Squad in 1972.[18] Systematic torture ordered by the military (and the guerrillas' violent response to it) caused political violence to spiral.

The first method used by the military dictatorship to manage corpses was returning the bodies to families while forbidding them to open the coffins to see them. This method was used between 1973 and 1974. In some cases families opened coffins and got a second expert forensic opinion.[19] This method was abandoned shortly after the coup. It was in this period that the systematic disappearing of political detainees began. The first disappeared detainees were opponents who were accused of being members of guerrilla groups, academics, trade unionists, or members of the communist parties.

As in Argentina, in Uruguay bodies were thrown into the sea and lakes. This included some bodies being thrown into the water along with stones and weights to prevent them resurfacing. In 1974 dozens of bodies thrown overboard by the Argentine air force began to reach the Uruguayan coast. It became a public issue, and the military authorities announced that they were the bodies of 'Oriental' sailors killed at sea. In central Uruguay, a body that had been cast into the Rincón del Bonete Lake also surfaced and was found.[20]

Between 1974 and 1981 political prisoners were 'transferred' and loaded onto military aircraft that had no destination at the Curbelo airbase (Maldonado) and Carrasco Airbase No. 1 (Montevideo).[21]

Between 1971 and 1974 bodies were left – or rather left out in the open – in the street. Leaving out savagely tortured and murdered bodies served as a deterrent and was a message to the enemy. This method was the first used by the Death Squad (which was made up of policemen, soldiers, and far-right civilians). In 1975, in response to the execution of the Uruguayan military attaché in France, seven bodies of Uruguayan disappeared detainees in Argentina were left, displaying signs of torture, in a small town close to Montevideo.[22]

The different methods of treating the bodies of the disappeared detainees each had a deliberate communicative effect and a semiology linked to the circumstances and events of each point in the conflict.

As a result of dozens of bodies of disappeared detainees from 'death flights' washing up on Uruguayan beaches in 1974, the dictatorship was forced to deal with dozens of bodies that had resisted being definitively disappeared. This situation led to a new form of concealment: anonymously depositing bodies in cemeteries under the classic label of 'unidentified'. This method was used both on bodies coming from the sea and also for others that had been subjected to different acts of violence. This episode of bodies of disappeared detainees failing to completely disappear reached the beaches of the River Plate region between Colonia and Montevideo and Maldonado.[23] Bodies were also recovered from the Atlantic Ocean between Punta del Este and the Brazilian border (Garzón, Rocha, Castillos, Cabo Polonio, Los Moros, and La Coronilla).[24]

As political repression became established in barracks, the most widespread method of concealing bodies began: that of burying bodies under military installations. In various barracks, though particularly in Battalion No. 13 (Instrucciones/Montevideo) and Battalion No. 14 (Toledo/Canelones) different places began to be set up where disappeared-detainee bodies were clandestinely gathered and began to accumulate.[25] In the paratrooper Battalion No. 14 this activity resulted in a clandestine military cemetery that soldiers called 'Arlington', apparently after the national cemetery in Arlington, Virginia. The bodies of detainees killed under different circumstances started to be taken to this location.

In 1983 (and until 1985) at the same time that democracy returned, and as a result of agreements between military figures and politicians,[26] the military began to look for bodies that had been clandestinely buried with the intention of exhuming them.[27] This process, known as Operation Carrot, was extended with different outcomes to various burial sites. The process was an organized one, involving planning and the use of machinery, as well as the participation of the military, which some years before had committed the crimes.

The aim of the operation was to make any skeletal remains permanently disappear. To this end the Engineers Battalion carried out the job, either by hand or with machines.[28] According to the reports that the military handed over to the Presidency of the Republic and the Peace Commission in 2004, all bodies appeared to have been burned and the remains thrown into the Bay of Montevideo.[29] However, the excavation works carried out by the GIAF managed to locate some bodies that the military had reported as destroyed during the operation.[30]

The archaeological work carried out by the GIAF succeeded in locating several material traces of Operation Carrot, whose explanation for the fate of the human remains had been fiercely contested by the families of disappeared detainees. Two new elements come into play from 2005. Firstly, studies of aerial photography show various renovation activities on existing buildings in these places.[31] Furthermore, new information from former military figures indicated that bodies recovered during Operation Carrot could have been reburied under different military buildings. Consequently, with bodies having been recovered and reburied shortly afterwards, this provisional typology came to an end for the time being. This provisional typology is interesting from both a criminological and chronological standpoint. Studying the treatment of the bodies of disappeared detainees has a methodological value in studying the conflict and helps researchers better understand the history and circumstances of the repression that took place.

Research challenges and the concealment of bodies

The systematic concealment of bodies had different aims, depending on the period of political repression. On the one hand, the practice repudiated the plan to exterminate enemies of the regime. At the same time, it prevented traces from being found and impeded the workings of the justice system. On the other hand, the physical *disappearing* of citizens was part of an overall strategy of long-term terror.

The disappearing of opponents was gradually phased in, but came about especially with the development and implementation of Operation Condor and the increasing concern of international public opinion over human-rights violations in Uruguay. Indeed, the United Nations was aware of what was going on and demanded specific answers from the military government.[32]

The search for the bodies of disappeared detainees has represented until now a complex and long-standing problem. Its challenges have required the input of more specific disciplinary fields such as archaeology and forensic anthropology. Archaeology has allowed the pursuit of searching for and finding bodies on the back of very fragmented (and sometimes false) information. It has also been a technical challenge to carry out searches over large tracts of land where it seemed probable discoveries would be made.

At the same time, technical developments in archaeological excavations made it possible to reconstruct crime scenes and identify some of the 'patterns' of criminal behaviour. Forensic anthropology has for its part allowed the torture – and in several cases, the causes of death – of bodies to be known and understood. There were clear patterns of peri-mortem fractures to the bones of the victims (to the ribs, legs, arms, and skulls), allowing inferences and theories about the conditions endured by disappeared detainees during their clandestine confinement to be made.[33]

DNA identification has brought one of the greatest scientific and legal developments by allowing bodies to be identified without the ambiguity of other commonly used methods such as 'facial reconstruction'. Misidentifications carried out by specialized judicial forensic services in Uruguay and Chile have created a moral and ethical debate about reliable identification.[34]

Field research conducted by the GIAF has allowed the identification of a succession of operations aimed at concealing bodies under Battalion No. 13 that were carried out systematically.[35] Burials in pits dug under the barracks that were covered with lime were also concealed with concrete slabs. A training area for tanks was subsequently set up over the bodies, and eventually the whole area was carefully forested.[36]

A large amount of false information was sent to the GIAF team in an attempt to mislead its research, something which amounts to another form of active concealment, this time in the democratic era.[37] In 2004 the Peace Commission created by President Jorge Batlle heard evidence from military figures which suggested that all of the missing bodies had been exhumed (in Operation Carrot), then burned and the ashes thrown into the Bay of Montevideo or disposed of at Battalion No. 14.[38] This false information also sought to continue concealment of the bodies and discourage any further search activity being demanded by relatives.

The active and systematic concealment of disappeared detainees' bodies that was carried out by the military was the biggest challenge faced by researchers, who were also vulnerable to the opportunism of politicians. The only possible response to active concealment was therefore the development of a research strategy that was moreover systematically and scientifically sound. The fact that the team was made up of university academics gave a guarantee that new information produced would be of a high quality and based on international protocols.

Testimonies were firstly classified based on their proximity to the scenes of the crimes, while priority was given to testimonies from people directly involved in the events under analysis (burials, exhumations, etc.). Throughout the research, getting a solid foundation of information on which to carry out the work was a critical problem. This same problem had led to the failure of President Batlle's Peace Commission.

A comparative study of (1:40,000 scale) aerial photographs from between 1966 and 2005 allowed the evolution of and significant changes to the landscape of military land during different moments of the dictatorship (and after the return to democracy) to be ascertained.[39] The technical overview this offered allowed us to recognize episodes of concealment (afforestation, building construction, renovations, etc.), as well as some episodes linked to Operation Carrot, such as the felling of trees carried out to facilitate the work of the machinery of the Engineers Battalion. This line of inquiry allowed us to identify the bodies of several disappeared detainees.[40]

The first strategic step was selecting quality witness accounts (direct ones) to allow the identification and delimitation of work areas. The second step was studying the changes and modifications (alterations and renovations) made to the landscape during the period under study. This controlled observation was then followed by archaeological studies aimed at directly surveying and examining large areas. The size of the study areas was different at each battalion and ranged between 1 and 40 hectares, meaning very careful strategic planning was required in the search for human bodies. The final step was to organize a team that was suitable for and capable of pursuing appropriate research over a long period of time.

In most cases the archaeological excavation technique used was that known as the 'open area or wide area' technique,[41] which was applied to units of between 1 metre by 2 metres and 10 metres by 10 metres. Applying geophysical 'prospecting' techniques was problematic in some places because of trees and proximity to water.

Systematic excavations facilitated the uncovering of 'primary archaeological contexts' containing material elements that had been present at the crime scenes at the moment atrocities took place. This functional association of objects (clothes, coins, bags, ropes, etc.) and traces of different kinds allowed inferences about the type of atrocity to be made, as well as profiles of their perpetrators. The following different levels of analysis were carried out at the graves of disappeared detainees: (a) the location of the grave site within the battalion; (b) the skeleton and the trauma it had been subjected to; (c) the pit and the techniques and methods used to produce it; and (d) any other associated elements.

The status of scientific evidence needed to be determined on a problem-by-problem basis and in coordination with the judges, prosecutors, and judicial forensic medical examiners. Through these methods, the bodies found, the 'incidents' established through archaeological techniques and the identification of abnormalities found on bones became legal evidence relating to specific instances of violations of human rights.

The archaeological and anthropological reconstruction of 'crimes against humanity'

Over the twentieth century mass crimes show common logistical challenges that cut across their considerable cultural diversity. For those responsible for repression in Uruguay, concealment came first, making bodies and all evidence disappear, and thus repudiating the crime. The magnitude of the horrors that had been committed highlighted the inability of the military to produce a narrative that could justify the levels of violence. The disappearing, torture, and execution of detainees was to take place outside of any moral or legal system and was to be set up beyond any jurisdictional reach.

The systematic disappearing of opponents was a crime that directly affected key segments of society. The disappearing of bodies, in turn, has an impact on historical memory and human rights. There was no battle, no trial, and no witnesses. No one actually knows what really happened. Procedures initially had to be improvised when the dictatorship unleashed its violence. However, the protocols implemented by military bureaucrats eventually standardized and harmonized the military and police procedures and conduct guidelines.

Among the activities that this research was able to verify, there were numerous episodes of concealment and intentional destruction of the bodies of political opponents. This 'dirty war' sought to destroy the evidence of what really happened. There were to be no records nor data to allow a historical reconstruction. However, the combining of archaeological and anthropological techniques allowed firsthand information of a good quality to be found. This information has been of critical importance in not just explaining the violence, but also in developing working hypotheses related to historical and legal problems. Testimony from the soldiers involved is still lacking today. But working hypotheses based on scientific rigour can at least shift research towards new areas. The heuristic value and complementary nature of the different lines of work have created a basis for an interdisciplinary approach. Reciprocity between scientific perspectives can develop a specific epistemology for the study of violence that is more suited to current social needs.

The concealment of bodies occurred at different times during the period of repression, but sometimes it took on a different significance. As we have seen, the first instance of concealment occurred at the moment of a disappeared detainee's death. From 1983 another episode of concealment began. This time it was a specific and specialized operation to ensure (through a supposed pact between politicians and the military) the definitive disappearing of bodies and their remains. All this occurred on the eve of the return to democracy. These were two unique historical moments with two different political objectives, but both had in common a strategy based on disappearing. The first, of a strictly military nature, prioritized the immediate physical disappearance of the enemy. The second prioritized the destruction of historical memory and the possibilities of judicial action against the genocide.

Mass murder occurred in a geographical space in which violence was territorially divided into various specialized areas of activity: secret prisons, places of torture, clandestine graves, and also the ocean (and beaches) into which many bodies were thrown. This cartography also offered a tool through which the itineraries for disappearing bodies could be reconstructed. In this map, the non-places (*sensu* Augé[42]) are those still-unknown spaces where the remains of disappeared detainees are still concealed.

Anthropological studies of modern scenarios of this complexity benefit from the contribution of interdisciplinary university teams because they are equal to the challenges of modern science. But academics also understand the social commitments involved in using research as a tool for improving quality of life.

Although in recent years there have been significant advances in the search for bodies, it seems that they are not enough. The final resolution of these socio-historical and political problems still requires input from all those involved in them. Research challenges of the identification process emerge directly from the kind of treatment given to the bodies of missing people by the perpetrator. In Uruguay, concealment and destruction were always the principal challenges for the identification of bodies. Analysed patterns of violence and the identification of corpses are both part of the same research process, which involves historic, genetic, archaeological, anthropological, and forensic approaches.

This very accurate archaeological undertaking in Uruguay has managed to recover some of the remains of bodies buried between 1973 and 1982, later exhumed and destroyed between 1983 and 1985. The great challenge of the identification of bodies is, however, dependent on the scientific protocol to obtain DNA material from an extremely small sample of bones.

Notes

1 Translation from the author's Spanish by Cadenza Academic Translations.
2 Madres y Familiares de D., *A todos Ellos*. (Montevideo: Caligráficos. S.A., 2004); V. Martínez, *Tiempos de dictadura* (Montevideo: Banda Oriental, 2005).
3 J. López Mazz, 'Las estructuras monticulares de las tierras bajas del este de Urugua', *Latin American Antiquity*, 12:3 (2001), 231–55.
4 J. López Mazz & F. Moreno, 'El cambio social en la prehistoria de las Tierras Bajas del este de Uruguay: la visibiidad arqueológica del conflicto', in J. López Mazz & M. Berón (eds), *Indicadores arqueológicos de conflicto y violencia* (Montevideo: CISC/Udelar, 2013), pp. 19–36.
5 D. Bracco & J. López Mazz, *La insurrección del año 1686* (Montevideo: Linardi y Risso, 2006); P. Clastres, *Arqueología de la violencia* (Sao Paulo: Brasiliense, 1980).
6 J. López Mazz & D. Bracco, *Minuanes* (Montevideo: Linardi y Risso, 2009).
7 P. Lozano, *Historia de la conquista del Paraguay, Río de la Plata y Tucumán* (Buenos Aires, 1873).

8   D. Bracco & J. López Mazz, *La insurrección del año 1686* (Montevideo: Linardi y Risso, 2006).

9   *Ibid.*, p. 111.

10 J. Barrán, *Apogeo y crisis del Uruguay pastoril y caudillesco* (Montevideo: Banda Oriental, 1980).

11 J. López Mazz, 'Approche historique et culturelle à la formation sociale et à l'identité uruguayenne' (doctoral thesis, Université de Lille, 1987).

12 *Ibid.*

13 V. Martínez, *Tiempos de dictadura* (Montevideo: Banda Oriental, 2005).

14 A. Rico (ed.), *Historia reciente*, Montevideo, PNUD/MEC, 2008.

15 E. Fernández Huidobro, *La tregua armada* (Montevideo: Ediciones Vintén, 1990); Rico, *Historia reciente*.

16 Fernández Huidobro, *La tregua armada*.

17 Rico, *Historia reciente*.

18 Fernández Huidobro, *La tregua armada*.

19 Madres y Familiares de D., *A todos Ellos*.

20 *Ibid.*

21 J. López Mazz (ed.), 'Informe de actividades del Grupo de Investigación en Antropología', FHCE, Presidencia de la República, 2011.

22 A. Rico (ed.), 'Informe final del equipo de historiadores', FHCE/UdelaR, Presidencia de la República, Manuscript, 2012.

23 *Ibid.*

24 López Mazz, 'Informe de actividades', 2011.

25 Comisión para la Paz, 'Informe final', Presidencia de la República Oriental del Uruguay, 2004; A. Díaz & E. Barneix, 'Informe del ejército sobre el destino de los detenidos desaparecidos', '*Diario la República*', Presidencia de la República Oriental del Uruguay, 2005; Madres y Familiares de D., *A todos Ellos*.

26 A. Alfonso, *Encontrando a los desaparecidos* (Montevideo: Caesare, 2006).

27 Comisión para la Paz, 'Informe final'.

28 López Mazz, *Informe de actividades*, 2011; J. López Mazz (ed.), 'Informe de actividades sobre los trabajos arqueológicos de búsqueda de los detenidos desaparecidos', FHCE, Presidencia de la República, 2012.

29 Comisión para la Paz, 'Informe final'.

30 López Mazz, 'Informe de actividades', 2011; López Mazz, 'Informe de actividades', 2012.

31 *Ibid.*

32 C. Demasi, A. Marchesi, V. Markarian, A. Rico & J. Yaffé, *La dictadura cívio-militar Uruguay 1973–1985* (Montevideo: Banda Oriental, 2009).

33 López Mazz, 'Informe de actividades', 2012.

34 R. Cáceres, 'Chile, operación retiro de televisores: desaparecer a los desaprecidos', in A. Zarankin, M. Salerno & M. Perosino (eds), *Historias desaparecidas* (Córdoba: Encuentro Grupo Editor, 2012), pp. 61–78; J. López Mazz, 'Archaeology of historical conflicts, colonial oppression and political violence', in A. Gonzalez-Ruibal & G. Moshenka (ed.), *Ethics and the Archaeology of Violence* (London: Springer, 2015).

35   J. López Mazz (ed.), 'Informe de actividades del Grupo de Investigación en Antropología Forense', Presidencia de la República, 2005; López Mazz & Bracco, *Minuanes*.
36   López Mazz, 'Informe de actividades', 2005.
37   *Ibid.*
38   Comisión para la Paz, 'Informe final'.
39   López Mazz, 'Informe de actividades', 2005; López Mazz, 'Informe de actividades', 2011; López Mazz, 'Informe de actividades', 2012.
40   *Ibid.*
41   E. Harris, *Principios de estratigrafía arqueológica* (Barcelona: Crítica, 1991).
42   M. Augé, *Les non lieux* (Paris: Éditions du Seuil, 1992).

Bibliography

Alfonso, A. *Encontrando a los desaparecidos* (Montevideo: Caesare, 2006)
Augé, M., *Les non lieux* (Paris: Éditions du Seuil, 1992)
Barrán, J., *Apogeo y crisis del Uruguay pastoril y caudillesco*, 3 vols (Montevideo: Banda Oriental, 1980)
Bracco, D. & J. López Mazz, *La insurrección del año 1686* (Montevideo: Linardi y Risso, 2006)
Cáceres, R, 'Chile, operación retiro de televisores: desaparecer a los desaprecido', in A. Zarankin, M. Salerno & M. Perosino (eds), *Historias desaparecidas* (Córdoba: Encuentro Grupo Editor, 2012), pp. 61–78
Clastres, P., *Arqueología de la violencia* (São Paulo: Brasiliense, 1980)
Comisión para la Paz, 'Informe final', Presidencia de la República Oriental del Uruguay, 2004
Demasi, C., A. Marchesi, V. Markarian, A. Rico & J. Yaffé, *La dictadura cívio-militar Uruguay 1973-1985* (Montevideo: Banda Oriental, 2009)
Díaz, A. & E. Barneix, 'Informe del ejército sobre el destino de los detenidos desaparecidos', '*Diario la República*', Presidencia de la República Oriental del Uruguay, 2005
Fernández Huidobro, E., *La tregua armada* (Montevideo: Ediciones Vintén, 1990)
Harris, E., *Principios de estratigrafía arqueológica* (Barcelona: Crítica, 1991)
López Mazz, J., 'Approche historique et culturelle à la formation sociale et à l´identité uruguayenne' (doctoral thesis, Université de Lille, 1987)
López Mazz, J., 'Archaeology of historical conflicts, colonial oppression and political violence', in A. Gonzalez-Ruibal & G. Moshenka (ed.), *Ethics and the Archaeology of Violence* (London: Springer, 2015), pp. 71–87
López Mazz, J., 'Las estructuras monticulares de las tierras bajas del este de Uruguay', *Latin American Antiquity*, 12:3 (2001), 231–55
López Mazz, J., 'Indicadores antropológicos y arqueológicos de violencia política en Uruguay (1973-1984)', in J. López Mazz & M. Berón (eds), *Indicadores arqueológicos de conflicto y violencia* (Montevideo: CISC/Udelar, 2013), pp. 209–22

López Mazz, J. (ed.), 'Informe de actividades sobre los trabajos arqueológicos de búsqueda de los detenidos desarpeecidos', Facultad de Humanidades y Ciencias de la Educación, IMPO, Presidencia de la República, Uruguay (Montevideo, 2005)

López Mazz, J. (ed.), 'Informe de actividades sobre los trabajos arqueológicos de búsqueda de los detenidos desarpeecidos', Facultad de Humanidades y Ciencias de la Educación, IMPO, Presidencia de la República, Uruguay (Montevideo, 2008)

López Mazz, J. (ed.), 'Informe de actividades sobre los trabajos arqueológicos de búsqueda de los detenidos desarpeecidos', Facultad de Humanidades y Ciencias de la Educación, IMPO, Presidencia de la República, Uruguay (Montevideo, 2011)

López Mazz, J. (ed.), 'Informe de actividades sobre los trabajos arqueológicos de búsqueda de los detenidos desaparecidos', Facultad de Humanidades y Ciencias de la Educación, IMPO, Presidencia de la República, Uruguay (Montevideo, 2012)

López Mazz, J. & D. Bracco, *Minuanes* (Montevideo: Linardi y Risso, 2009)

López Mazz, J. & F. Moreno, 'El cambio social en la prehistoria de las Tierras Bajas del este de Uruguay: la visibiidad arqueológica del conflicto', in J. López Mazz & M. Berón (eds), *Indicadores arqueológicos de conflicto y violencia* (Montevideo: CISC/Udelar, 2013), pp. 19–36

López Mazz, J. & M. Berón (eds), *Indicadores arqueológicos de conflicto y violencia* (Montevideo: CISC/Udelar, 2013)

Lozano, P., *Historia de la conquista del Paraguay, Río de la Plata y Tucumán* (Buenos Aires, 1873)

Madres y Familiares de D., *A todos Ellos* (Montevideo: Caligráficos. S.A., 2004)

Martínez, V., *Tiempos de dictadura* (Montevideo: Banda Oriental, 2005)

Rico, A. (ed.), *Historia reciente* (Montevideo, PNUD/MEC, 2008)

Rico, A. (ed.), 'Informe final del Equipo de Historiadores', Facultad de Humanidades y Ciencias de la Educación/UdelaR, IMPO/Presidencia de la República, 4 vols (Montevideo, 2005)

Rico, A. (ed.), 'Informe final del Equipo de Historiadores', Facultad de Humanidades y Ciencias de la Educación/UdelaR, Presidencia de la República, unpublished manuscript (2011)

Rico, A. (ed.), 'Informe final del Equipo de Historiadores', Facultad de Humanidades y Ciencias de la Educación/UdelaR, Presidencia de la República, unpublished manuscript (2012)

5

State secrets and concealed bodies: exhumations of Soviet-era victims in contemporary Russia[1]

Viacheslav Bitiutckii

Introduction

This chapter discusses the search for, exhumation, and identification of the remains of victims of mass political repression during the Stalinist Great Terror (1937–38) in the USSR. It does not consider those who died in the concentration camps and prisons of the Gulag system, but concentrates rather on those who were subjected to the severest form of repression, that is, those who were shot following sentencing during judicial or extrajudicial processes.

Such sentences were, as a rule, carried out in the place where the investigation had occurred and the sentence was passed, i.e. in those cities that had prisons where the people under investigation could be held. In particular, these tended to be administrative centres at the district, regional, or republic level.

The need to conceal the facts and the locations of these unlawful executions, combined with their large scale during the years of the Great Terror, when in a single night several dozen or even several hundred people might be killed, led to the creation of a network of unmarked burial pits into which the corpses of the executed were thrown, and then covered over.[2] These pits are known to be widespread, a fact corroborated by the accidental discovery of such mass graves in many regions of the former Soviet Union. There were many discoveries during the periods of *glasnost'* and *perestroika* at the end of the 1980s. The best known of these are: the Butovo and

Kommunarka cemeteries in the Moscow region, the Levashosvkii religious sanctuary and Kovalevskii forest in the St Petersburg region, the Kuropaty rocks near Minsk, the village of Bykovnia near Kiev, the Rutchenkovskoe field in Donetsk, Piatikhatki in Kharkov, Zolotaya Gora in Chelyabinsk, Kolpashevskii ravine near Tomsk, and the Medvedevskii forest near Oryol.[3]

As such, it is unsurprising that in 1989 such burial pits were discovered in the Voronezh region and in Voronezh itself. Voronezh was the administrative centre of the 6-million-strong Central Black Earth region of the Russian Soviet Federative Socialist Republic, which existed between 1928 and 1934, 500 kilometres to the south of Moscow. Within the modern-day boundaries of the region, such burials are to be found in the regional centres of Boguchar, Bobrov, Borisoglebsk, Ostrogozhsk, and Novokhopersk. However, to date, only in Boguchar and Voronezh have any burial pits been opened and remains exhumed.[4]

In the Voronezh region, a memorial zone in the small village of Dubovka marks the main location in which the remains of victims shot during the period of political repression and mass state terror have been discovered and exhumed. Dubovka is located 35 kilometres from the city centre, in its Zheleznodorozhnyi region, in the urban district of Somovo. Between 1989 and 2013, sixty-two pits were opened. From these, the remains of 2,890 people have been exhumed and reburied in the memorial zone.[5]

In the early 1990s, the remains of victims of repression were disinterred from pits in the city of Bobrov. No attempt at research was made and the remains were conveyed to dedicated ground outside the city, where a monument now stands. In 1989, in the village of Podgornoe (which stands within the city limits of Voronezh) two pits were discovered, from which the remains of sixty-nine people were disinterred.[6] In June 2007, in Boguchar in the south of the Voronezh region, five pits were opened, from which the remains of twenty-one people were disinterred. They were reinterred on 3 August 2007, in the city's public cemetery.[7]

As this then shows, the scale of work done in Voronezh is sufficiently impressive to be worthy of our attention in this chapter.

The discovery of mass graves at in Voronezh and the investigation of their contents

For the sake of brevity, we will consider issues of searching for, disinterring, identifying, and reinterring remains disinterred from concealed burial pits all to be aspects of exhumation, thus giving the latter term a broad construction.

Ever since the collapse of Soviet power in the USSR and the beginning of democratization, those events have been the constant object of public attention, being among the most important events in the twentieth-century history of the country. Political and legal assessments of the communist terror plus the question of how to destalinize society were the subject of unceasing discussions between their respective supporters and opponents.

However, in this instance, it is to a great extent the 'technical' side of the matter that will be of most interest; in particular, the following questions:

- Why – to what end were the exhumations carried out, and how were their results then used?
- Who – who was the driving force behind the exhumations, and who carried them out?
- How – how did the exhumations occur? What techniques were used in searching for, disinterring, and identifying the remains of victims of political repression in Voronezh?

These questions are closely interlinked, and answering them will prove easier by following an outline of what, and when it, happened.

Seventy-five years ago, during the so-called Great Terror, the Politburo of the Central Committee of the Communist Party issued a decree dated 3 July 1937 and entitled 'On Anti-Soviet elements', which was signed by Stalin. There followed an operational order made by the then head of the People's Commissariat for Internal Affairs (the law enforcement agency of the Soviet Union, hereafter NKVD), Nikolai Ezhov, introducing a simplified judicial process to be implemented by the troikas on the ground. This ushered in a period of mass murder, in which as many as several dozen people could be shot over the course of a single night.[8]

By far the largest proportion of victims in Voronezh were shot in the cellars of the NKVD building in the centre of the city. Their corpses were secretly transferred to specially selected sites outside the city, and thrown into pits. One such site was hilly, sandy, and in places marshy, being part of the flood-plain of the River Usmanka, which adjoins the territory of NKVD training camps in the village of Dubovka. In the early 1950s, these sites were planted with pine forest, which formed a natural camouflage for burial pits containing the bodies of several thousand people.[9]

These burials remained secret for fifty years. In 1989, several residents of the village of Somovo wrote to a local newspaper describing how in February 1938 they had witnessed bodies being dumped into a pit somewhere near Dubovka. Journalists picked up on the story, and ran a campaign calling for the Voronezh mass graves to be investigated.[10]

On 3 August 1989, a group consisting of local newspaper correspondent V. M. Kotenko, deputy chief of the Committee for State Security (KGB) A. K. Nikiforov, searchers from an organization called Rif (Reef), the local historical museum in Voronezh, and members of the civil organization Memorial, together with I. A. Tekutev, one of the original witnesses, examined the forest at Dubovka. On 6 September 1989, the first pit was discovered by searchers from Rif.[11]

Clearly, the 1989 discovery of human remains in this area necessitated their disinterment in the interests of an investigation, and so an exhumation in the narrow sense of the word took place. For precisely this reason, on 9 September 1989, in the presence of a great number of journalists, as well as Voronezh region KGB officers and members of interested civil organizations (namely Rif and Memorial), the pit discovered on 6 September was opened and the remains of forty-two people were removed.[12]

On 13 September 1989, A. V. Kosyakin, an investigator from the State Prosecutor's Office in the Zheleznodorozhnyi region of Voronezh, examined the material pertaining to the discovery of these human remains in the forest near Somovo. The nature of the gunshot wounds (without exception, these were to the back of the head) pointed clearly to the cause of death being execution. Analysis of shell-cases found in the pits established that some of them were designed for the 1895 pattern 7.62 calibre Nagan revolver, and that all of them were made in the Tula ammunition factory no later than 1936.[13]

Incontrovertible proof of the fact that the victims of mass Stalinist terror discovered were peaceful residents, ordinary Soviet citizens, came from the fact that the Somovo district was not occupied during the war. Furthermore, the nature of clothing and footwear remnants ruled out the possibility that this might be a military burial site, such as for prisoners of war who had died of their wounds in hospital or the like. Indeed, the most widespread finds were of rubber overshoes from small manufacturers, which were worn over felt boots or leather shoes in rain and snow. There was a variety of shoes, including women's shoes, home-made footwear, and even bast sandals.[14]

Since there were indications that a crime had been committed at the sites which had been examined, the investigator concluded that a criminal investigation should take place, which he proposed to pursue himself, and that preliminary enquiries should begin. After this, the searches and excavations were on an official footing, although they took place with active public support, from members of Rif, the local historical museum and Voronezh Memorial, joined by teaching staff from Voronezh State University and a large group of employees from the Voronezh regional history museum. By 18 October 1989, eleven pits had been discovered.[15]

Given the large scale and public importance of the investigation, on 2 November it was handed over to the Voronezh Regional State Prosecutor's Office, where it was taken up by senior investigator V. D. Likhachev on 20 November. The investigation had as its objectives: to establish the causes and circumstances of death; to establish the particular crimes committed; and to identify those responsible.

A Voronezh KGB inquiry established that 252 personnel from the Voronezh region NKVD were directly implicated in signing off and carrying out unlawful sentences of capital punishment, death by shooting: investigators, warders, administrative staff, drivers, and others.[16] Investigations and evidence further suggested that twenty-seven former NKVD personnel were directly implicated in the actual shootings. But, as the investigator declared, '8 of these are dead, while the location of 18 is unknown'. For this reason, the case was closed.

Of the ninety-seven former NKVD personnel in the Voronezh region who may, as a result of the nature of their role, have known the burial locations of those who had been shot, ten had died. The whereabouts of sixty-six were unknown. Seven were questioned, with no result, while questioning of the others 'proved impossible due to their advanced age and poor health'. Charges were not brought against anyone following the death of those responsible, and on 14 June 1992 the criminal investigation into the mass burials discovered in the Somovo region was closed 'due to the absence of perpetrators'.[17]

Nonetheless, the investigations that followed the exhumations established the burials as arising from the execution of victims of political repression by NKVD organs in Voronezh during the Great Terror of 1937–39.[18] This carried great socio-political importance during a period in which Soviet dictatorship was being overthrown in the USSR. As the investigation continued, information was received about the existence of similar secret burial sites in other cities in the Voronezh region: Borisoglebsk, Boguchar, and Bobrov. The lack at that time of documentary evidence supporting the fact of mass executions in the provinces greatly increased the role of exhumation in the formation of public awareness of the methods of governmental control to which the communists had resorted. And this can be understood as one of the purposes behind the exhumation of the victims of political repression.

Meanwhile, digging continued. By the end of 1989, eleven pits had been discovered, and the remains of 465 people had been disinterred. Voronezh city council decree no. 174-R, dated 23 June 1990, entitled 'On the conduct of work connected with investigations into the mass executions of people between 1930 and 1950' not only allowed such excavations to continue, but also obliged public institutions to provide transport, tools, and materials for such work.[19] At the same time, council decree no. 276, dated 16 September 1990, created a commission to organize a commemorative rally and the reinterment of the remains of victims of political repression.

The first reinterments took place on Saturday 13 October 1990. Through the efforts of regional and city commissions for the restoration of justice for the victims of political repression, and of the general public, 437 people were reinterred. They were interred in coffins which were lowered back into the pits from which the remains had been exhumed. Memorial plaques were placed on the burial mounds, bearing the inscription 'Here lie the remains of 437 people'.[20]

The ceremony was accompanied by a large-scale commemorative rally and an Orthodox service amidst a great throng of people. Metropolitan Mefodija of Voronezh and Lipetsk attended, while the city and regional leadership were represented by A. N. Tsapin and I. M. Shabanov, respectively.

Work in Dubovka continued in 1990 and 1991, overseen by the young and energetic deputy chairman of the city council, B. A. Artemov. At his suggestion, on 6 November 1991, the city council created a temporary committee for the commemoration of the victims of mass repression, to be headed by Artemov himself. At the same time, the scientific research and investigative group Memorial was created, working directly on the excavations in Dubovka. The group was joined by members of Rif; by the legal expert I. M. Porokhnevich, deputy head of the search team centre; by regional history museum staff N. V. Dushutin and A. V. Kirianov; by engineer K. A. Ratushnyi and by students from Voronezh State University. On October Days in 1991 and 1992, the burial ceremonies were repeated. By this stage, in all, twenty-four pits had been opened, and the remains of 924 people had been exhumed.[21]

Disillusionment with the results of the country's experimentation with democracy in the middle and late 1990s led to diminishing public interest in criticizing the communist regime and commemorating its victims. The exhumations in Dubovka ceased. Questions as to the whole point of the exercise took on exaggerated importance.

However, after a delay of fourteen years, in 2006, digging resumed. To a great extent, this was linked to the ousting of communists from positions of authority, and the arrival in office as the governor of the Voronezh region of V. G. Kulakov, who, as unlikely as it sounds, was a former head of the NKVD; also to the ascendance of Metropolitan Sergei of Voronezh and Borisoglebsk, who ran the diocese, and likewise the appearance in post of a conscientious secretary to the regional administration's commission for the restoration of rights to rehabilitated victims of political repression: the dynamic V. A. Sych. At his initiative, and with the active participation of search organizations and Memorial, on 4 August 2006 the remains of 255 people,[22] exhumed from six pits, were reinterred in tombs in the newly created Alley of Sorrow, in the central section of the memorial zone.

On that same day, at the burial site, Metropolitan Sergei blessed the foundation stone of a chapel to be built in memory of the blameless victims of execution. In all, in 2006, the remains of 399 people were exhumed from nine pits and reinterred.[23]

In autumn 2007, thanks to the efforts of the civilian search organizations Brig and Don,[24] and with the untiring participation of Memorial, the remains of 336 people were disinterred from six pits in Dubovka. The name of one of the innocent victims was established. This was a priest, I. A. Dukhovskoi, born in 1887. A document pertaining to his arrest that by some chance had been preserved and then discovered in the pit allowed the names of forty-seven other people shot alongside him on 17 December 1937 to be established.[25] In this manner, one of the tombs in Dubovka ceased to be anonymous.

On 8 August 2008, 206 people found their final resting places in three graves, and a further eighty-nine did so on 30 October, 2009. On 30 October 2010, the date which had been officially designated back in 1991 as the date of commemoration for the victims of political repression, 238 people were buried, while a further 170 were buried on 18 August 2011. Their total number now stood at 2,362.[26]

The forest fires of the hot summer of 2010 did not bypass the memorial zone. The fire passed along a strip from the main road to the Usmanka River, a tributary of the River Don. The great majority of the graves, including the Alley of Sorrow, remained practically untouched. But several pits were revealed on the site of the burnt forest, which had taken on the look of a lumber yard. The majestic forest had been transformed into an ugly wasteland of burnt tree stumps and timber waste, useless for building with.

The future of the memorial zone, which is a unique historical monument to the Stalin era, is a cause for serious concern. Following its transformation into a lifeless timber desert, it faces being chopped down. This process has already begun. And yet there are dozens of unmarked mass graves here remaining to be discovered. What will happen on the plots of land that have been hived off from the forest? In whose ownership will they end up? Is economic activity not likely to destroy this sacred place of commemoration of the victims of repression? These questions remain unanswered.

The opening of three pits in 2010 was marked by a grisly record: the remains of sixty-four, eighty, and as many as ninety-four people in the last, were disinterred from them. Work in 2011 was carried out in accordance with the 'Memory' project, drawn up by the Voronezh city commission on restoring the rights of the victims of political repression, and agreed with the corresponding Voronezh regional government commission, with input from the historical and patriotic association Don and from the civic organization Voronezh Memorial. The plan for this year was not only to exhume remains from several pits that had been located, but also to establish the boundaries of the entire memorial zone – no easy task, but of the utmost importance if the cemetery is to receive official status as a historical monument. The first part of the work was completed: the Don association excavated five pits in the memorial zone, from which the remains of 170 people were exhumed. By this stage, in total, fifty-three pits had been discovered, and as of 18 August, the remains of 2,362 executed prisoners had been reinterred.[27]

In 2012, that same Don association, led by M. M. Sigodin, and Voronezh Memorial worked together on the excavation of seven burial pits, from which were exhumed the remains of Voronezh residents shot by the Voronezh NKVD during the Great Terror. As usual, items associated with day-to-day existence in prison were recovered from the pits: mugs, toothbrushes, remnants of rotted clothes and footwear. Also, several dozen shell-cases, buttons, and small Orthodox crosses of the executed. But one particular find can only be described as curious – a rusty Nagan revolver in its holster. Most likely, it belonged to one of the executioners.

In one of the pits, a crumpled, half-rotted sheet of paper was discovered. This was a copy of a search report, filled out during the arrest and given to the person who was subsequently executed. The printed text on the paper fragment can be easily made out (it transpires printer's ink lasts very well), in particular, the headline of a table, which reads 'Description of items, valuables and documents'. There was also a fragment which read 'Everything is correctly listed in the warrant, and has been read to us, in attestation of which, we sign', followed by the signatures of witnesses.[28] It can be asserted with some confidence that the first name of the condemned began with the letter 'M'. This could greatly ease the search for the full name of the victim, by comparing the recovered fragment with the original document, which will be in the archived dossier on the as-yet unidentified victim. However, the fact that the archive of such dossiers is closed will not allow this identification work to proceed.

On 30 October 2012, the remains of a further 320 martyrs were laid to rest following an Orthodox ceremony. The overall total of people interred, in sixty tombs, now reached 2,681. Finally, 2013, saw the recovery of a further 208 sets of remains, to be interred in October. The total has now reached 2,890. A grim new record of 108 people in one pit has been set.[29]

Such is the story of how this unique memorial cemetery came to exist, while still not having official status or clear perimeters, nor yet even a fence.

Techniques used in searching for and opening burial pits: removing, researching, and identifying objects and reinterring human remains

Even the brief description of events surrounding the exhumation of the victims of political repression in Voronezh allows us to begin formulating answers to the questions posed earlier, namely: why? To what end were the exhumations carried out, and how were their results then used? Who? Who was the driving force behind the exhumations, and who carried them out? How? How were the exhumations carried out? What techniques were used in searching for, recovering, and identifying the remains of victims of political repression?

Searching for pits is done using the very simplest of apparatus to inspect the 6 square kilometres of the memorial zone, namely: two right-angled lengths of 3-millimetre-diameter aluminium wire ('dowsing rods'), and flexible steel probes which are 8 millimetres in diameter and 2 metres in length. The searcher holds one dowsing rod in each hand, in a loose pistol grip. Places where the soil density changes can be established by observing their behaviour, suggesting the existence of sites where a burial pit may potentially be located. Further exploration of the site is done using the probe, which penetrates the upper layer of the soil until it comes into contact with a skeleton. The presence of any remains, the depth at which they lie, and the extent of the pit is established by listening for characteristic sounds and by the sensation of hardness of the object with which the probe has made contact. Further checks are made by means of an inspection shaft: two ditches running at right angles to each other are dug down to the depth at which the upper layer of remains lies. After this, it is possible to embark on the opening of the pit.[30]

Notwithstanding the primitive nature of the techniques just described, they almost never lead to errors being made. We do not know of a single instance when the probe has indicated the presence of a pit, only for this not to be corroborated by the presence of human remains. A different matter is the possibility of overlooking unmarked burial pits, and it must not be assumed that all pits in the zone explored up to now have been completely accounted for.

We are undertaking attempts to establish the positions of pits using aerial photographs of the memorial zone, taken by German reconnaissance aircraft in 1942 and now held by the National Archives and Records Administration in New York.

Once it is clear that there are remains, the searchers begin to remove the top layer of soil, and to extract tree stumps. Then begins the gradual removal of skeletal remains and other objects (fragments of clothing and footwear, and the day-to-day objects of prison life: mugs, spoons, combs, toothbrushes, soap dishes, coins, cigarette holders and pipes, etc.). Small metallic objects are recovered from the soil with the aid of a metal detector.

Skeletal remains are photographed and analysed with the aim of identifying bullet wounds in the skull. The number of executed people in the pit is calculated according to the quantity of thigh bones.

Identifying individuals is only possible if fragments of documentation are discovered. Such cases have occurred; however, they are exceptionally rare. And so we have begun attempts to develop a method of group identification, i.e. to associate the contents of burial pits with individuals named in lists of those condemned.[31] For such identification to be possible, it is necessary to determine the gender and age of the executed through features of the skeleton, which can in principle be done as part of medical/judicial post-mortem examinations. On the other hand, it is necessary to have access to the execution lists, but these are held in archives which are closed to us. It is also necessary to have knowledge of the regulations governing executions, and the transportation of corpses.

Given these conditions and, perhaps, a little good will, in those situations where the executions and burials involved groups of people, hope may be preserved that the 'curse of anonymity' might one day be lifted from the memorial cemeteries of the victims of political terror. This applies to the memorial cemetery in the village of Dubovka.

The implications of the graves for contemporary Russian society

From the point of view of legality and due process, any report of crime, and still more the discovery of human remains, demands investigation in order to establish the identity of the person, the cause of death, whether there are any clear signs of crime, and whether, in the interests of justice, a criminal investigation should be launched.

However, in the context of contemporary Russia, which is still searching to discover the direction its future development will take, the exhumation of victims of repression at the hands of the previous regime has special significance for both the public and the leadership in the country. The faith in the rightness and ideals of communist ideology that was implanted in the minds of Soviet citizens, along with the idealization of the actual communist past and the significant effort to draw a veil over its darker sides, transforms exhumation into a political act aimed at enabling a deeper understanding of the historical processes of the past. The exhumation of burial pits containing the victims of mass communist terror and the creation of a memorial cemetery to the victims allows us to put a completely different slant on the words of Mayakovsky in his poem 'To Comrade Nette – the steamship and the man':

> Communism on paper seems dreary,
> All sorts of old nonsense gets printed.
> What you did gives sudden life to dry theory:
> The true nature of Communism unstinted.[32]

In the awareness of the burial pits, the poet's panegyric to individual belief in the communist idea turns its monstrous side to us, a side which has become impossible to conceal or deny, no matter which theoretical tracts might be resorted to. Linked with this aim is also the goal of forming objectivity in the public's memory of past events, in particular of communist terror, as a real consequence of the use of extrajudicial violence as a means of exerting state control.

It should likewise not be forgotten that the results of exhumations can act as primary sources for further historical research into the Great Terror, and, given the continuing lack of access to archives, they are in fact often the sole sources. In the Russian context of continued secrecy surrounding the burial sites of executed victims of political repression, and constant resistance from the relevant state institutions to their archived material being used for research into this matter, exhumations are almost the sole source of data available when researching issues around the mass imposition of capital punishment during the years of the Great Terror. By way of illustration, when conducting searches for burial sites in the Voronezh region, searchers have been unable to consult any documents at all, relying instead exclusively on the testimony of a handful of witnesses and their own experience of surveying and inspecting potential sites where the remains of executed victims may be concealed.

On the other hand, the results of the exhumations have posed many questions to the researchers, such as, for example, how secrecy was maintained around the executions given the necessity of large-scale earth-moving and transportation operations in order to bury the victims; how it was that objects have been discovered in the mass graves which could not have been in the cells of the accused. One example of such objects is a large silver cross discovered in one of the pits.[33]

Despite the exceptionally rare nature of those instances where a set of remains has been identified or the exact name and place of burial of an executed victim has been established, we still cannot deny the significance of such outcomes for the relatives of the deceased.

There is also an ethical and moral imperative to exhumation, linked to the awareness of the need to return human remains to the earth in accordance with the customs and creeds that obtain in society. In particular, in Russia, the tenets of Orthodoxy that have taken root dictate that an unmarked pit may not be considered a proper place of burial for an Orthodox Christian, and that any remains within one require reinterment with all due ceremony, which in turn requires exhumation.

For twenty-three years in a row, now, on the Russian day of commemoration for the victims of political repression, 30 October, memorial services have been held at the Dubovka cemetery. These are organized by the city administration with the help of the clergy, of Voronezh Memorial, and with support from search teams, civic organizations, Cossack associations, students at the military aviation institute, Voronezh cadets, and with the participation of relatives of the deceased and of other victims of political repression. And every year, on 30 October, everyone in whom the memory of repression is still alive – the now-adult children and grandchildren of the tortured and executed, members of Memorial, schoolchildren, and students – all gather at the Spartak cinema in Voronezh, from where they set out for Dubovka to take part in the sombre reinterment ceremony, and in the rally commemorating the victims of political repression. And this, too, is to be understood as one outcome of the searches and exhumations.

As is clear from what has been said, from 1989 to the present, the driving force behind the exhumation and reinterment of the victims of political repression has undoubtedly been democratic society: journalists, civic groups and repressed people's organizations, and search organizations, including Voronezh Memorial. It is on these groups that the city and regional administrations rely, providing public funds for them to conduct searches, exhumations, and reinterments. Annual expenditure on these activities does not exceed 500,000–700,000 roubles ($20,000–25,000). No more than 40 per cent of this amount goes on search and exhumation work.[34]

Regarding the organization of the reinterments, transportation for the participants in the rally at Dubovka is provided by the Voronezh city administration. The memorial plaques on the tombs are made possible by funds from the regional budget. Technical help with the organization of the reinterments comes from the Somovo district management committee, and public utility services in the city of Voronezh. The ceremonial aspect of the reinterment is overseen by the Voronezh diocese of the Russian Orthodox Church.

The people actually conducting the searches for the unmarked burial pits are members of civilian organizations, whose main focus is searching for the remains of soldiers from both the Soviet army and the enemy army who were killed during the Second World War and remained where they fell on the battlefield. These organizations include those mentioned earlier: the diving and search club Rif, which was actively involved in the search for burial pits between 1989 and 1992; the Voronezh city youth organization Brig took part in searches and excavations until 2010. After this date, such work has been done exclusively by the historical and patriotic search association Don, a Voronezh regional civic organization, and the Centre of Search Technology. None of these organizations is professional, although they possess both the necessary permits and plenty of experience in conducting searches and exhumations. They are focused on the search for victims and places of interest from the war of 1941–45, and so digging for the victims of political repression is not one of their regular activities. The Don association has its own premises where discovered items can be preserved and exhibited.

Between 1989 and 1992, the Voronezh regional history museum took an active part in the excavations, collecting and exhibiting finds from burial pits.[35] Unfortunately, the museum has in effect ceased to take an active role following the resumption of digs in 2006. A regular participant on a voluntary basis is the Voronezh city historical and educational organization Memorial. Its aims include observing and describing excavations, and publishing information gained as a result of the digs, as well as archival work on findings from previous excavations.

The future for the Dubovka memorial zone and the excavations' legacy

What are the outcomes and the prospects for further searches, exhumations, and identifications in the memorial zone we have been describing?

The Dubovka memorial zone has transformed into a unique memorial cemetery for the victims of political repression in Russia. The significance of such historical places for commemorating victims of political repression in central Russia is indisputable. According to both researchers and searchers there still remain at least several thousand more people buried in the region in unmarked pits. It should be borne in mind that in the 1930s, Voronezh region also included the Tambov, Lipetsk, Kursk, and Belgorod regions. Voronezh was, in the 1930s, a place of exile for many figures who had been repressed for political reasons, including those exiled from the Central Asian republics, Georgia, and Armenia.[36] Those on Stalin's lists of condemned people found their final resting-place here: Party members, Soviet officials, and economic managers in the Central Black Earth region, as well as members of the intelligentsia, from both arts and sciences, plus thousands of ordinary workers from the villages and towns of the region.

Meanwhile, despite the efforts of the Voronezh region the proper ratification of the Dubovka cemetery's status as a historical monument has proven impossible: the scale of the work required for this is too large: there needs to be a thorough search made, using modern search methods, in order to conclusively discover all the burial pits and to reinter all the remains found within. By this means, the precise boundaries of the memorial zone will be established, which will provide a solid justification for removing cemetery land from the property market and transferring it into the care of appropriate institutions.

The land assigned for the memorial cemetery must be given a suitable appearance. A border fence is vital. The tombs should be renovated, and then maintained in an appropriate manner. A structure should be erected within the cemetery on which the names of the executed can be read.

Furthermore, the natural destruction and neglect of the memorial zone (from forest fires and construction work on commercial and private residential buildings) is leading to the loss of a unique monument to the victims of political repression in central Russia.

Judging by the experience of the past twenty-three years, it seems that this outcome can only be avoided if Dubovka is included in the list of Russian memorial sites which are supported by the 'Federal Programme to Commemorate the Victims of Political Repression'.[37] Following a presidential decree, under the auspices of this programme, a working group on historical memory is being developed within the Russian President's council for the development of civil society and human rights. A proposal to include Dubovka in this programme has been made to the working group by Voronezh Memorial and the Voronezh regional government. And we hope that the publication of this chapter will further increase the likelihood that this monument to the victims of communist terror will be added to the list of sites supported by that federal programme.

Notes

1 Translation from the author's Russian by Dr Ian Appleby.
2 M. Iunge, G. Bordiugov & R. Binner, *Vertikal' bol'shogo terrora* (*The Great Terror Vertical*) (Moscow: Novyi Khronograf, 2008); A. G. Tepliakov, *Protsedura ispolneniia smertnykh prigovorov v 1920–1930-kh godakh* (*Execution Procedure in the 1920s and 1930s*) (Moscow: Vozvrashchenie, 2007).

3 A list of monuments to the victims of political repression. Database 'Pamiatniki zhertvam politicheskikh repressii na territorii byvshego SSSR' (Monuments to the victims of political repression on the territory of the former USSR), The Andrei Sakharov 'Peace, Progress and Human Rights' Museum and Social Centre. www.vainahkrg.kz/e/2382177-spi-sok-pamyatnoikov-zhertv-politrepressiy (accessed 17 February 2014).

4 A. N. Akin'shin, V. I. Bitiutckii, O. G. Lasunskii & K. B. Nikolaev (eds), *Obnaruzhenie skhronov v VO: Politicheskie repressii v Voronezhe. Putevoditel'* (*Discovering Mass Graves in the Voronezh Region. Political Repressions in Voronezh: A Guide*) (Krasnoyarsk: PIK 'Ofset', 2011); V. I. Bitiutckii, 'Kak rasstrelivali na rodine vozhdia mirovogo proletariata' (How they used to shoot the leader of the international proletariat in his homeland), 'Postskriptum' (Postscript), *Voronezhskii kur'er* (Voronezh Courier), no. 122 (2619), 30 October 2007, p. 3.

5 A. N. Akin'shin, V. I. Bitiutckii, O. G. Lasunskii & K. B. Nikolaev (eds), *Politicheskie repressii v Voronezhe* (*Political Repressions in Voronezh*) (Krasnoyarsk: PIK 'Ofset', 2011).

6 *Voronezhskii kur'er* (Voronezh Courier), 'Tikhii 'Don' vershit bol'shie dela' (The 'Don' may flow quietly, but serious matters are afoot), no. 130 (1276), 19 November 1998.

7 Bitiutckii, 'Kak rasstrelivali na rodine vozhdia mirovogo proletariata', p. 3.

8 *Operativnyi prikaz NKVD SSSR No. 00447 ob repressirovanii byvshikh kulakov, ugolovnikov i antisovetsuikh elementov* (USSR NKVD Operational Order No. 00447: The repression of former kulaks, criminals and anti-Soviet elements), 30 July 1937, in *Lubianka: Stalin i GUGB NKVD 1937–1938: Documents.* 'Democracy' International Fund (Moscow: Materik, 2004), pp. 273–81.

9 Akin'shin *et al.*, *Politicheskie repressii*.

10 V. M. Kotenko, 'Kakoi les khranit tainu?' (Which forest conceals a secret?), *Kommuna* (The Commune), Voronezh, 7 July 1989.

11 Akin'shin *et al.*, *Politicheskie repressii*, p. 129.

12 *Ibid.*, p. 129.

13 *Ibid.*, p. 130.

14 B. K. Bukharina, *Ushel v bessmertie* (*Departed into Immortality*) (Moscow: Iuridicheskaia Literatura, 1991).

15 Akin'shin *et al.*, *Politicheskie repressii*, p. 134.

16 *Ibid.*, pp. 129–30.

17 *Ibid.*, p. 134.

18 *Ibid.*, pp. 129–31.

19 *Ibid.*, p. 134.

20 E. Timofeeva, 'Upokoi, Gospodi, ikh dushi ...' (Oh Lord, grant peace to their souls ...), *Voronezhskii kur'er* (Voronezh Courier), 17 October 1990, no. 20, p. 1; I. Skorikov, 'I bezvinnaia korchilas' Rus'' (And innocent Russia writhed in pain), *Molodoi kommunar* (Young Communard [newspaper]), no. 124 (9466), 16 October 1990, p. 1; W. Millinship, 'Peace at last for Stalin's victims', *Observer*, 14 November 1990, p. 15.

21 V. G. Glebov, *Konveier smerti voronezhskogo Upravleniia NKVD* (*The Voronezh NKVD Execution Conveyor Belt*) (Voronezh: Voronezhskaia oblastnaia tipografiia, 2012), pp. 79, 311.
22 *Ibid.*, p. 84.
23 V. I. Bitiutckii, *Voronezhskie stalinskie spiski. Kniga pamiati zhertv politicheskikh repressii Voronezhskoi oblasti* (*Stalin's lists in Voronezh. The Book of Remembrance for the Victims of Political Repression in the Voronezh Region*), vol. 2 (Voronezh: Tsentr dukhovnogo vozrozhdeniia Chernozemnogo kraia, 2007), p. 231.
24 Glebov, *Konveier smerti voronezhskogo Upravleniia NKVD*, pp. 79, 311.
25 Akin'shin *et al.*, *Politicheskie repressii*, p. 147–50.
26 Glebov, *Konveier smerti voronezhskogo Upravleniia NKVD*, pp. 78, 311.
27 Akin'shin *et al.*, *Politicheskie repressii*, p. 138.
28 V. I. Bitiutckii, 'Zhertvy terrora' (The victims of terror), *Voronezhskii kur'er* (Voronezh Courier), no. 121 (3360), 27 October 2012, p. 3.
29 V. I. Bitiutckii, 'Dubovka. God 2012. Bez imeni, bez granits, bez ogrady' (Dubovka in 2012: No name, no border, no fence), *30 Oktiabria* (30 October), no. 109, MOO Memorial. 2012–13, p. 8.
30 Akin'shin *et al.*, *Politicheskie repressii*, pp. 163–8.
31 E. Iu. Sadovskaia & E. A. Tolokonnikov, 'Metod gruppovoi identifikatsii ostankov zhertv massovykh rasstrelov' (A method for the group identification of the remains of mass shooting victims), in *Korni trav* (*Grass roots*) (Moscow: Zven'ia, 1996), pp. 176–84.
32 V. V. Mayakovsky, *Sochineniia v 3-kh tomakh* (*Selected Works in Three Volumes*), vol. 2 (Moscow: Khudozhestvennaia Literatura, 1970), p. 67.
33 B. K. Bukharina, *Ushel v bessmertie* (*Departed into Immortality*) (Moscow: Iuridicheskaia Literatura, 1991), p. 249.
34 G. Poltaev, 'Poterpevshie pretenzii ne imeiut' (The victims have no complaints), *Voronezhskii kur'er* (Voronezh Courier), no. 81 (2877), 23 July 2009, p. 2.
35 The participation of Voronezh Region Memorial in digs in 1991–92. E. Timofeeva, 'O tekh, kto tam lezhit na dne ovraga' (About those who lie at the bottom of the ravine), *Voronezhskii kur'er* (Voronezh Courier), no. 12, 5 September 1990, p. 5.
36 T. G. Kuderina-Nasonova & L. D. Kuderina, *Nedalekoe proshloe* (*The Recent Past*) (Moscow: obshchestvo Feniks, 1994), p. 296.
37 'Sobranie zakonodatel'stva Rossiiskoi Federatsii', 2012, No. 1 (Collected Legislation of the Russian Federation, 2012, No. 1). *Rasporiazhenie Prezidenta Rossiiskoi Federatsii ot 27 dekabria 2011 g. N 819-rp 'Ob obrazovanii rabochei gruppy po podgotovke predlozhenii, napravlennykh na realizatsiiu programmy uvekovecheniia pamiati zhertv politicheskikh repressii'* (Russian Federation Presidential Directive dated 27 December 2011, No. 819-gr: 'On the creation of a working group to design proposals for the implementation of programmes to immortalise the memory of the victims of political repression'), p. 89.

Bibliography

Akin'shin, A. N., V. I. Bitiutckii, O. G. Lasunskii & K. B. Nikolaev (eds), *Obnaruzhenie skhronov v VO: Politicheskie repressii v Voronezhe. Putevoditel'* (Krasnoyarsk: PIK 'Ofset', 2011)

Akin'shin, A. N., V. I. Bitiutckii, O. G. Lasunskii & K. B. Nikolaev (eds), *Politicheskie repressii v Voronezhe* (Krasnoyarsk: PIK 'Ofset', 2011)

Bitiutckii, V. I., 'Dubovka. God 2012. Bez imeni, bez granits, bez ogrady', *30 Oktiabria*, no. 109, MOO Memorial, 2012–13

Bitiutckii, V. I., 'Kak rasstrelivali na rodine vozhdia mirovogo proletariata. Postskriptum', *Voronezhskii kur'er*, no. 122 (2619), 30 October 2007

Bitiutckii, V. I., *Voronezhskie stalinskie spiski: Kniga pamiati zhertv politicheskikh repressii Voronezhskoi oblasti*, vol. 2 (Voronezh: Tsentr dukhovnogo vozrozhdeniia Chernozemnogo kraia, 2007)

Bitiutckii, V. I., 'Zhertvy terrora', *Voronezhskii kur'er*, no. 121 (3360), 27 October 2012

Bukharina, B. K., *Ushel v bessmertie* (Moscow: Iuridicheskaia Literatura, 1991)

Glebov, V. G., *Konveier smerti voronezhskogo Upravleniia NKVD* (Voronezh: Voronezhskaia oblastnaia tipografiia, 2012)

Kotenko V. M., 'Kakoi les khranit tainu?', *Kommuna*, Voronezh, 7 July 1989

Kuderina-Nasonova, T. G. & L. D. Kuderina, *Nedalekoe proshloe* (Moscow: obshchestvo Feniks, 1994)

Iunge, M., G. Bordiugov & R. Binner, *Vertikal' bol'shogo terrora* (Moscow: Novyi Khronograf, Moscow, 2008)

Mayakovsky, V. V., *Sochineniia v 3-kh tomakh*, vol. 2 (Moscow: Khudozhestvennaia literatura, 1970)

Millinship, W., 'Peace at last for Stalin's victims', *Observer*, 14 October 1990

Operativnyi prikaz NKVD SSSR No. 00447 ob repressirovanii byvshikh kulakov, ugolovnikov i antisovetsuikh elementov, 30 July 1937, in *Lubianka: Stalin i GUGB NKVD, 1937–1938: Documents*. 'Democracy' International Fund (Moscow: Materik, 2004)

'Pamiatniki zhertvam politicheskikh repressii na territorii byvshego SSSR', Database, The Andrei Sakharov 'Peace, Progress and Human Rights' Museum and Social Centre, www.vainahkrg.kz/e/2382177-spisok-pamyatnoikov-zhertv-politrepressiy (accessed 17 February 2014)

Poltaev, G., 'Poterpevshie pretenzii ne imeiut', *Voronezhskii kur'er*, no. 81 (2877), 23 July 2009

Sadovskaia, E. Iu & E. A. Tolokonnikov, 'Metod gruppovoi identifikatsii ostankov zhertv massovykh rasstrelov', in *Korni trav* (Moscow: Zven'ia, 1996)

Skorikov, I., 'I bezvinnaia korchilas' Rus'', *Molodoi kommunar*, no. 124 (9466), 16 October 1990

Sobranie zakonodatel'stva Rossiiskoi Federatsii, 2012, No. 1. *Rasporiazhenie Prezidenta Rossiiskoi Federatsii ot 27 dekabria 2011 g. N 819-rp 'Ob obrazovanii rabochei gruppy po podgotovke predlozhenii, napravlennykh na realizatsiiu programmy uvekovecheniia pamiati zhertv politicheskikh repressii'*

Tepliakov, A. G., *Protsedura ispolneniia smertnykh prigovorov v 1920–1930-kh godakh* (Moscow: Vozvrashchenie, 2007)

Timofeeva E., 'O tekh, kto tam lezhit na dne ovraga', *Voronezhskii kur'er*, no. 12, 5 September 1990

Timofeeva, E., 'Upokoi, Gospodi, ikh dushi …', *Voronezhskii kur'er*, no. 20, 17 October 1990

Voronezhskii kur'er, 'Tikhii 'Don' vershit bol'shie dela', no. 130 (1276), 19 November 1998

6

A mere technical exercise? Challenges and technological solutions to the identification of individuals in mass grave scenarios in the modern context

Gillian Fowler and Tim Thompson

Introduction

The identification of individuals from mass grave contexts is a difficult process which is made more challenging by a variety of taphonomic and situational variables, such as cause of death, number of bodies present, disturbance of the grave, climatic conditions, and the time since death. Clothing, personal effects, and type of burial have traditionally been used as an identification tool where the victims are recognized by family members and identified in the field; a practice that is frequently used in Latin America. Commingling of human remains is a common occurrence in large mass graves. Here an added challenge is that these burials are often 'open context cases' where the list of actual victims is unknown and the search for families of the dead has to be conducted on a national and sometimes international level. This is especially difficult in situations where populations have been displaced or disappeared by the state and records remain classified or unobtainable. An additional complication is the issue of body parts that cannot be identified and, therefore, cannot be returned to the family, which has societal repercussions on national reconciliation policies. Further, it is imperative to identify the victim group if charges of genocide are being pursued.

Forensic scientists, including anthropologists, have been exploring the potential of new methods and processes in the resolution of such contexts. The introduction of DNA to contexts where these challenges exist has had some success in the Balkans and in Guatemala, two areas that have experienced brutal civil wars for a number of years. More recently, the analysis of elemental and osteometric measures on the body have demonstrated potential in attempts to reassociate remains. Ultimately however, technological developments complement extensive ante-mortem investigation and the two cannot be utilized independently if the required end result is to successfully identify victims.

The search for and identification of corpses and human remains in post-genocide and mass violence contexts presents a particularly pressing aim for the twenty-first century. The interest in this work stems from a number of different sources. From an academic perspective this may include legal scholars, forensic archaeologists and anthropologists, historians, sociologists, and so on. This chapter is an example of such academic interest. From a social perspective this may include those directly affected by the violent and traumatic events that require investigating, or those with the responsibility to scrutinize such events. This chapter will focus on one particular aspect of the search and identification of corpses and human remains, namely the application of technical methods to the examination of bodily remains recovered from mass graves.

Why bother with human identification?

One of the primary issues to be addressed when investigating these contexts is the question of why to bother making the effort to identify the victims held within a mass grave. The very fact that clandestine mass graves exist means that the circumstances of the death of the victims within this context is evidence that an illicit act took place. Massacres of innocent civilians and extrajudicial executions are a violation of the Third and Fourth Geneva Conventions and Additional Protocol I which govern the proper burial, identification, and registration of those killed in conflict.[1] During an armed conflict perpetrators may attempt to hide their crimes by creating mass graves. Surviving family members can be left ignorant about the whereabouts of their loved ones and can only assume that they have been killed or are still being detained. Therefore, identifying victims of mass graves can bring closure to family members, and the very process of the investigation brings an acknowledgement of the terrible crimes that took place. Identifying victims can support prosecutions, especially if charges of genocide are sought. Article 6 of the

Rome Statute defines genocide as five acts with the intent to destroy, in whole or part, a national, ethnical, racial, or religious group. The five acts are: killing members of the group; causing serious bodily or mental harm to members of the group; imposing conditions on the group calculated to destroy it; preventing births within the group; and forcibly transferring children from one group to another.[2]

Investigation of mass graves in this context can be used as a means of creating a 'truth and reconciliation tool',[3] which may at times be linked to a sense of a state owning up to the crimes of its past. Included within this process are reparation payments to the families of victims, where the need for a positive identification and subsequent issue of a death certificate adds pressure to investigators to identify victims. Other reasons for identification may also exist. One of the consequences of the use of mass graves can be to further cause insult by effectively excluding the victims from their communities of death.[4] Thus the primary factor governing the search and identification of victims of the armed conflict in Guatemala is to bury their loved ones in cemeteries reflecting the funerary practices of the indigenous culture, a religious blend of Catholic and Mayan rituals.

The second key issue to be addressed is how these identifications are to be achieved. Technological solutions have in some cases given false hope to family members who perceive DNA technology as an all-encompassing solution. They are then disappointed if an identification is not possible, and may feel misled by the whole process. In his recent work, Francisco Ferrándiz highlights this very issue with the identification of victims of the Spanish Civil War.[5] The science of identification is fallible and care must be taken not to present these advances as a solution with a guaranteed outcome. There are numerous challenges that exist that hinder an identification being made.

Traditional approaches to identification

Before the advent of DNA technology in human rights violation contexts, identifications of human remains in mass graves were carried out using a variety of methods. The cornerstone of these presumptive identifications was extensive ante-mortem investigation and the subsequent comparison of the ante-mortem profile of a suspected victim with a post-mortem profile of a cadaver.[6] The circumstances surrounding the death of an individual was usually provided by a witness interview, and corroboration of this testimony would be sought through archaeological and anthropological evidence. An identification would then be made if the two profiles matched. Official documents can also prove to be significant here.[7] Archaeological evidence can include the type of grave and the position of the bodies within the grave, along with clothing and personal artefacts which are recognized by family members during the remains' archaeological recovery. The post-mortem description provides a biological profile (sex, age at death, height, ancestry, and dental characteristics) of the victim, which, when including any individualizing features (such as an ante-mortem injury or pathological disease that the individual may have experienced in life), can help to narrow down or confirm the identity of the victim. This emic approach to identification is often used in developing countries, where ante-mortem data is not available in the form of medical and dental records,[8] or has been subsequently destroyed.[9] Clothing and personal effects recovered within the grave are compared to descriptions of what the person was wearing when they were 'disappeared' or killed, details of which form an important stage of the ante-mortem interview.[10] Despite the passage of time, family members present when a loved one was kidnapped or killed tend to remember exactly what their loved one was wearing at the time the incident occurred. One woman who was kidnapped as a 14-year-old alongside her mother during the Civil War in Spain remembered exactly what her mother was wearing as she was driven off in a truck by paramilitary groups in 1936.[11] All of these constitute a 'traditional' identification and have their place in certain contexts where DNA analysis is not available, either through a lack of resources or because a long period of time has elapsed since the event occurred and degradation of bone inhibits successful DNA analysis.

Context is paramount, and these types of identifications can only be used in what are termed 'closed' context cases or a 'closed synchronic system' as defined by Baraybar.[12] This constitutes a finite group of victims at a single point in time and space. The situation is much more challenging in 'open' context cases where the number and identity of victims is unknown. This may occur when individuals are brought to a central place for detention purposes, may occur over a longer period of time, and may not be confined to one location. In Guatemala the largest mass graves are found within ex-military bases that served as detention and execution centres throughout the armed conflict. People were transported there from both urban (where they became more commonly known as 'the disappeared') and rural areas (where rebel groups were operating).

Challenges to the identification of individuals in mass graves

Unfortunately the very nature of a mass grave, that it involves multiple bodies, means that identification of specific individuals can be difficult. This can be a result of a number of variables, from the location and size of the mass grave to the number of bodies placed inside and whether it is subsequently disturbed.

Therefore there are a number of issues to address which derive from the actual process of identification. The first issue to consider is the quantity of remains that must be sampled before identification of an individual person can be confirmed – for example, does the identification commission require identification from just one or multiple bodily elements? This is relatively straightforward if the bodies still have considerable soft tissue present, but is more complicated if the remains are skeletonized. The identification process can be further complicated if the particular mass grave in question is an 'open' context. As noted above, this means that the identities of the individuals within the grave are unknown, and indeed the actual number of people placed there may also be uncertain. This differs from a 'closed' context in which the identities of the victims within the grave are already known, and the identification process focuses more on individual verification. Clearly the former requires greater resource investment, such as through a national campaign of DNA collection. Any investigation of mass graves requires coordinated and well-thought-out legal and institutional structures, at both regional and national levels. Examples of the problems that can occur when this is not the case abound.[13] It should also be noted that the opposite can be a hindrance, too – a multitude of influential international bodies and organizations can also bring confusion and impact the identification process.[14]

Time is a complicating factor with all of these issues. The longer the time since initial deposition, the more difficult the remains will be to identify. As Komar notes, it is not uncommon to have a significant time delay between conflict and recovery, and recovery and identification.[15] Such identification problems include the increased decomposition of the remains, the greater degree of soil activity, and the passing away of witnesses. Location of the mass grave will also be instrumental in determining the success of body recovery and identification. In their retrospective study of cases from Croatia, Šlaus et al. noted that the identification of bodies found in wells was significantly more difficult than those recovered from other contexts.[16]

Experience has also shown that different bones within a single skeleton will degrade at differing rates, further compounding the identification and recovery of individuals.[17] Ultimately, in the field, preservation of the remains correlates with the probability of positive identification.[18] Very short time periods can also be challenging, since the conflict that caused the mass grave may still be ongoing, thus making it difficult or dangerous to access the graves (as is the case in Afghanistan).

A key problem associated with multiple individuals in a single grave is commingling. This is a process where body parts from one person become associated with another. This can lead to problems when trying to determine the minimum number of individuals in a grave context and when attempting to reassociate body parts. Work in the field has shown that increased commingling of remains will cause increased problems with identification.[19] Commingling within a grave can be the result of a number of factors, such as natural processes like flooding or animal activity, or due to human intervention as a strategy to prevent identification of the remains in the future. In some contexts, intentional dismemberment was performed on the victims prior to burial[20] and this would also increase the degree and complexity of any commingling present.[21] In a similar vein, it was seen in the Balkans, for example, that large machinery was used to remove sections of graves which were then transported to different parts of the country and placed in new graves (which are termed secondary burials). Damage by large machinery, whether used to move bodies to secondary burial sites or as part of the excavation process, has also been noted as causing additional challenges associated with commingling and identification. Ensuring that bodies are composed of parts from only one individual is important for a variety of reasons, including humanitarian considerations and the success of DNA identification of the remains.[22]

It should be noted that the origins of mass graves can vary. Although they are often associated with genocide, they can also be a consequence of other forms of mass violence – such as wars[23] or criminal activity[24] – or originate from non-violent events such as mass disasters[25] or epidemics.[26] The latter examples associate mass graves with the managing of large numbers of the deceased with local resources that cannot manage the scale of event, rather than hiding the evidence of crimes. Nonetheless, subsequent identification of the deceased, perhaps to allow for more culturally appropriate funerary practices, may still be problematic. It is also worth noting here that although our focus is the mass grave context, the issues and potential solutions we discuss are also applicable to many other forensic contexts where multiple or fragmented remains are recovered.[27]

There are potentially a number of solutions to the issues and concerns discussed above. Traditionally the mass grave management process involves sorting out the osseous material (from bones) and the non-osseous material (such as debris or vegetation), removing the non-human bone and teeth, ensuring that the remains in question are indeed modern and not of archaeological origin, and then sorting the remaining skeletal material.[28] It is this sorting of skeletal material into specific and identifiable individuals that gives rise to the greatest challenges. This chapter will explore some of the more technical approaches to managing this identification of individuals from mass graves.

Technical solutions

DNA profiling

The techniques used by anthropologists to identify individuals in mass grave scenarios through traditional or classical methods and the challenges these bring have already been discussed in this chapter. The introduction of DNA technology to the identification process has certainly changed the way practitioners identify the missing. In Serbia, for example, identification rates of bodies from mass graves increased noticeably following the implementation of a thorough DNA profiling process.[29] There are two ways that DNA can be used for mass grave identifications; the first is that a DNA profile taken from a family member is used to confirm a traditional identification in a small, closed context. The second, and perhaps more important, way is to attempt a blind match between a victim's DNA extracted from soft tissue (or more frequently bone and dental samples) from exhumed remains compared against a family reference database which comprises profiles from donated buccal (mouth) or blood samples.[30]

For a number of reasons the application of DNA analysis is not always as successful as is perceived and can present severe limitations.[31] One limitation is that it is not always possible to achieve a DNA profile from bone that has gone through a lengthy process of diagenesis (the term used to describe the structural and chemical changes to bone after death). In Guatemala, some of the bone samples did not produce a workable DNA profile because of the destructive burial environment, and as a result more traditional methods of identification had to be relied upon. Another limitation is that the family must have donated a reference sample in the first instance, and be included on the database, for a match to be made. A further reason why a match cannot sometimes be made between a victim and family member is that a genealogical link does not exist in the first place. If this is the case, it is essential that social anthropologists are at the forefront of the ante-mortem investigation, because they have the skills required in dealing with sensitive situations that a DNA scientist may not possess. In another case in Guatemala, a mother and her three daughters were identified in a mass grave as members of the same family, but the fourth daughter had a different genetic profile despite the father insisting that it was his child. Social anthropologists skilled in dealing with specific cultures in this community were able to establish that the child had been 'adopted' unofficially, and that the father did not want to admit this fact in case he got into trouble with the authorities, as he had previously registered the child as his own. In his worldview she was his daughter, as he had raised her from an early age, and therefore the father's insistence is understandable. This is just one example of how DNA analysis can add a complication to already extremely sensitive issues within the community. Finally, if there are several siblings in one mass grave who cannot be individually identified through a DNA profile, a post-mortem biological profile must be relied upon if individual identification is to be achieved. In some cases, such as in Rwanda, whole families were massacred and it was not possible to trace surviving family members for DNA identification purposes.[32]

Methods employed by anthropologists to remove the soft tissues in preparation for a full anthropological examination can also have an effect on the quality and quantity of DNA recovered from a body or body part.[33] Over a period of time, soft tissue decomposes and the likelihood of obtaining usable DNA decreases as the soft tissue is compromised.[34] Eventually bone or dental tissue becomes the only tissue available from which a DNA sample can be taken. Unfortunately, it may be necessary to remove the overlying soft tissues to access this material. With this in mind, a study by Steadman *et al.* which compared ten different maceration techniques involving heat or chemical treatments on pig ribs, found that the highest yield of DNA were with methods that involved macerating at high temperatures (above 90 degrees centigrade) for short periods of time. Mitochondrial DNA (mtDNA), which is found in large numbers in the cells of the body, is less useful for unique identification (since it derives only from the maternal line and therefore is shared by all siblings), is not affected by maceration techniques.[35] A later study by Lee *et al.*,[36] this time using human lower-leg long bones and nine heat and chemical maceration methods, replicated the results found by Steadman *et al.* and concluded that of the main maceration techniques, heat treatments of high temperatures and short duration produce the highest of levels of nuclear DNA amplification.

The use of DNA for identifications in mass grave contexts has been used since the mid-1990s. Mitochondrial DNA profiles are more easily produced in ancient or degraded bones than nuclear DNA because it has a high copy number per cell.[37] However, nuclear DNA is more useful in forensic identification contexts because it is inherited from both parents.[38] In Guatemala mitochondrial DNA was utilized after an exhumation in 1992 of twelve skeletons in two mass graves.[39] Mitochondrial DNA was chosen over nuclear DNA because the victims were men and only one maternal relative to donate a DNA sample was necessary. Nine of the twelve skeletons were identified using traditional techniques, but three proved more difficult because of a lack of ante-mortem data. Only six families were willing to donate a DNA sample, and of these six, four had a common maternal lineage. In small, traditional, and isolated villages such as are found in Guatemala, with little admixture between settlements, using mtDNA may not be the best option. Since then in Guatemala, a Short Tandem Repeat (STR) population allele frequency database was created from 451 Guatemalans.[40] In the Balkans, where it was estimated that 40,000 people went missing, the first DNA-led strategy for identification was proposed and implemented by the International Commission for Missing Persons (ICMP) Forensic Science Department.[41] However, in all of these contexts, traditional techniques are still necessary to corroborate the identification.

Bone and teeth are the more reliable sources for DNA and provide higher success rates,[42] but the extraction methods are more complicated and time-consuming than for soft tissues.[43] Nevertheless, there are very real problems associated with contamination in commingling contexts. Usually, this is of greatest concern when sampling the soft tissues; however, following the tsunami in Southeast Asia it was noted that samples taken from bone tissue also exhibited contamination.[44] The source of the contamination is uncertain, especially considering that the samples were extracted from within the bone tissue rather than the surface, but putrefaction fluids or contaminated formalin preservative fluids have been suggested.[45] One way to address this issue is to clean the bones using various chemical washing solutions, UV radiation, or removal of the surface. Unfortunately, it has also been noted that this may not entirely remove the risk of contamination.[46] Nonetheless, the challenges of using DNA profiling in the field should not detract from the fact that it can be an extremely successful and potent tool for identification in commingled and mass grave contexts.[47]

Elemental analysis

The chemistry of the human skeleton has been shown to hold great potential in terms of identification and understanding our actions and activities during life. Yet despite this existing knowledge, anthropologists have been slow to apply it to the investigation and resolution of mass graves in the modern context.

One such elemental tool is the use of stable isotope analysis. This has had wide application in forensic science generally, but in terms of the study of human skeletons, is largely limited to the archaeological context. Stable isotopes are atoms of a given chemical element which vary in their number of neutrons, do not decay over geological timescales, and are subject to fractionation.[48] It is this fractionation which is useful in forensic science, since it causes slight variations in the ratios of these elements within a given material. Stable isotopic analysis therefore has the ability to help with the study of mass graves in two key ways. First, it is possible to learn information about diet and migration through changes in isotopic ratios, and this can be used to suggest the status or geographical origin of the deceased. This has been used very successfully in archaeological mass graves, such as those in Britain[49] and the USA.[50] In all of these examples it was possible to comment on the relationship between the victims and those living in the local regions associated with the mass graves. The second potential use is referred to as stable isotope profiling. In this analysis, the ratios of a number of elements are examined, not with a view to interpreting life history, but simply to create a unique chemical signature which differs from those of other individuals. Forensically this approach has already been used to study non-human evidence such as drugs, explosives, paper, and wood.[51] Stable isotope profiling would be particularly useful in cases of commingled remains where the combination of ratios for a collection of elements from one individual should differ from other bodies. Juarez has tried to address this issue in the USA and has carried out a pilot study which analysed strontium isotopes from the dental enamel of individuals originating from four states in Mexico.[52] The results demonstrated that individuals could indeed be associated with originating from distinct regions in Mexico. This research can then hopefully be applied to unidentified border crossers found on the US side of the frontier so that their remains can be identified and repatriated back to Mexico.[53]

X-ray fluorescence is a method of analysis that utilises a material's response to exposure to X-rays in order to determine the elemental or chemical composition of that material. It has been proposed as a potential solution to reassociating disarticulated remains in a mass grave context,[54] having already been used in other forensic contexts to identify bone from other non-osseous material.[55] Initial research using medieval articulated skeletons[56] has indicated that trace elemental composition differs between individuals and can be used through chemometric analysis to literally identify 'which bone' belongs to 'which person'. The idea behind this technique is to establish a method that is non-destructive, portable, easy to use, and less costly than DNA analysis – the more conventional way of reassociating remains in challenging commingling circumstances. In the first instance, individual elements were chosen which are considered to be associated with diet or physiological importance. Individual elements were successful in separating two individual skeletons but when further skeletons were included it became more difficult to differentiate between individuals. Therefore, bone element ratios have been used to differentiate between skeletons in an attempt to increase separation and reduce chemical noise. Five ratios were used: Pb/C, K/Fe, Zn/Fe, Sr/Ca, and Sr/Pb, with the most effective being Pb/Ca, Zn/Fe, and Sr/Pb.[57] One of the issues that emerged from this research was the question of whether bone diagenesis is affected by the results and whether the length of time that the bones are in contact with the soil affects the separation of the bone element ratios. In modern mass grave contexts, however, diagenesis may be less of an issue and all skeletal elements are likely to be subjected to the same elements and processes within the soil, therefore it could be possible that any variation in elemental analysis is related to the individual's diet.

Other analytical methods have also been proposed as a means of resolving commingling of skeletal remains using the elemental composition of the bones themselves. Dillane et al. have demonstrated the ability of inductively coupled plasma-atomic emission spectroscopy, a form of spectroscopy which detects trace metals in a material (when combined with subsequent discriminant analysis), to differentiate between bones of different origins.[58] This method is really designed for speciation but would prove to be particularly useful when dealing with highly fragmented remains, which can be challenging to analyse macroscopically.

Caution must be applied when using any of these elemental methods since bone will continue to exchange certain elements with its surrounding environment even after death.[59] This is problematic, as it may mean that the original elemental signature may be altered and thus no longer suitable for individualization.

Osteometric approaches

Osteometric methods of studying the skeleton rely on the application of measurements and statistics to the bones of the body, with the aim of contributing to the biological profile of the deceased, or addressing ancillary questions such as a minimum number of individuals and commingling. Crucially they are used to maximize objectivity in the study of the skeleton.[60] With regard to commingled remains, osteometric methods aim to associate body parts through the analysis of size and shape relationships of said body parts, and these methods can contribute to the resolution of complicated mass grave scenarios in a number of ways. Often the use of such measures is enhanced by the application of statistical methods, such as Principal Components Analysis and logarithmic transformations, which can provide a stronger understanding of these osteometric relationships.[61]

One of the more straightforward means of addressing commingled remains is to group left and right bones into pairs. This process works by assuming that the left and right bones of a person are essentially a mirror image. Traditionally this would be performed visually, with the anthropologist assessing size and general shape alongside other variables such as colour and degree of decomposition. More recently, this approach has become increasingly quantitative with a drive to reduce potential observer error. In 2013 Thomas *et al.* published the results of their research into pair-matching of the skeleton and introduced the new M statistic as a measure of asymmetry in the skeleton, therefore allowing one to comment on the likelihood that a pair of elements came from the same individual. They concluded that the differences between the sexes was minor, with only three of the fifty-one measures that they investigated showing signs of statistically significant sexual dimorphism.[62] This is advantageous for a method which seeks to investigate remains where biological profiling may be difficult. In addition to size differences, there are also shape-based asymmetrical differences which can be used for examining the skeleton. Although shape-based methods are currently focusing on other aspects of biological profiling, these very statistical measures should also be able to assist in cases of commingling.[63]

Asymmetry within the skeleton has been noted for a long time, and understanding the nature of this in humans is critical to resolving issues of commingled remains. Although asymmetry is in essence the difference between the left- and right-hand sides of the body, or the deviation from a mirror image, it should be noted that there are different forms of asymmetry with different aetiologies, and that the degree of asymmetry will vary between different geographic and temporal populations.[64]

Skeletal remains can also be reconstructed by assessing the articulation of adjoining elements.[65] Since adjoining bones grow and develop together and in a related manner, their size and shape should correlate to form a functioning moving joint. It should be noted that the effectiveness of this method is influenced by the fact that some articulations are anatomically tighter than others and by the presence of pathologies.[66] Research has shown that articulations with a good degree of confidence with regard to fit include the cranium and mandible, vertebrae, humerus and ulna, and the metacarpals/tarsals.[67] Low confidence can be seen, for example, with the ribs and the humerus and scapula.

One challenging aspect of the use of osteometric approaches is when dealing with fragmented remains. Indeed, Adams and Konigsberg suggest that bone preservation is the most critical limiting factor when selecting the appropriate quantitative method for sorting commingled remains.[68] Clearly the relationships discussed above still exist, but the broken nature of the bone increases the degree of inaccuracy likely to be experienced and complicates or makes impossible the measurement of the bones. Nevertheless, detailed recording of the remains *in situ* combined with delicate and careful recovery can allow the spatial relationships between fragments to be understood, thus potentially facilitating conjoining of the pieces.[69] Currently there is interest in the ability of computer software to match bone fragments together following their scanning through non-contact methods.[70] This may be a way to resolve some of the issues associated with working on fragmented bony remains.

On occasion there are additional challenges faced when attempting to decipher commingled remains and these require specific methods. An example of this is when the remains have also been burned. Here the technical approaches discussed above will likely be even more problematic to implement, since the process of burning can cause DNA to denature, may result in shifts to the elemental composition of the skeleton, and can cause shrinkage and warping of bones.[71] In resolving these issues, traditional osteological analysis is generally still of use, but some workers have also demonstrated the benefit of examining the weight of the burned remains. It has been argued that the weight of the burned remains will correlate with the number of individuals present.[72] The use of such metric measures has been applied to burned commingled remains in both archaeological[73] and forensic contexts.[74]

Conclusions

Although highly technical approaches to the identification of victims in mass graves, such as those discussed above, have real scientific potential, it has also been noted that the realities of the field may inhibit their use and application. In her reflection of the identification process in Bosnia, Komar notes that the scale of bodies to be examined combined with time pressures may negate the use of more labour-intensive methods.[75] Klonowski implies this for the same country in a later work.[76] She also adds that there are issues with the experience and training of the anthropologists in the field, and we could extend her conclusion with regard to the methods discussed here. In this situation, osteometric approaches may be preferable since they are easier and less expensive to apply,[77] yet there are times when these methods will struggle to resolve mass grave issues – which explains the more recent exploration of more technical approaches. We also acknowledge that there are other approaches to resolving these issues in mass graves than the ones discussed above, but our focus here is on more technical and quantitative methods. Nonetheless, the availability of expertise, equipment, and the necessary standards are real limiting factors in the wide-spread application of advanced analytical methods in forensic anthropology. And of course, despite the methodological developments within the discipline, there are times when complete reassociation of remains will still be impossible.[78]

Good local knowledge and witness testimony is key to a high identification rate. Although technological solutions have assisted in these efforts, effective ethnographic investigation is still the crux of any mass grave investigation. Yet this raises many questions. From an ethical perspective, is it always appropriate to investigate mass graves? We could think of this from the perspective of the local community (whose support for exhumation should not be assumed, and is discussed further below) or from that of the forensic practitioners, where the investigating bodies have an ethical duty to ensure the safety of their personnel.[79] Is there a strategy in place to deal with the remains once they are exhumed? Is the DNA-led identification process targeted correctly? The work by Ferrándiz in Spain demonstrates the problems that can occur further down the line of the investigation if this is not thoroughly considered at the start.[80] Is the solution a traditional approach corroborated by DNA or a DNA-led process that uses traditional techniques if necessary? Naturally, the answers to these questions entirely depend on the context and the legal authority of the country involved and the resources available. Further, the application of more technical identification methods in commingling contexts may be welcomed, but should balance the needs of the families as well as those of the scientists and politicians. This is more complicated than it seems, since the evidential needs of each group will vary and shift.[81] In some contexts, family members and next of kin are actively involved in the application and management of the identification methods and processes.[82] These new technical methods can be complicated and rather abstract to explain to non-experts, without the additional difficulties of applying them in the field.

We should also note, as alluded to above, that identification of the victims of mass graves is not always supported or desired. Examples exist of pressures to keep mass graves undisturbed (such as displayed in Crossland's 2002 work in Argentina) or to emphasize the broader political or community-based identities of the victims over their individual ones.[83] There are also examples of families opting to rebury their identified loved ones in a communal mass grave with the other victims with whom they were originally buried (such as in Chile).[84] In extreme cases the perpetrator of the crime may still live in the village or town. When this occurs the grave may be tampered with or 'disappeared', and the family threatened if they insist on pursuing an exhumation. One such case in Guatemala resulted in the double tragedy of the family losing their loved ones twice.

It is imperative to identify the missing for many worthy reasons, including the right to a dignified burial being a basic human condition that transcends cultures, and the will to prosecute the guilty in order to create a better future for those communities that have suffered as a result of armed conflict. However, we conclude with a note of caution which should be borne in mind before embarking on a mass grave exhumation. An identification strategy that is achievable and affordable must be in place before any soil is removed. Misidentifications must not happen, and any combination of traditional and technological techniques must work when applied in the field in order to achieve the best possible outcome and the maximum number of correct identifications.

Notes

1   E. Neuffer, 'Mass graves', in R. Gutman, D. Rieff & A. Dworkin (eds), *Crimes of War 2.0: What the Public Should Know* (New York and London: W. W. Norton, 2007), pp. 238–40.
2   W. A. Schabas, *An Introduction to the International Criminal Court* (Cambridge: Cambridge University Press, 2007).
3   F. Ferrándiz, 'Exhuming the defeated: Civil War mass graves in 21st-century Spain', *American Ethnologist*, 40 (2013), 39.
4   *Ibid.*
5   *Ibid.*
6   J. P. Baraybar, 'When DNA is not available, can we still identify people? Recommendations for best practice', *Journal of Forensic Sciences*, 53 (2008), 533–40.
7   L. Ríos, A. García, A. Rubio, B. Martínez, A. Alonso & J. Puente, 'Identification process in mass graves from the Spanish Civil War II', *Forensic Science International*, 219 (2012), e4–e9.
8   Baraybar, 'When DNA is not available'.
9   E.-E. Klonowski, 'Forensic anthropology in Bosnia and Herzegovina: theory and practice amidst politics and egos', in R. Ferllini (ed.), *Forensic Archaeology and Human Rights Violations* (Springfield, IL: Charles C. Thomas Publisher, 2007), pp. 148–69.
10   M. Djuric, D. Dunjic, D. Djonic & M. Skinner, 'Identification of victims from two mass-graves in Serbia: a critical evaluation of classical markers of identity', *Forensic Science International*, 172 (2007), 125–9.
11   Ferrandiz, 'Exhuming the defeated'.
12   Baraybar, 'When DNA is not available'.
13   Ferrandiz, 'Exhuming the defeated'; A. M. Gómez López & A. Patiño Umaña, 'Who is missing? Problems in the application of forensic archaeology and anthropology in Colombia's conflict', in Ferllini (ed.), *Forensic Archaeology and Human Rights Violations*, pp. 170–204.
14   Djuric *et al.*, 'Identification of victims'.

15 D. Komar, 'Lessons from Srebrenica: the contributions and limitations of physical anthropology in identifying victims of war crimes', *Journal of Forensic Sciences*, 48 (2003), 1–4.

16 M. Šlaus, D. Strinović, N. Pećina-Šlaus, H. Brkić, D. Baličević, V. Petrovečki & T. Cicvara Pećina, 'Identification and analysis of human remains recovered from wells from the 1991 War in Croatia', *Forensic Science International*, 171 (2007), 37–43.

17 Ríos *et al.*, 'Identification process in mass graves'.

18 M. Šlaus, D. Strinović, V. Petrovečki, D. Mayer, V. Vyroubal & Z. Bedic, 'Identification and analyses of female civilian victims of the 1991 war in Croatia from the Glina and Petrinja areas', *Forensic Science International Supplement Series*, 1 (2009), 69–71.

19 *Ibid.*

20 Gómez López & Patiño Umaña, 'Who is missing?'.

21 *Ibid.*

22 C. Garrido Varas & M. Intriago Leiva, 'Managing commingled remains from mass graves: considerations, implications and recommendations from a human rights case in Chile', *Forensic Science International*, 219 (2012), e19–e24.

23 For example, in relation to the First World War, see D. Gaudio, A. Betto, S. Vanin, A. De Guio, A. Galassi & C. Cattaneo, 'Excavation and study of skeletal remains from a World War I mass grave', *International Journal of Osteoarchaeology*, DOI: 10.1002/oa.2333 (2013); R. Howard, V. Encheva, J. Thomson, K. Bache, Y.-T. Chan, S. Cowen, P. Debenham, A. Dixon, J.-U. Krause, E. Krishan, D. Moore, V. Moore, M. Ojo, S. Rodrigues, P. Stokes, J. Walker, W. Zimmermann & R. Barallon, 'Comparative analysis of human mitochondrial DNA from World War I bone samples by DNA sequencing and ESI-TOF mass spectrometry', *Forensic Science International: Genetics*, 7 (2013), 1–9.

24 For example in Mexico, see G. Moore, 'Mexico's massacre era: gruesome killings, porous prisons', *World Affairs*, 175 (2012), 61–8.

25 The Southeast Asian tsunami, see R. Rohan, M. Hettiarachchi, M. Vidanapathirana & S. Perera 'Management of dead and missing: aftermath tsunami in Galle', *Legal Medicine*, 11 (2009), s86–s88.

26 R. Gowland & A. T. Chamberlain, 'Detecting plague: palaeodemographic characterisation of a catastrophic death assemblage', *Antiquity*, 79 (2005), 146–57.

27 See, for example, M. B. Brickley & R. Ferllini (eds), *Forensic Anthropology: Case Studies in Europe* (Springfield, IL: Charles C. Thomas Publisher, 2007); T. Delabarde & B. Ludes, 'Missing in Amazonian jungle: a case report of skeletal evidence for dismemberment', *Journal of Forensic Sciences*, 55 (2010), 1105–10; T. Delabarde, C. Keyser, A. Tracqui, D. Charabidze & B. Ludes, 'The potential of forensic analysis on human bones found in riverine environment', *Forensic Science International*, 228 (2013), e1–e5.

28 D. H. Ubelaker, 'Methodology in commingling analysis: an historical overview', in B. J. Adams & J. E. Byrd (eds), *Recovery, Analysis, and Identification of Commingled Human Remains* (New York: Humana

Press, 2008), pp. 1–6; D. H. Ubelaker & J. L. Rife, 'Approaches to commingled issues in archaeological samples: a case study from Roman
era tombs in Greece', in Adams & Byrd (eds), *Recovery, Analysis, and
Identification*, pp. 97–122.

29 Djuric *et al.*, 'Identification of victims'.

30 *Ibid.*

31 R. Ferllini, R., 'Forensic anthropological interventions: challenges in the
field and at mortuary', in Ferllini (ed.), *Forensic Archaeology and Human
Rights Violations*, pp. 122–47.

32 *Ibid.*

33 *Ibid.*

34 A. Mundorff, R. Shaler, E. Bieschke & E. Mar-Cash, 'Marrying anthropology and DNA: essential for solving complex commingling problems
in cases of extreme fragmentation', in Adams & Byrd (eds), *Recovery,
Analysis, and Identification*, pp. 285–99.

35 D. W. Steadman, L. Diantonio, J. Wilson, K. Sheridan & S. Tammariello,
'The effects of chemical and heat maceration techniques on the recov-
ery of nuclear and mitochondrial DNA from bone', *Journal of Forensic
Sciences*, 51 (2006), 11–17.

36 E. J. Lee, J. G. Luedtke, J. L. Allison, C. E. Arber, D. A. Merriwether
& D. W. Steadman, 'The effects of different maceration techniques on
nuclear DNA amplification using human bone', *Journal of Forensic
Sciences*, 55 (2010), 1032–8.

37 *Ibid.*

38 T. C. Boles, C. C. Snow & E. Stover, 'Forensic DNA testing on skeletal remains from mass graves: a pilot project in Guatemala', *Journal of
Forensic Sciences*, 40 (1995), 349–55.

39 *Ibid.*

40 M. Garcia, L. Martinez, M. Stephenson, J. Crews & F. Peccerelli, 'Analysis
of complex kinship cases for human identification of civil war victims
in Guatemala using M-FISys software', *Forensic Science International:
Genetics*, 2 (2009), 250–2.

41 L. Yazedjian & R. Kešetović, 'The application of traditional anthropological methods in a DNA-led identification process', in Adams & Byrd
(eds), *Recovery, Analysis, and Identification*, pp. 271–84.

42 Ferllini, 'Forensic anthropological interventions'.

43 R. Zehner, '"Foreign" DNA in tissue adherent to compact bone from tsunami victims', *Forensic Science International: Genetics*, 1 (2007), 218–22.

44 *Ibid.*

45 *Ibid.*

46 S. M. Edson & A. F. Christensen, 'Field contamination of skeletonized
human remains from exogenous DNA', *Journal of Forensic Sciences*, 58
(2013), 206–9.

47 Klonowski, 'Forensic anthropology in Bosnia and Herzegovina'.

48 W. A. Brand & T. B. Coplen, 'Stable isotope deltas: tiny, yet robust signatures in nature', *Isotopes in Environmental and Health Studies*, 48 (2012),
393–409; Y. Oulhote, B. Le Bot, S. Deguen & P. Glorennec, 'Using and

interpreting isotopes data for source identification', *TrAC – Trends in Analytical Chemistry*, 30 (2011), 302–12.

49 C. Chenery, G. Müldner, J. Evans, H. Eckardt & M. Lewis, 'Strontium and stable isotope evidence for diet and mobility in Roman Gloucester, UK', *Journal of Archaeological Science*, 37 (2010), 150–63.

50 S. H. Ambrose, J. Buikstra & H. W. Krueger, 'Status and gender differences in diet at Mound 72, Cahokia, revealed by isotopic analysis of bone', *Journal of Anthropological Archaeology*, 22 (2003), 217–26.

51 See, for example, S. Benson, C. Lennard, P. Maynard & C. Roux, 'Forensic applications of isotope ratio mass spectrometry – a review', *Forensic Science International*, 157 (2006), 1–22; N. Gentile, L. Besson, D. Pazos, O. Delémont & P. Esseiva, 'On the use of IRMS in forensic science: proposals for a methodological approach', *Forensic Science International*, 212 (2011), 260–71; Oulhote *et al.*, 'Using and interpreting isotopes data'.

52 C. A. Juarez, 'Strontium and geolocation, the pathway to identification for deceased undocumented Mexican border-crossers: a preliminary report', *Journal of Forensic Sciences*, 53 (2008), 46–9.

53 *Ibid.*

54 J. Gonzalez-Rodriguez & G. Fowler, 'A study on the discrimination of human skeletons using X-ray fluorescence and chemometric tools in chemical anthropology', *Forensic Science International*, 231 (2013), 1–3.

55 A. M. Christensen, M. A. Smith & R. M. Thomas, 'Validation of X-ray fluorescence spectrometry for determining osseous or dental origin of unknown material', *Journal of Forensic Sciences*, 57 (2012), 47–51.

56 Gonzalez-Rodriguez & Fowler, 'A study on the discrimination'.

57 *Ibid.*

58 S. Dillane, M. Thompson, J. Meyer, M. Norquay & R. C. O'Brien, 'Inductively coupled plasma-atomic emission spectroscopy (ICP-AES) as a method of species differentiation of bone fragments', *Australian Journal of Forensic Sciences*, 43 (2011), 297–312.

59 Dillane *et al.*, 'Inductively coupled plasma-atomic emission spectroscopy'.

60 J. E. Byrd & B. J. Adams, 'Osteometric sorting of commingled human remains', *Journal of Forensic Sciences*, 48 (2003), 717–24.

61 For example, E. Anastasiou & A. T. Chamberlain, 'The sexual dimorphism of the sacral-iliac joint: an investigation using geometric morphometric techniques', *Journal of Forensic Sciences*, 58, (2013), s126–s134; Byrd and Adams, 'Osteometric sorting of commingled human remains'.

62 R. M. Thomas, D. H. Ubelaker & J. E. Byrd, 'Tables for the metric evaluation of pair-matching of human skeletal elements', *Journal of Forensic Sciences*, 58 (2013), 952–6.

63 Anastasiou and Chamberlain, 'The sexual dimorphism of the sacral-iliac joint'; D. Franklin, A. Cardini, A. Flavel & A. Kuliukas, 'The application of traditional and geometric morphometric analyses for forensic quantification of sexual dimorphism: preliminary investigations in a Western Australian population', *International Journal of Legal Medicine*, 126 (2012), 549 58.

64 Byrd & Adams, 'Osteometric sorting of commingled human remains';
    C. Garrido Varas & T. J. U. Thompson, 'Metric dimensions of the prox-
    imal phalanges of the human hand and their relationship to side, pos-
    ition and asymmetry', *HOMO – Journal of Comparative Human Biology*,
    62 (2011), 126–43.
65 Byrd and Adams, 'Analysis of commingled human remains'; M. Cox, A.
    Flavel, I. Hanson, J. Laver & R. Wessling (eds), *The Scientific Investigation
    of Mass Graves: Towards Protocols and Standard Operating Procedures*
    (Cambridge: Cambridge University Press, 2008), pp. 174–86.
66 Byrd & Adams, 'Analysis of commingled human remains'.
67 Byrd & Adams, 'Osteometric sorting of commingled human remains'.
68 B. J. Adams & L. W. Konigsberg, 'How many people? Determining the
    number of individuals represented by commingled human remains', in
    Adams & Byrd (eds), *Recovery, Analysis, and Identification*, pp. 241–55.
69 Byrd & Adams, 'Analysis of commingled human remains'; Cox *et al.*, *The
    Scientific Investigation of Mass Graves*.
70 M. Friess, 'Scratching the surface? The use of surface scanning in phys-
    ical and paleoanthropology', *Journal of Anthropological Sciences*, 90
    (2012), 7–31; S. C. Kuzminsky & M. S. Gardiner, 'Three-dimensional
    laser scanning: potential uses for museum conservation and scientific
    research', *Journal of Archaeological Science*, 39 (2012), 2744–51.
71 T. J. U. Thompson, 'Burned human remains', in S. Blau & D. H. Ubelaker
    (eds), *Handbook of Forensic Anthropology and Archaeology* (Walnut
    Creek, CA: Left Coast Press, 2009), pp. 295–303.
72 For a discussion of this, and specific examples, see D. Gonçalves, E. Cunha
    & T. J. U. Thompson, 'Weight references for burned human skeletal remains
    from Portuguese samples', *Journal of Forensic Sciences*, 58 (2013), 1134–40.
73 Ubelaker & Rife, 'Approaches to commingled issues'.
74 M. Warren, 'Detection of commingling in cremated human remains', in
    Adams & Byrd (eds), *Recovery, Analysis, and Identification*, pp. 185–97.
75 D. Komar, 'Lessons from Srebrenica: the contributions and limitations
    of physical anthropology in identifying victims of war crimes', *Journal of
    Forensic Sciences*, 48 (2003), 1–4.
76 Klonowski, 'Forensic anthropology in Bosnia and Herzegovina'.
77 Byrd & Adams, 'Osteometric sorting of commingled human remains'.
78 Cox *et al.*, *The Scientific Investigation of Mass Graves*.
79 See, for example, the discussion of the response in Iraq, S. Cordner, R.
    Coupland, 'Missing people and mass graves in Iraq', *The Lancet*, 362
    (2003), 1325–6.
80 Ferrandiz, 'Exhuming the defeated'.
81 Z. Crossland, 'Evidential regimes of forensic archaeology', *Annual
    Review of Anthropology*, 42 (2013), 121–37.
82 See, for example, Varas & Intriago Leiva, 'Managing commingle remains
    from mass graves'; Klonowski, 'Forensic anthropology in Bosnia and
    Herzegovina'.
83 Such as in Ferrandiz, 'Exhuming the defeated'.
84 Garrido Varas & Intriago Leiva, 'Managing commingled remains from
    mass graves'.

Bibliography

Adams, B. J. & J. E. Byrd, 'Resolution of small-scale commingling: a case report from the Vietnam War', *Forensic Science International*, 156 (2006), 63–9

Adams, B. J. & L. W. Konigsberg, 'How many people? Determining the number of individuals represented by commingled human remains', in B. J. Adams & J. E. Byrd (eds), *Recovery, Analysis, and Identification of Commingled Human Remains* (New York: Humana Press, 2008), pp. 241–55

Ambrose, S. H., J. Buikstra & H. W. Krueger, 'Status and gender differences in diet at Mound 72, Cahokia, revealed by isotopic analysis of bone', *Journal of Anthropological Archaeology*, 22 (2003), 217–26

Anastasiou, E. & A. T. Chamberlain, 'The sexual dimorphism of the sacral-iliac joint: an investigation using geometric morphometric techniques', *Journal of Forensic Sciences*, 58 (2013), s126–s134

Baraybar, J. P., 'When DNA is not available, can we still identify people? Recommendations for best practice', *Journal of Forensic Sciences*, 53 (2008), 533–40

Benson, S., C. Lennard, P. Maynard & C. Roux, 'Forensic applications of isotope ratio mass spectrometry – a review', *Forensic Science International*, 157 (2006), 1–22

Boles, T. C., C. C. Snow & E. Stover, 'Forensic DNA testing on skeletal remains from mass graves: a pilot project in Guatemala', *Journal of Forensic Sciences*, 40 (1995), 349–55

Brand, W. A. & T. B. Coplen, 'Stable isotope deltas: tiny, yet robust signatures in nature', *Isotopes in Environmental and Health Studies*, 48 (2012), 393–409

Brickley, M. B. & R. Ferllini (eds), *Forensic Anthropology: Case Studies in Europe* (Springfield, IL: Charles C. Thomas Publisher, 2007)

Byrd, J.E. & B. J. Adams, 'Analysis of commingled human remains', in S. Blau & D. H. Ubelaker (eds), *Handbook of Forensic Anthropology and Archaeology* (Walnut Creek, CA: Left Coast Press, 2009), pp. 174–86

Byrd, J. E. & B. J. Adams, 'Osteometric sorting of commingled human remains', *Journal of Forensic Sciences*, 48 (2003), 717–24

Chenery, C., G. Müldner, J. Evans, H. Eckardt & M. Lewis, 'Strontium and stable isotope evidence for diet and mobility in Roman Gloucester, UK', *Journal of Archaeological Science*, 37 (2010), 150–63

Christensen, A. M., M. A. Smith & R. M. Thomas, 'Validation of X-ray fluorescence spectrometry for determining osseous or dental origin of unknown material', *Journal of Forensic Sciences*, 57 (2012), 47–51

Cordner, S. & R. Coupland, 'Missing people and mass graves in Iraq', *The Lancet*, 362 (2003), 1325–6

Cox, M., A. Flavel, I. Hanson, J. Laver & R. Wessling (eds), *The Scientific Investigation of Mass Graves: Towards Protocols and Standard Operating Procedures* (Cambridge: Cambridge University Press, 2008)

Crossland, Z., 'Evidential regimes of forensic archaeology', *Annual Review of Anthropology*, 42 (2013), 121–37

Crossland, Z., 'Violent spaces: conflict over the reappearance of Argentina's disappeared', in J. Schofield, C. Beck & W. G. Johnson (eds), *The Archaeology of 20th Century Conflict* (London: Routledge, 2002), pp. 115–31

Delabarde, T., C. Keyser, A. Tracqui, D. Charabidze & B. Ludes, 'The potential of forensic analysis on human bones found in riverine environment', *Forensic Science International*, 228 (2013), e1–e5

Delabarde, T. & B. Ludes, 'Missing in Amazonian jungle: a case report of skeletal evidence for dismemberment', *Journal of Forensic Sciences*, 55 (2010), 1105–10

Dillane, S., M. Thompson, J. Meyer, M. Norquay & R. C. O'Brien, 'Inductively coupled plasma-atomic emission spectroscopy (ICP-AES) as a method of species differentiation of bone fragments', *Australian Journal of Forensic Sciences*, 43 (2011), 297–312

Djuric, M., D. Dunjic, D. Djonic & M. Skinner, 'Identification of victims from two mass-graves in Serbia: a critical evaluation of classical markers of identity', *Forensic Science International*, 172 (2007), 125–9

Edson, S. M. & A. F. Christensen, 'Field contamination of skeletonized human remains from exogenous DNA', *Journal of Forensic Sciences*, 58 (2013), 206–9

Ferllini, R., 'Forensic anthropological interventions: challenges in the field and at mortuary', in R. Ferllini (ed.), *Forensic Archaeology and Human Rights Violations* (Springfield, IL: Charles C. Thomas Publisher, 2007), pp. 122–47

Ferrándiz, F., 'Exhuming the defeated: Civil War mass graves in 21st-century Spain', *American Ethnologist*, 40 (2013), 38–54

Franklin, D., A. Cardini, A. Flavel & A. Kuliukas, 'The application of traditional and geometric morphometric analyses for forensic quantification of sexual dimorphism: preliminary investigations in a Western Australian population', *International Journal of Legal Medicine*, 126 (2012), 549–58

Friess, M., 'Scratching the surface? The use of surface scanning in physical and paleoanthropology', *Journal of Anthropological Sciences*, 90 (2012), 7–31

Garcia, M., L. Martinez, M. Stephenson, J. Crews & F. Peccerelli, 'Analysis of complex kinship cases for human identification of civil war victims in Guatemala using M-FISys software', *Forensic Science International: Genetics*, 2 (2009), 250–2

Garrido Varas, C. & M. Intriago Leiva, 'Managing commingled remains from mass graves: considerations, implications and recommendations from a human rights case in Chile', *Forensic Science International*, 219 (2012), e19–e24

Garrido Varas, C. & T. J. U. Thompson, 'Metric dimensions of the proximal phalanges of the human hand and their relationship to side, position and asymmetry', *HOMO – Journal of Comparative Human Biology*, 62 (2011), 126–43

Gaudio, D., A. Betto, S. Vanin, A. De Guio, A. Galassi & C. Cattaneo, 'Excavation and study of skeletal remains from a World War I mass grave', *International Journal of Osteoarchaeology*, DOI: 10.1002/oa.2333 (2013)

Gentile, N., L. Besson, D. Pazos, O. Delémont & P. Esseiva, 'On the use of IRMS in forensic science: proposals for a methodological approach', *Forensic Science International*, 212 (2011), 260–71

Gómez López, A. M & A. Patiño Umaña, 'Who is missing? Problems in the application of forensic archaeology and anthropology in Colombia's conflict', in R. Ferllini (ed.), *Forensic Archaeology and Human Rights Violations* (Springfield, IL: Charles C. Thomas Publisher, 2007), pp. 170–204

Gonçalves, D., E. Cunha & T. J. U. Thompson, 'Weight references for burned human skeletal remains from Portuguese samples', *Journal of Forensic Sciences*, 58 (2013), 1134–40

Gonzalez-Rodriguez, J. & G. Fowler, 'A study on the discrimination of human skeletons using X-ray fluorescence and chemometric tools in chemical anthropology', *Forensic Science International*, 231 (2013), 1–3

Gowland, R. & A. T. Chamberlain, 'Detecting plague: palaeodemographic characterisation of a catastrophic death assemblage', *Antiquity*, 79 (2005), 146–57

Howard, R., V. Encheva, J. Thomson, K. Bache, Y.-T. Chan, S. Cowen, P. Debenham, A. Dixon, J.-U. Krause, E. Krishan, D. Moore, V. Moore, M. Ojo, S. Rodrigues, P. Stokes, J. Walker, W. Zimmermann & R. Barallon, 'Comparative analysis of human mitochondrial DNA from World War I bone samples by DNA sequencing and ESI-TOF mass spectrometry', *Forensic Science International: Genetics*, 7 (2013), 1–9

Juarez, C. A., 'Strontium and geolocation, the pathway to identification for deceased undocumented Mexican border-crossers: a preliminary report', *Journal of Forensic Sciences*, 53 (2008), 46–9

Klonowski, E.-E, 'Forensic anthropology in Bosnia and Herzegovina: theory and practice amidst politics and egos', in R. Ferllini (ed.), *Forensic Archaeology and Human Rights Violations* (Springfield, IL: Charles C. Thomas Publisher, 2007), pp. 148–69

Komar, D., 'Lessons from Srebrenica: the contributions and limitations of physical anthropology in identifying victims of war crimes', *Journal of Forensic Sciences*, 48 (2003), 1–4

Kuzminsksy, S. C. & M. S. Gardiner, 'Three-dimensional laser scanning: potential uses for museum conservation and scientific research', *Journal of Archaeological Science*, 39 (2012), 2744–51

Lee, E. J., J. G. Luedtke, J. L. Allison, C. E. Arber, D. A. Merriwether & D. W. Steadman, 'The effects of different maceration techniques on nuclear DNA amplification using human bone', *Journal of Forensic Sciences*, 55 (2010), 1032–8

Moore, G., 'Mexico's massacre era: gruesome killings, porous prisons', *World Affairs*, 175 (2012), 61–8

Mundorff, A., R. Shaler, E. Bieschke & E. Mar-Cash, 'Marrying anthropology and DNA: essential for solving complex commingling problems in cases of extreme fragmentation', in B. J. Adams & J. E. Byrd (eds), *Recovery, Analysis, and Identification of Commingled Human Remains* (New York: Humana Press, 2008), pp. 285–99

Neuffer, E. 'Mass graves', in R. Gutman, D. Rieff & A. Dworkin (eds), *Crimes of War 2.0: What the Public Should Know* (New York and London: W. W. Norton, 2007), pp. 238–40

Oulhote, Y., B. Le Bot, S. Deguen & P. Glorennec, 'Using and interpreting isotopes data for source identification', *TrAC – Trends in Analytical Chemistry*, 30 (2011), 302–12

Ríos, L., A. García, A. Rubio, B. Martínez, A. Alonso and J. Puente, 'Identification process in mass graves from the Spanish Civil War II', *Forensic Science International*, 219 (2012), e4–e9

Rohan, R., M. Hettiarachchi, M. Vidanapathirana & S. Perera, 'Management of dead and missing: aftermath tsunami in Galle', *Legal Medicine*, 11 (2009), s86–s88

Schabas, W. A., *An Introduction to the International Criminal Court* (Cambridge: Cambridge University Press, 2007)

Šlaus, M., D. Strinović, N. Pećina-Šlaus, H. Brkić, D. Baličević, V. Petrovečki & T. Cicvara Pećina, 'Identification and analysis of human remains recovered from wells from the 1991 War in Croatia', *Forensic Science International*, 171 (2007), 37–43

Šlaus, M., D. Strinović, V. Petrovečki, D. Mayer, V. Vyroubal & Z. Bedic, 'Identification and analyses of female civilian victims of the 1991 war in Croatia from the Glina and Petrinja areas', *Forensic Science International Supplement Series*, 1 (2009), 69–71

Steadman, D. W., L. Diantonio, J. Wilson, K. Sheridan & S. Tammariello, 'The effects of chemical and heat maceration techniques on the recovery of nuclear and mitochondrial DNA from bone', *Journal of Forensic Sciences*, 51 (2006), 11–17

Thomas, R. M., D. H. Ubelaker & J. E. Byrd, 'Tables for the metric evaluation of pair-matching of human skeletal elements', *Journal of Forensic Sciences*, 58 (2013), 952–6

Thompson, T. J. U., 'Burned human remains', in S. Blau & D. H. Ubelaker (eds), *Handbook of Forensic Anthropology and Archaeology* (Walnut Creek, CA: Left Coast Press, 2009), pp. 295–303

Ubelaker, D. H., 'Methodology in commingling analysis: an historical overview', in B. J. Adams & J. E. Byrd (eds), *Recovery, Analysis, and Identification of Commingled Human Remains* (New York: Humana Press, 2008), pp. 1–6

Ubelaker, D. H. & J. L. Rife, 'Approaches to commingled issues in archaeological samples: a case study from Roman era tombs in Greece', in B. J. Adams & J. E. Byrd (eds), *Recovery, Analysis, and Identification of Commingled Human Remains* (New York: Humana Press, 2008), pp. 97–122

Warren, M., 'Detection of commingling in cremated human remains', in B. J. Adams & J. E. Byrd (eds), *Recovery, Analysis, and Identification of Commingled Human Remains* (New York: Humana Press, 2008), pp. 185–97

Yazedjian, L. & R. Kešetović, 'The application of traditional anthropological methods in a DNA-led identification process', in B. J. Adams & J. E. Byrd (eds), *Recovery, Analysis, and Identification of Commingled Human Remains* (New York: Humana Press, 2009), pp. 271–84

Zehner, R., '"Foreign" DNA in tissue adherent to compact bone from tsunami victims', *Forensic Science International: Genetics*, 1 (2007), 218–22

7

Disassembling the pieces, reassembling the social: the forensic and political lives of secondary mass graves in Bosnia and Herzegovina

Admir Jugo and Sari Wastell

Introduction

In a powerful documentary film entitled *Statement 710399*, director, activist, and former employee of the International Criminal Tribunal for the Former Yugoslavia (ICTY) Refik Hodzić follows a trail of clues that he hopes will lead to the discovery of the fate of four young men (one a boy of only fifteen), who escaped the Srebrenica massacres only to be recaptured, interrogated, and later 'disappeared'. Escaping through a forest in the dark of the night, the youngest boy slips from his father's hand, and he and the other three can not be relocated by the escaping group. Once separated, the boys are later helped by a Serb family, who supply them with food, clothes, and directions – a family in whom the Serb authorities would later take a great interest. It is for this reason that the boys are interrogated when recaptured, in order to locate the family that attempted to offer them aid in their escape. The fate of the four is never fully ascertained by the end of the film, thanks to obstructive police officers (themselves still employees of the state despite their possible complicity in the wartime events the film depicts), and the families of the four young men fail in their attempt to gain some measure of closure over the loss of their loved ones.

While not an intentional narrative ploy by any means, the film offers a potent example of the ever-reassembling network of memory politics in Bosnia and Herzegovina. A legal artefact (the witness statement) acts as an entry point through which the viewer can slowly unwind a skein of closely associated human actors, legal forms, political institutions and agendas, technical practices, and material objects that create the platform for both the constitution of collective memory in the aftermath of BiH's history of mass atrocity and – as importantly – its sites of blockage. In short, it is a perfect Latourian 'actor-network'.[1]

There is probably little need to rehearse the basic tenets of actor-network theory here. Suffice to say, it is a constructivist and agency-based approach, where both human and non-human 'actants' are understood to hold similar forms of agency in networks of relational ties. These networks are fluid and performative, constantly in a state of making and remaking, and through this ongoing process of poesis, materiality and concepts, people and institutions, technologies and techniques, come together in a network of associations that demands 'the social' cannot be understood as a distinct domain of reality (in contraposition to 'the natural', for example), but exists as the 'glue' that fixes together distinct elements. That is to say, 'the social' is not a constellation of elements itself, but rather the assembling of the relational ties of heterogeneous elements.[2]

So in the case of *Statement 710399*, the viewer enters the network through a node (actant) that is both a material artefact (the particular document that is statement 710399) and a conceptual legal form – (such statements/documentation generally). The latter is a 'punctualization' of the former, a point we will return to briefly in the conclusion.[3] The document exists in relation to the actors who created it and their agendas, but also in relation to the ICTY and a particular case in which it is brought into evidence. It is fodder for Hodzić's own agenda and its lengthy network of associations, even as it is connected to the plethora of actants that surround the investigation of the events in Srebrenica in 1995 more generally – actants that include forensic techniques, political organizations, individuals and families, mortal remains, material artefacts, and most importantly for our purposes, a unique sort of post-genocidal phenomenon, *the secondary mass grave*.

This chapter aims to explore the particular agency of *the phenomenon* of the secondary mass grave in the network of associations that constitutes the contested ground of BiH's memory politics. Why might a secondary mass grave play a distinct role from a primary mass grave, and in what ways, and for whom? Through an (admittedly implicit) description of the actor-network in which these graves are embedded, and the many sorts of actants with which they are in relation, the authors will attempt to describe the precarious and shifting place of Bosnia's secondary mass graves in the country's processes of social reconciliation and peace-building.

A definition of the mass grave

Over the course of time, ever since the first excavations of mass graves, there have always been attempts at defining what constitutes a mass grave. Currently, there are several definitions and typologies of mass graves that have been put forward. Some of these definitions are based solely on the minimum number of bodies buried, while others try to define a mass grave not only by the number of bodies buried, but by the processes of creation and formation of the grave, the physical relationship between the bodies, and, especially in cases of mass graves of forensic importance, the legal and societal aspects of the burial.

The earliest definitions were given in 1987. Mant, after working on excavations of Second World War mass graves related to the Nuremberg trials, defined a mass grave rather nominally as a grave where two or more bodies in physical contact are buried together.[4] This minimal definition has more recently been reiterated by Ruwanpura et al.[5] By contrast however, Skinner defined a mass grave as one with a minimum of half a dozen bodies placed randomly and tightly together, but went on to note that the bodies were buried 'with no reverence to the individual', introducing a decidedly social aspect to the definition.[6] Skinner et al. elaborated further on Skinner's original definition, distinguishing organized group graves, in which bodies are laid out side by side, and mass graves, where placement of the bodies is disorganized and they are buried with no regard to the dignity of their disposal.[7] Of particular interest to the current discussion is the definition proffered by *The Final Report of the United Nations Commission of Experts to the Former Yugoslavia*, where a mass grave is defined as two or more individuals sharing the same permanent internment, the physical characteristics of which prevent movement of the bodies by natural elements within the grave, returning to a concern for numbers and forensics, but to the exclusion of social concerns like those intimated in Skinner's definition.[8] Whether this definition foreshadowed or even prefigured the legal and political agendas that would surround the exhumation of mass graves across the former Yugoslavia can only be a matter of speculation.

However, the concern for numbers has remained something of a constant in this naming game. Connor defined a mass grave as containing more than six bodies, admitting that her discrimination of a 'multiple burial' (two to six individuals) from a 'mass grave' was arbitrary.[9] Haglund presented a view that every grave is unique and different, and he rejected any oversimplifying definition, instead advocating for the number of bodies within the grave to define the grave itself,[10] further emphasizing the view that a 'mass, of course, means a large quantity or aggregate, usually of considerable size' and thus a 'mass grave' should be left as a relative term.[11] These definitions, as Juhl points out, implicitly exhibit the common denominator that a mass grave contains human remains in close contact, packed tightly with no regard for the dignity involved in burial[12] – perhaps even where questions of dignity (i.e., social concerns around the *modus operandi* of burial) remain unenunciated. It was predominantly in the context of a rise in the number of exhumations and excavations of mass graves involving victims of human rights abuses that authors started defining mass graves by considering the manners of death visited upon the individuals buried within the grave, as well as the legal aspects of burials.

One of the earliest definitions taking into account the legal aspects of burial is that used by Bacre Waly Ndiaye, a UN Special Rapporteur on extrajudicial, summary, or arbitrary executions. Ndiaye defined mass graves as 'locations where three or more victims of extrajudicial, summary or arbitrary executions were buried, not having died in combat or armed confrontations'.[13] This definition was later taken up by the International Criminal Tribunal for the Former Yugoslavia (hereafter ICTY) and is still in use.[14] Jesse and Skinner unified this definition with earlier ones, defining a mass grave in terms of the number of bodies (two or more), their placement within the feature (indiscriminate and deliberate), and the legal aspect of their death (extrajudicial, summary, or arbitrary executions only).[15]

Schmitt argues that these definitions are incomplete as they rely on physical and technical characteristics and proposes a holistic approach to defining mass graves be taken by considering the anthropological context of human remains within the grave as well.[16] For Schmitt, a mass grave contains remains of more than one victim which share a common trait related to the cause and manner of their death. He also went on to distinguish mass graves of forensic importance and interest (criminal mass graves), and those that are not.[17] It is very important to distinguish these graves, as not all mass graves merit forensic investigation, and not every grave is created for the same purpose. Criminal mass graves here constitute graves that are a result of a burial of extrajudicial, summary, or arbitrary executions that break international humanitarian law and human rights laws. Non-criminal mass graves are for the practical purpose of temporary storage of human remains after disasters and crises, before the remains can be properly disposed of and buried at a later date. Remains placed in these mass graves are often tagged with a specific identification reference code, as was the case with the victims of the 2004 Asian tsunami.[18]

It is important to highlight these differences in the social contexts of criminal and non-criminal mass graves. Non-criminal mass graves are places where remains are buried for temporary, but sometimes even permanent storage. These are remains of people that died as a result of natural disasters, but because of the high number of bodies involved and the sanitary conditions on the scene, they were buried in mass graves, most often after the documentation and attachment of an identifying code. If looking at earlier definitions involving 'no reverence to the individual', these graves do not qualify as mass graves in the sense with which this chapter is concerned, as in these cases it is highly important to respect the dead, and to take steps to minimize the trauma of them being buried in a mass grave that might be experienced by their families.[19] Such mass graves often become places of pilgrimage and commemoration,[20] where large numbers of people come together in their grief and mourning. Likewise, there are examples of non-criminal mass graves of individuals executed and disposed of in criminal mass graves that are later exhumed, but reburied and memorialized collectively. The social and political decision to rebury the dead together creates a very different sort of actant, to return to our previous discussion of Latour, than either the criminal mass grave or the identified and reinterred mortal remains of *individuals* reclaimed by their loved ones or families.

Doubtless, criminal mass graves are those that most divide. Mass graves in Bosnia and Herzegovina (hereafter BiH) were made for the purpose of hiding crimes committed. By their very nature, these mass graves already divide people into victims and perpetrators. The mass graves of Srebrenica, for example, are the result of ethnic genocide, and as such, articulate and materialize mutually exclusive relations of sociality between groups according to their ethnic affiliation. Thus, survivors of the victims are called upon by the grave itself to isolate, distance, and differentiate themselves from the perpetrators of the crime. The division is further exacerbated where there are attempts to obscure the past, usually through intimidation and/or the undermining of the survivors,[21] especially where efforts have been taken to keep the graves concealed, which is where the distinct social valence of secondary (and tertiary, etc.) mass graves derives. Unlike the case of non-criminal mass graves, where creators of graves and families unite in the aim to alleviate distress and pain, the social aspects surrounding criminal mass graves combine to form a set of circumstances that make creators and relatives bifurcate into two very distinct groups on opposite sides of interest with respect to these graves.

The mass graves discussed in this chapter are criminal mass graves requiring medico-legal investigation. Despite the plethora of definitions put forward, we will be using the definition provided by Skinner *et al.*, which defines them as those that contain the bodies of many persons murdered and concealed by state actors or civilians during war.[22] An important aspect of this definition is that for the first time, mass graves are viewed as also containing 'bodies that are often jumbled and incomplete'.[23] All definitions prior to this one dealt with bodies, victims, and/or individuals, definitions which imply completeness of the human remains buried. In the case of BiH, as will be shown later, mass graves, more often than not, contain partial, commingled, and/or disarticulated human remains, and this definition is especially reflective of this fact, and thus appropriate to our further discussion. It also anticipates the extent to which the mass graves under consideration in this chapter, and the mortal remains they reveal, must be understood as distinct sorts of actants in the networks that conceptualize memory and justice in the aftermath of BiH's wartime atrocity.

To find a grave

The war in BiH broke out on 1 March 1992, and included several factions. However, the main warring parties were the Army of Bosnia and Herzegovina (ABiH) against the Army of Republika Sprska (VRS) and between ABiH and the Croatian Territorial Defence (HVO). The crude rendering of the conflict thus was that ABiH represented Bosniak Bosnians (presumed Muslim), the VRS represented Serb Bosnians (presumed Orthodox), and the HVO represented Croat Bosnians (presumed Catholic).[24] Mobilization surely happened along these lines, but 'inevitable' ethnic antagonisms were more the object and *modus operandi* of the conflicts than their cause.

While outside the remit of this chapter, this vulgarized version of events disappears numerous other forms of identification that added multiple other factions to the conflicts, even as it occludes the intra-ethnic fighting that also occurred. In so doing, the overly facile account that suggests that there were three main factions that left a legacy of three histories of the conflicts becomes part of the ethno-nationalist memory politics about which we will be speaking – a form of memory management in which the international community has been entirely complicit.

The Army of Republika Srpska, in collaboration with the Yugoslav People's Army (JNA), the Ministry of Internal Affairs of Serbia, and various paramilitary units had an aim 'to implement the objective of ethnic separation by force'[25] of all non-Serbs, but mainly Bosniaks (Bosnian Muslims). The first attempts at preventing the war were undertaken as early as 1992, when Portuguese Foreign Minister José Cutiliero proposed a plan which, although providing for a sovereign Bosnia and Herzegovina, would divide it into three distinct, ethnically divided territories.[26] This agreement fell through and led to the establishment of a Bosnian Serb police force, and later, on 12 May 1992, to the formation of VRS,[27] as a separate entity from the official state military force which fought ABiH.

Throughout the conflicts, reports of grave breaches of the Geneva conventions were documented on the territory of BiH. The UN Security Council adopted Resolution 780 (1992) on 6 October 1992, establishing an impartial Commission of Experts to analyse and examine allegations of these alleged breaches and violations of international humanitarian law in the territory of Former Yugoslavia, especially in BiH.[28] After the Commission submitted their First Interim Report, the UN Security Council established the ad hoc criminal tribunal – the ICTY – on 25 May 1993 to prosecute the perpetrators of the crimes uncovered by the Commission.[29] In its Final Report, published in 1994, the Commission provided the first list of 187 alleged mass graves they had uncovered across the territories of BiH and Croatia, among others several graves in Prijedor and one grave in Srebrenica.[30]

Srebrenica, the UN safe area, fell on 11 July 1995, and men were separated from the elderly, women, and children, taken to the nearby Bratunac and were joined by thousands of men who were captured from the column of people trying to flee the area. They were kept in several locations, including a school building and an abandoned warehouse. Thousands of men were killed in 'carefully orchestrated executions' on 13 July 1995. Those not killed on this day were executed between 14 and 17 July 1995, with only a few wounded surviving and later testifying at the ICTY trials.[31] During the month of July 1995 these men were buried in mass graves throughout the Donje Podrinje area (an area around the towns of Srebrenica, Bratunac, Konjević Polje, Nova Kasaba, Cerska, and Zvornik), in an attempt by the Army of Republika Srpska to hide the crimes, especially in light of the ever-increasing presence of international reporters and investigators showing more interest in these crimes.

These mass graves might never have been found had it not been for the American CIA. After the fall of Srebrenica, the survivors started sharing stories of what they had witnessed in Srebrenica. A CIA analyst took notice and referred to overhead aerial spy images taken by US military U-2 airplanes in July 1995, and on 2 August 1995 he recognized three disturbances he identified as potential mass graves near the village of Nova Kasaba. The information was confidentially passed on to the US President at the time, Bill Clinton.[32] The then US Secretary of State, Madeleine Albright, in a closed session, presented the UN Security Council with aerial images that she claimed showed mass graves in and around Srebrenica.[33] Albright showed the UN Security Council a 'before' image of prisoners crowded in a football field, and an 'after' image revealing three areas of disturbed earth where she claimed that up to 2,700 Bosnian Muslims had been killed and buried.[34]

This revelation was originally received with scepticism, until David Rhode, a journalist for the *Christian Science Monitor*, visited the location identified by the analyst. After a two-hour search, Rhode uncovered freshly overturned earth and what he presumed to be a decomposing leg sticking out of the ground, together with empty ammunition boxes, and diplomas, photographs, and various other personal effects that he identified as belonging to 'Srebrenica Muslims',[35] finally providing evidence and support for claims of violence in Srebrenica. During the summer of 1996, the ICTY exhumation team excavated thirty-three bodies from this location from four separate graves in two fields near the village of Nova Kasaba.[36]

The use of aerial imagery in locating mass graves in BiH proved very successful. The United States authorities provided the ICTY with aerial imagery of various locations in Donje Podrinje where they had noticed soil changes indicative of possible grave locations. Through aerial photography, thirty-nine mass graves related to the 1995 Srebrenica massacre have been identified, and all of them have been excavated.[37]

Figure 7.1 Mass burial at Branjevo farm: Donje Pilica area, Bosnia and Herzegovina. Courtesy of the ICTY.

Forensic puzzle or forensics of a puzzle: groups and persons

The public discovery of mass graves led to Serb forces attempting to hide their crimes. During the months of September and October 1995, the VRS started digging up most of these mass graves, and reburying the bodies within them in several smaller graves in more remote locations, creating assemblages of related mass graves.[38]

These would become a new and even more powerful node in the network of associations and the political afterlife of the Srebrenica massacres.

VRS held their victims in several different locations in lower Podrinje. Victims were either killed at the detention centre or taken to another location and killed. After the killings they buried their victims *en masse*. These locations are marked as 'primary' mass graves as they are the original places of burial. As news of the existence of these graves broke out, the graves were dug up by heavy machinery, a process that has since been termed 'robbing', and remains were transported elsewhere. Once dug up, primary graves are known as 'disturbed' or 'robbed' primary mass graves. The location where the dislocated remains are subsequently buried is known as a 'secondary' mass grave.[39] On rare occasions these secondary mass graves have been robbed, and the remains redistributed to other locations to make a tertiary mass grave.[40] This phenomenon of robbing mass graves and the subsequent reburial of remains from within them in secondary and tertiary locations in order to hide the crimes is unique to Bosnia and Herzegovina and is not encountered, in this form, almost anywhere else.

In a forensic sense, these graves are very different, and primary graves are easy to distinguish from subsequent graves. Primary graves, generally, are characterized by including complete human remains. There might be some commingling and repositioning of remains as a result of decomposition and a lack of reverence for their deposition within the grave feature, but generally they contain complete remains and artefacts.[41] Once the grave is made, the content of a primary mass grave includes mixed natural soil from the location with inclusions of the original local soils. After a few months, during which the remains decompose naturally (leading to disarticulation of body parts as the flesh dissipates), these graves were robbed using heavy machinery, thus creating 'robbed primary mass graves'. This process destroys bodies as they become additionally disarticulated, and bones fracture and break as the machine digs the grave fill. Human remains and the grave fill are loaded onto trucks that will transport them to secondary locations, up to 50 kilometres away, initiating the process of commingling of human remains. Given such distances between graves, investigators from the ICTY's Prosecutors Office estimated that 'it would have taken at least two full nights and several trucks to move the bodies to the secondary gravesite'.[42] From the prosecutorial point of view, this process of exhumation and reinterment suggests the systematic nature of the project, the number of people and quantity of resources that would have been marshalled to conceal the crime, the possibility of using this evidence to corroborate other forms of evidence and testimony, and most importantly, the fact that the people ordering the robbing of primary mass graves knew that they had committed a crime. All of these inferences may be equally potent to the families of the victims, but the subsequent incompleteness of mortal remains when later exhumed creates new meanings for families in this network of association. Whereas the criminal proceedings might be content with the quantification of remains, an ability to establish 'command responsibility' or the presence of a 'joint criminal enterprise', and (perhaps) some evidence of the *mens rea* of the perpetrator, families might be at least equally concerned with the identification of remains and the ability to bury their loved ones as complete and reassembled – *reassociated* – remains of a person. As one of the leaders of The Mothers of Srebrenica once poignantly said: 'I did not marry a man without hands or a head. I did not give birth to sons without hands or a head. But I buried them that way.'

Fournet argues that in cases of genocide, bodies are often completely destroyed by the perpetrators so as to be unrecognizable. This is done for two reasons: to erase all traces of the crime, so as to be able to continue the destructive behaviour, but also to destroy the group as a social entity.[43] This is at the very core of what genocide is. The actual victim of the genocidal act is the group, but the group is eradicated in part or in whole through acts visited on the bodies of discrete persons. The individual and the group become mutually constitutive insofar as the burial of corpses in mass graves destroys individual identities and in so doing, denudes the victim of all belonging to any group – including the collectivity of humanity, as they become unrecognizable and unidentifiable as consummate 'once-persons'. Therefore, victims disappear as a whole, their various erasures slowly defacing and denying the existence of the 'once-group'. In the case of BiH, burial of remains in secondary mass graves can very specifically be construed as what Fournet calls *genocidal death*, a death that aims 'to destroy the existence of the victims as individual human beings, to annihilate their identities and, therefore, to erase them from both individual memories and collective memory'.[44] And yet, in the case of BiH, even as families struggle to 'presence the dead'[45] loved ones through the identification of mortal remains now made visible to the world, the real intended target of genocide – the group – re-emerges with ferocity from the very existence of the secondary mass grave.

Not only do secondary mass graves index an implicit recognition of guilt for illegal acts ordered by political and military elites, but the existence of these graves and the coordinated effort required to realize them, suggests a further story to survivors. While it is not countenanced in international criminal law, in extralegal contexts, the graves betray a great level of corporate responsibility: Enter the spectre of 'us' versus 'them' and the entrenchment of ethnic division – materialized and revealed – in the phenomenon of the grave itself. Even as the histories of individual victims become obscured by the co-mingled remains of incomplete 'once-persons' in the secondary mass grave, the very grave itself reasserts new grounds for narrative and meaning. The narrative enabled by the secondary mass grave in its network of associations tells a seemingly more invidious meta-story that encompasses discrete, individual traumas. One person can command the exhumation, removal, and reinterment of hundreds or thousands of bodies, but numerous people must enact it. In this way, secondary mass gravesites inscribe a different kind of history, not just legally for the few people who will be prosecuted for the lives taken and the mortal remains disassembled, removed, and redistributed across multiple sites, but for a society that needs to grasp the reasons and mechanisms through which such atrocities happened. Secondary mass gravesites are a confirmation that the people doing the killing and the burying, and the un-burying – not just their leaders – were aware that they were doing something wrong. This was not just war, which involves killing and is governed by its own laws. It is what Mark Osiel once termed the 'administrative massacre' of the Other.[46]

Bodies on the move: the complexity of the Srebrenica genocide

The relationship between primary and secondary mass graves has been established through various methods. Original linking of graves was conducted on the basis of evidence and artefacts uncovered during excavations, ballistic evidence, and ligatures. Ballistic evidence was examined by the US Bureau of Alcohol, Tobacco, Firearms, and Explosives (ATF) with reports submitted to the ICTY.[47] Linking of graves was also realized through the work of Anthony Brown and his analysis of soil and pollen samples collected from different locations.[48] Finally, and most conclusively, the relationship of primary to secondary mass grave sites has been verified through results of DNA analysis conducted by the International Commission on Missing Persons (ICMP).[49]

Since 2001, the ICMP have been in charge of the exhumation process in Bosnia and Herzegovina. Since 2009, this has been under the auspices of the state-level Missing Persons Institute (MPI). ICMP has been implementing its DNA-led identification process in BiH since 2001, and results of these identifications have been used for linking mass graves within assemblages.[50] These links determined that there are five separate assemblages of graves related to the genocide in Srebrenica of July 1995. Out of over eighty mass graves related to the fall of Srebrenica,[51] forty-nine mass graves in these assemblages have been located and excavated by late 2011.[52] It has been established that from 5,557 unique DNA profiles obtained by the ICMP for Srebrenica related mass graves, over 1,700 individuals have been recovered from more than one grave,[53] with a single individual being reassociated from as many as four different grave sites.[54]

Kravica warehouse related mass graves

Between 1,000 and 1,500 Bosniak people were bussed or marched from Sandići meadow, where they were held, and forced into the Kravica warehouse in the late afternoon of 13 July 1995. Kravica warehouse was a building of prefabricated concrete construction with brick or concrete interior walls and Styrofoam insulation sheets, a floor and ceiling also made from concrete, and brick and paint used in the construction of the interior and exterior of the building. During the killings several partially wrecked vehicles, grass, straw bales, and mechanical parts were located inside the building.[55]

Once the warehouse was full, at around 6 p.m., the soldiers started killing the prisoners using machine-guns and automatic weapons, which were discharged amongst the packed prisoners, followed by hand-grenades thrown into the huddled crowds. Any prisoners trying to escape through the windows were caught and shot by the guards surrounding the building, and any survivors were called out the next day and also killed. A very few prisoners managed to survive by pretending to be dead.[56]

Kravica warehouse was examined by the US Naval Criminal Investigative Service (NCIS) at the request of the ICTY on 30 September 1996. NCIS uncovered evidence of bullet strikes both on the inside and the outside of the building, evidence of blood spatter, and explosive residue along with human blood, bone and tissue adhering to the walls and floors of the building.[57] These samples were later examined by the Netherlands Forensic Science Laboratory, and proved to contain human DNA and traces of trinitrotoluene (TNT).[58] The warehouse was also examined by the ICTY investigators on 12 April 1996 and 17 August 1997. During these visits ICTY investigators collected shell casings, bullets, personal identifications, and belongings, and eleven grenade handles supporting findings regarding the manner of these killings. Following the executions, a wheeled front-end loader was used to break through the entire concrete section of the warehouse wall containing the double entrance door to gain access to the bodies inside the warehouse. These were loaded onto trucks and transported to primary locations.

It is believed through forensic information that the bodies outside the warehouse were transported to Ravnice and the bodies within the warehouse to Glogova,[59] where they were buried. The remains were buried in four primary mass graves: Ravnice 01 and Ravnice 02, and Glogova 01 and series of interlinked sub-graves marked as Glogova 02. The mass graves in Ravnice were undisturbed and later excavated by the ICTY in 2000 and 2001, revealing graves containing remains of 175 bodies and 324 body parts. Almost all of the complete bodies were determined to be male, and 92 per cent of these cases were determined to have had gunshot injury as the cause of death. Some remains showed signs of burning.[60]

The Glogova graves were exhumed by the ICTY in 1999, 2000, and 2001. Most of these graves were determined to have been robbed.[61] Furthermore, some of the graves in the Glogova 02 series were undisturbed, but still contained body parts. The expert report on the excavation of Glogova 02 stresses that this fragmentation of remains was not due to taphonomic processes or grave environment, but was a result of a blast injury, i.e. events surrounding the death of the victims.[62]

During the excavation of the Ravnice graves, the ICTY investigators uncovered plaster, concrete, and other building materials that were identical to the same material from Kravica warehouse (the execution point), Glogova 01 and Glogova 02 mass graves, and later secondary mass graves called Zeleni Jadar 05 and Zeleni Jadar 06. Investigators also highlighted the recovery of a piece of polystyrene that was indistinguishable from the polystyrene lettering on the outside facade wall of the Kravica warehouse, linking Ravnice mass graves to the Kravica warehouse executions.[63] ATF also established forensic links between shell casings recovered from Kravica warehouse and the secondary mass grave Zeleni Jadar 05,[64] while soil and pollen analysis linked Glogova 02 robbed primary mass grave to the secondary grave mass grave, Zeleni Jadar 05.[65]

Through DNA links, primary mass graves from Glogova have now been linked to secondary mass graves in the areas of Zeleni Jadar (seven graves), Blječeva (three graves), Budak (two graves), and Zalazje (two graves), with evidence of robbing of at least one secondary mass grave[66] and subsequent deposition of its contents into a presumed tertiary grave Zalazje 04.[67] The Zalazje graves had, by 2010, only presumptively been linked to Glogova primary mass graves.

The secondary graves definitively linked to Glogova primary mass graves are: Zeleni Jadar 1A, 1B, 2, 3, 4, 5, and 6; Blječeva 1, 2, and 3; Budak 1 and 2; and Zalazje 01 and 04. By the end of 2011, 1,374 Srebrenica victims had been identified from the Kravica warehouse assemblage.[68] This case also demonstrates the intent of the perpetrators in hiding their crimes as the secondary mass graves are kilometres away from the primary graves in Glogova, with secondary graves in Blječeva being roughly 11–12 kilometres away, secondary graves in Budak being some 10.5 kilometres away, and Zeleni Jadar secondary graves being even further away, with Zeleni Jadar 1A and 1B being about 25 kilometres away and Zeleni Jadar being some 34 kilometres south of Glogova. Most of these graves have been uncovered through aerial images showing their creation during September and October 1995. The secondary mass graves are not only linked to the primary mass graves, but are also inter-linked to various levels.

A very interesting aspect of this assemblage is the fact that even the primary mass graves, Glogova 01 and Glogova 02, are linked by DNA. This fact further supports the findings of excavations where bodies have been determined to have been partly destroyed prior to their burial.

While one would expect to find destruction of corpses during the robbing of mass graves and transport of bodies to secondary and tertiary locations, in the case of Kravica warehouse, destruction of corpses started during the killing of victims. As noted during excavations, use of RPGs and hand-grenades caused blast injuries and the bodily destruction of victims held at Kravica warehouse, and thus body parts and destroyed corpses got buried in primary locations, and not just complete bodies, as is usually the case.

Lazete mass graves assemblage

On the morning of 14 July 1995, a group of about 1,000 prisoners held in Bratunac the night before were transported in thirty buses to Grbavci school in Orahovac, already half-full with prisoners that had been arriving that morning. With the arrival of buses, the building filled up within a few hours, and there were about 2,000–2,500 prisoners in total. After being held there for a few hours, the prisoners were taken out in groups, loaded onto trucks, and led to execution in a field less than a kilometre away. The prisoners were lined up and shot in the back. While the executions were in progress heavy machinery was digging the two primary mass graves where the bodies of the killed were buried.[69]

These primary graves are Lazete 01 and Lazete 02. Mass grave Lazete 01 was excavated in 2000 and contained the remains of 130 males, and Lezet 02 was excavated in 1999 and 2000 and included the remains of 243 males. Aerial imagery shows that Orahovac was originally constructed between 5 and 27 July 1995, when comparing images across that window of time. Aerial images further showed that the robbing of these primary graves occurred between 7 and 27 September 1995.[70]

Links between Lazete 01 and 02 primary mass graves have been established to a series of graves in the Hodžići Road area 8–12 kilometres away, with both evidentiary and DNA links being confirmed. The US ATF linked shell casings from primary Lazete 02 grave to Hodžići Road 03, Hodžići Road 04, and Hodžići Road 05 secondary graves. Furthermore, the ATF linked shell casings recovered on the surface around primary graves, the area where the executions occurred, to the same secondary mass graves.[71] Soil and pollen analysis also linked Lezete 02 to Hodžići Road 03, 04, and 05, as did the recovery of piping from the original primary location,[72] which was disturbed during excavation and robbing and then transferred to secondary locations. The ATF also examined blindfolds and ligatures recovered by the ICTY teams during exhumations and those collected from the Grbavci school, and through this analysis has positively linked Lazete 02 mass grave with the secondary mass graves Hodžići Road 03, 04, and 05.[73]

Through DNA links the primary mass grave, Lazete 01, has been linked to a single secondary mass grave, Hodžići Road 05, while the primary mass grave Lazete 02 has been linked to 6 Hodžići Road graves: Hodžići Road 01, 02, 03, 04, 06, and 07, and by the end of 2011 841 individuals had been identified from this assemblage.[74]

Petkovci dam mass graves assemblage

On 14 July 1995 about 1,500 to 2,000 people were brought to and held at Petkovci school. After being held in deplorable conditions, they were taken out in small groups, ordered to strip to the waist and take their shoes off, and then had their hands bound behind their backs. During the night they were taken in trucks to nearby Petkovci dam. Once there, they were taken off of the trucks in small groups, lined up, and shot. The bodies were collected and buried by heavy machinery at the plateau in front of the dam.[75] The ATF's analysis of shell casings from the Petkovci dam grave and shell casings on the surrounding surface showed that this was the site of both the executions and primary burial.[76]

As with Lazete primary mass graves, aerial imagery shows that the Petkovci dam grave was originally constructed between 5 and 27 July 1995, when comparing images across these days. Aerial images further showed that the robbing of these primary graves occurred between 7 and 27 September 1995.[77] A team of ICTY experts exhumed the site in April of 1998, and concluded that the grave was robbed using heavy machinery. This robbing resulted in 'grossly disarticulated body parts' in the grave.[78]

DNA links between Petkovci dam primary mass grave have been established to a series of graves in the Liplje area roughly 18 kilometres south from Petkovci dam. Through DNA links, Petkovci dam has been linked to Liplje 01, 02, 03, 04, and 07 secondary mass graves. Furthermore, secondary mass graves have also shown interlinking: Liplje 01 links to Liplje 02 and 03, Liplje 02 additionally links to Liplje 04 and 07, Liplje 03 links to Liplje 01 and 04, while Liplje 04 links to Liplje 02, 03, and 07. By the end of 2011, 815 individuals had been identified from this assemblage.[79]

Branjevo military farm graves assemblage

About 1,000 to 1,200 men were bussed from Bratunac to a school in Pilica near Zvornik on 14 July 1995, and were held there for two nights. On 16 July 1995, these men were bussed to a Branjevo military farm where they were to be executed. After being held with no food, water, or latrines, they were called out, had their hands bound behind their backs and were taken to the execution site, while some men had already died from dehydration when being held in Pilica school. Men started arriving on trucks at Branjevo around 10 a.m. and, once at Branjevo, prisoners were lined up in groups of ten and shot in the back. Heavy machinery was used to dig the grave while the executions were still ongoing and later to bury the corpses in the grave.[80] During the Krstić trial, it was noted that over the course of the executions, 'when some of the soldiers recognized acquaintances from Srebrenica, they beat and humiliated them before killing them', and that machine-guns were used for the killings, the gunfire often 'mortally wounded the prisoners, but did not cause death immediately and prolonged their suffering'.[81]

Aerial images of the Branjevo farm area show large numbers of corpses lying in the nearby field, as well as excavators moving them on 17 July 1995, with the robbing of Branjevo primary grave and the creation of the related secondary Čančari Road graves between 7 and 27 July 1995. These graves were then backfilled before 2 October of the same year.[82] Branjevo military farm mass grave, also known as Pilica, was excavated by the ICTY between 10 and 24 September 1996, with 132 remains being uncovered, with almost all being established to have died from gunshot wounds.[83]

Pilica Dom was also examined by the US NCIS and the ICTY on 27 September and 2 October 1996. NCIS uncovered evidence of bullet strikes on the inside of the building, evidence of blood spatter, and explosive residue along with human blood and human bones.[84] These samples were later examined by the Netherlands Forensic Science Laboratory and proved to contain human DNA and traces of trinitrotoluene (TNT).[85] The ATF also examined blindfolds and ligatures recovered by the ICTY teams during exhumations and those collected from the Branjevo military farm, and through this analysis positively linked Lazete 02 mass grave with the secondary mass graves Čančari Road 03 and 12,[86] while similar links have also been established by the ICMP during their excavation of Čančari Road 08 secondary mass grave.[87] Additional links were provided through the presence of hay in secondary mass graves, as it was established that Branjevo-related mass graves contained hay as the bodies buried in the Branjevo primary grave were covered with it.[88]

DNA links between Branjevo military farm primary mass grave have been established to a part of a series of thirteen graves in the Čančari Road area roughly 45 to 50 kilometres south. Thus, through DNA links, Branjevo has been linked to Čančari Road 04, 05, 06, 08, 09, 11, and 12 secondary mass graves. Čančari Road 10 secondary mass grave does not directly link to Branjevo primary mass grave, but through its links to Čančari Road 06, 11, and 12, it has been established that it is also a secondary mass grave related to Branjevo military farm.[89] Furthermore, other Čančari Road secondary mass graves have also shown inter-linking. By the end of 2011, 1,735 individuals had been identified from this assemblage.[90]

Kozluk graves assemblage

About 500 men were killed and buried at the edge of the Drina river, near the Vitinka bottled-water factory between 15 and 16 July 1995. Information on this event was provided to the ICTY by Bosnian refugees in Germany. The prisoners were loaded onto trucks, and while being driven to Kozluk for execution, they were forced to sing Serb songs. Heavy machinery was used to dig the graves, with burials taking place between 17 and 18 July 1995.[91]

Aerial images of the Kozluk area show that Kozluk primary mass grave was created between 5 and 17 July 1995, with the robbing of Kozluk primary grave and creation and backfilling of related secondary Čančari Road graves between 27 September and 2 October of the same year. Kozluk primary mass grave was excavated by the ICTY between 27 May and 10 June 1998, with at least 340 individuals being excavated. As the executions and burials occurred in the vicinity of a bottled-water factory, both primary and secondary mass graves included green bottle glass and bottle labels in the grave fill.[92]

The ATF linked shell casings from the primary mass grave at Kozluk to the Čančari Road 03 secondary mass graves.[93] DNA links between Kozluk primary mass grave have been established as part of a series of 13 graves in the Čančari Road area roughly 45 to 50 km south. Through DNA links, Petkovci Dam has been linked to Čančari Road 01, 02, 03, and 13 secondary mass graves. Furthermore, other Čančari Road secondary mass graves have also shown inter-linking. By the end of 2011, 813 individuals had been identified from this assemblage.[94]

Destruction of corpses: forensic and social aspects

The forensic work in the identification of these remains and their return to families for proper burial is complex in the case of the missing from the fall of Srebrenica as they, in anthropological terms, represent a very homogenous group. All of those excavated from these mass graves have similar demographics: they belonged to a displaced, economically underdeveloped population, with a large number reported missing (over 8,000) who are mostly males between seventeen and forty-five,[95] men commonly referred to as men of a fighting age, and there is generally inconclusive information in terms of ante-mortem medical and dental records because of the victims' social, cultural, and/or economic status.[96] Dental records are available for less that 10 per cent (roughly 600) of those reported missing.[97] All of these factors severely limit the use of non-DNA-based (or more 'traditional' forensic) methods normally useful in the process of 'reassociation' (reassembling mortal remains) and identification,[98] and indeed had DNA not been utilized as a powerful tool in the forensic arsenal of the Srebrenica exhumations, these remains might never have been identified.

Through ICMP's implementation of a DNA-led process of tracing, excavating, and exhuming missing persons in the Balkans, the search and recovery of the missing and their return to the families has changed. DNA has started being used for reassociations of body parts within graves and between graves, but also for the identification of remains that allow for their return to family members. To this end, ICMP formed the Podrinje Identification Project (PIP) located in Tuzla in 1999 and the Lukavac Re-association Center (LKRC), in Lukavac, near Tuzla, in 2005. Their task was to examine remains recovered from mass and other graves sites, identify them and return them to their families, by combining 'traditional' forensic anthropology and DNA analysis. LKRC also conducted bone-to-bone DNA matching in order to resolve a high volume of cases of disarticulation and commingling, as well as to expedite the whole process and make it more efficient.[99]

However, after the complex process of identification, which can exist in tension with the needs and resource requirements of the forensic evidence sought by prosecutorial institutions, there enters yet another actant into this network of competing agendas. In a country where ethnic, political, and religious identities are fused, the commingled remains of the secondary mass graves might prove a particular sort of conundrum for the religious communities that seek to represent both the individual dead and the groups from which they come. While families might want to commemorate their individual murdered loved ones, they will likely hope to do so in many cases in ways that conform to practices that identify those individuals as members of a specific collectivity. This might not be for political reasons (although on the part of religious and political leaders, it often is), but because of matters of personal belief. As Tunjo Stanić, a family member from Orašje, points out: 'If it is possible somehow to find the body, to bury it, so that there is a place to go at the cemetery, to light a candle and so forth', the perpetrators have not entirely succeeded as they thought they had.[100] Here, the commingled remains of the disassociated person are mirrored by the commingled preoccupations of individual and group identities.

As one Mother of Srebrenica says:

> Even today we are searching, we are looking, hoping that they will appear. I would always prefer to live in hope, to expect that someone will appear somewhere, regardless of whose child, not only mine, anyone's child. If any child might still return, we will keep searching as long as we are still standing on our feet, and it seems to me that I would walk, I would look, with whatever God gives us.[101]

These are the bodies of the twice dead. These bodies underwent a process of anonymous death (on the individual level) and sacrilegious burial (in terms of group concerns). The phenomenon of secondary mass graves twins the defilement and destruction of both physical being and any kind of shared identity in a particularly powerful form. As a result, Wagner notes in her book, *To Know Where He Lies*, that in contemporary Bosnia, interring and commemorating victims of genocide or crimes against humanity relies on both following Bosnian Muslim traditions, and also on improvising from them. Thus, communities must reconcile the initial conditions of death and burial of their loved ones with the return of the (usually partial) remains and identities through consecrated funerals.[102]

The Bosnian Islamic Community (IZ) responded to this need by consulting Sharia law, in order to make sense of the destruction of bodies through repeated sacrilegious burials. A leading Bosnian Islamic cleric weighed in on the issue, and at a roundtable discussion in March 2003, the only open forum to have dealt with this particular problem, the current head of Bosnia's IZ, and then Tuzla *mufti*, Husejn ef. Kavazović, explained that

> Sharia law considers a missing person as a person who went missing for some reason and for whom we do not know current whereabouts or their status; whether they are alive or dead. ... Bearing in mind the circumstances leading to mass executions of Muslims from Srebrenica and Žepa, which are confirmed by the verdicts of [the] ICTY as well as the discovery of mass graves, it is assumed that the victims who are still missing are presumed to be dead. They would be considered dead if more than four years have passed since their disappearance[103]

if they have gone missing during circumstances of war. Kavazović went on to explain that Srebrenica victims have the status of a *šehid* (martyr) and this determines the religious practice that was to be accorded to both excavated and unexcavated remains. This finally resolved the question of the treatment of skeletonized remains encountered in mass graves, which get washed in mortuaries by technicians and not according to religious practices, as a *šehid* in him/herself is clean and thus would not require the 'usual cleansing ritual nor will the remaining clothing be removed from them'.[104] Kavazović also addressed the burial practices by stating that each of the identified remains, whether complete or incomplete, should be marked with a *nišan* (a tombstone) with the person's identity, as is the custom in the Bosnian Islamic tradition and 'the same treatment should be used for incomplete body parts for which identity is known'.[105] He added that incomplete remains should be treated as if they were complete during prayers and markings of the graves and also that bones of multiple individuals can be buried within a collective tomb, while reminding listeners that they do not just have strictly religious obligations to these remains, but that they also have a duty of commemorating them.[106]

In this way, the Bosnian Muslim community and its 'improvised' or reinterpreted doctrines have served as new actants in the network of BiH's memory politics around the crimes committed during the conflicts of the 1990s. On the one hand, the identification of all the missing as having the status of a *šehid* serves to counteract some of the most disruptive ethno-nationalist associations posed by the phenomenon of the secondary mass grave. This rendering of the disappeared and the disarticulated creates what Latour referred to as a 'de-punctualization', whereby a whole (here the secondary mass grave) is broken down into its parts (the partial remains of individual persons of faith, as well as the absences instantiated by what is still missing). This is much the same process as when a machine, upon breaking down, is recognized as an aggregation of its various parts and systems. If at first we throw up our hands and say, 'my laptop is broken', we later reassess the situation to recognize that it is either the electronics or the mechanics, this discrete component or that one. So, too, does the insertion of the concept of the *šehid* into the overall network disaggregate (de-punctualize) and disrupt the initial meaning that the secondary mass grave has in association with other actants from the network. However, it cannot be ignored that this new node in the network must necessarily also recapitulate the centrality of collective identities as well (here the Bosnian Muslim identity of the victims against the shared identities of the perpetrators), and in so doing, it reiterates the divisions that criminal mass graves always instantiate.

Some concluding remarks

Much of the point of this chapter has been to argue for the secondary mass grave as a particular kind of actant in a post-conflict network of memory politics. Because of its mode of coming into being and the fact that the persons in the grave remain incomplete assemblages of mortal remains, often even after DNA identification, these graves divide even more than other mass graves. They create clear delineations along ethnic group lines because of the kind of phenomenon they are. The makers of the graves are seen as collective perpetrators because of the systematic, concerted, and resource-intensive processes involved in the graves' production. The incompleteness of what can be found in the graves pulls in sometimes conflicting directions – towards identifying the shared fate of the commingled partial remains as a targeted *group*, even as families seek to materialize the absence of their *particular* lost members. These processes lead to changing significance for other nodes in the network, for example where material objects found in a grave or left behind before the loved one was taken come to serve as a stand-in for either the parts of the person that will for ever remain missing or as a placeholder for someone disappeared and never identified at all. And all of these processes are inflected by the agency of actants that are not necessarily persons or objects, but include the forensic practices we have described, the political organizations that have motivated exhumation and/or identification, and the religious concepts mobilized when faced with secondary mass graves (for example). So rather than talk blandly about the '*social context*' that allows for BiH's current, overheated ethnonationalist politics, this chapter has sought to describe the 'social' as the connections between the multi-various nodes in a network, turning attention not to what is 'socially exceptional' about BiH, but how certain entities in its network of memory politics provide for unanticipated patterns of connection and reassemblage – like that of the phenomenon of the secondary mass grave.

Notes

This research was supported from the European Research Council and was undertaken as part of the project 'Bosnian Bones, Spanish Ghosts: "Transitional Justice" and the Legal Shaping of Memory after Two Modern Conflicts' (grant no. 241231).

1 B. Latour, *Reassembling the Social: An Introduction to Actor Network Theory* (Oxford: Oxford University Press, 2005).
2 *Ibid.*, p. 5.

3   B. Latour, *Pandora's Hope: Essays on the Reality of Science Studies* (Cambridge, MA: Harvard University Press, 1999).

4   A. Mant, 'Knowledge acquired from post-war exhumations', in A. Boddington, A. N. Garland & R. C. Janaway (eds), *Death, Decay and Reconstruction: Approaches to Archaeology and Forensic Science* (Manchester: Manchester University Press, 1987), pp. 65–78.

5   P. R. Ruwanpura, U. C. Perera, H. T. Wijayaweer & N. Chandrasiri, 'Adaptation of archaeological techniques in forensic mass grave exhumation: the experience of "Chemmani" excavation in northern Sri Lanka', *Ceylon Medical Journal*, 51:3 (2006), 98–102.

6   M. Skinner, 'Planning the archaeological recovery of evidence from recent mass graves', *Forensic Science International*, 34:4 (1987), 267–87.

7   M. Skinner, H. York & M. Connor, 'Postburial disturbances of graves in Bosnia-Herzegovina', in W. Haglund & M. H. Sorg (eds), *Advances in Forensic Taphonomy: Method, Theory and Archaeological Perspective* (Boca Raton, FL: CRC Press, 2002), pp. 293–308; W. Haglund, 'Recent mass graves, an introduction', in Haglund & Sorg (eds), *Advances in Forensic Taphonomy*, pp. 243–62.

8   UN Doc S/1994/674/Add.2 (vol. V), *Final Report of the United Nations Commission of Experts Established Pursuant to Security Council Resolution 780 (1992). Annex X: Mass graves*, 28 December 1994, http://ess.uwe.ac.uk/comexpert/ANX/X.htm#II (accessed 28 October 2012).

9   M. Connor, *Forensic Methods: Excavation for the Archaeologist and Investigator* (Plymouth: Altamira Press, 2007), p. 157.

10 *Ibid.*

11 W. Haglund, M. Connor & D. Scott, 'The archaeology of contemporary mass graves', *Historical Archaeology*, 35:1 (2001), 57–69.

12 K. Juhl, *The Contribution by (Forensic) Archaeologists to Human Rights Investigations of Mass Graves*, AmS-NETT 5 (Stavanger: Museum of Archaeology, 2005), p. 15, http://am.uis.no/getfile.php/Arkeologisk%20museum/publikasjoner/ams-nett/Mass_Graves2.pdf (accessed 28 October 2012).

13 UN Doc E/CN.4/1993/50, *Situation of Human Rights in the Territory of the Former Yugoslavia. Report on the situation of human rights in the territory of the former Yugoslavia submitted by Mr. Tadeusz Mazowiecki, Special Rapporteur of the Commission on Human Rights, pursuant to Commission resolution 1992/S-1/1 of 14 August 1992. Annex I: Summary of the report of the Special Rapporteur on extrajudicial, summary or arbitrary executions on his mission to investigate allegations of mass graves from 15 to 20 December1992*, 10 February 1993 www.unhchr.ch/huridocda/huridoca.nsf/0811fcbd0b9f6bd58025667300306dea/313049964d7549ec80256790 0054cf88?OpenDocument#more (accessed 28 October 2012).

14 International Criminal Tribunal for the Former Yugoslavia (ICTY), 'Special: exhumations', *ICTY-Bulletin*, no. 8, 1996, p. 1.

15 E. Jesse & M. Skinner, 'A typology of mass grave and mass grave-related sites', *Forensic Science International*, 152:1 (2005), 55–9.

16 S. Schmitt, 'Mass graves and the collection of forensic evidence: genocide, war crimes and crimes against humanity', in Haglund & Sorg (eds), *Advances in Forensic Taphonomy*, pp. 277–92.

17 *Ibid.*
18 C. Perera & C. Briggs, 'Guidelines for the effective conduct of mass buri-
    als following mass disasters: post-Asian tsunami disaster experience in
    retrospect', *Forensic Science, Medicine and Pathology*, 4:1 (2008), 1–8.
19 *Ibid.*
20 H. Simanjuntak, 'Jainab shuttles between mass graves', *Jakarta Post*, 27
    December 2011, www.thejakartapost.com/news/2011/12/27/jainab-
    shuttles-between-mass-graves.html (accessed 1 November 2012).
21 E. Williams & J. Crews, 'From dust to dust: ethical and practical issues
    involved in the location, exhumation, and identification of bodies from
    mass graves', *Croatian Medical Journal*, 44:3 (2003), 252.
22 M. F. Skinner, D. Alempijevic & M. Djuric-Srejic, 'Guidelines for inter-
    national forensic bio-archaeology monitors of mass grave exhumations',
    Forensic Science International, 134:2–3 (2003), 82, note 4.
23 *Ibid.*
24 However, it is important to note that even were one to accept this character-
    ization of the fighting, it has to be recognized that each of the three named
    armies comprised conscripts and volunteers that were not 'co-ethnic'.
25 Sentencing Judgment, *Prosecutor v. Biljana Plavšić* (IT-00-39&40/1-S),
    Trial Chamber, 27 February 2003, § 15.
26 D. Campbell, 'Apartheid cartography: the political anthropology and
    spatial effects of international diplomacy in Bosnia', *Political Geography*,
    18:4 (1999), 404.
27 Sentencing Judgment, *Prosecutor v. Biljana Plavšić* (IT-00-39&40/1-S),
    §§ 15–17.
28 UN Doc S/RES/780, *Resolution 780*, http://daccess-dds-ny.un.org/
    doc/UNDOC/GEN/N92/484/40/IMG/N9248440.pdf?OpenElement
    (accessed 28 October 2012).
29 UN Doc S/1994/674/Add.2 (vol. V), *Final Report of the United Nations
    Commission of Experts Established Pursuant to Security Council
    Resolution 780 (1992). I. Mandate, structure and methods of work*, 28
    December 1994, www.his.com/~twarrick/commxyu3.htm#II (accessed
    28 October 2012).
30 UN Doc S/1994/674/Add.2 (vol. V), *Final Report*.
31 Judgment, *Prosecutor v. Radislav Krstic* (IT-98-33-T) 'Srebrenica-Drina
    Corps', Trial Chamber, 2 August 2001, §§ 66–70.
32 M. Dobbs, 'Memo to the CIA: share your secrets', Foreign Policy Blog:
    Mladic in The Hague – Michael Dobbs Explores the Origins of Evil,
    2012, http://dobbs.foreignpolicy.com/posts/2012/01/27/memo_to_cia_
    share_your_secrets (accessed 28 October 2012).
33 N. Kempster, 'Photos show mass graves of civilians from "safe areas"
    U.S. tells U.N: Bosnia: the American ambassador to the United
    Nations charges "wide-scale atrocities" by rebel Serbs', *Los Angeles
    Times*, 11 August 1995, http://articles.latimes.com/1995-08-11/news/
    mn-33948_1_bosnian-serb (accessed 28 October 2012).
34 L. Parks, 'Satellite views of Srebrenica: tele-visuality and the politics of
    witnessing', *Social Identities: Journal for the Study of Race, Nation and
    Culture*, 7:4 (2001), 561–85.

35 D. Rhode, 'Evidence indicates Bosnia massacre', *Christian Science Monitor*, 18 August 1995, www.columbia.edu/itc/journalism/nelson/rohde/p-8181.html (accessed 25 September 2012).

36 W. Haglund, 'Forensic investigation of four graves in the area of Nova Kasaba Bosnia and Herzegovina – exhumation: July 20, 1996 through July 26, 1996, examination: August 27, 1996 through September 1, 1996', Report to the ICTY, 15 June 1998.

37 D. Manning, 'Srebrenica investigation. Summary of forensic evidence – execution points and mass graves', Report to United Nations International Criminal Tribunal for Former Yugoslavia, 16 May 2000.

38 A. Jugo, 'Primena forenzičkih tehnika na masovne grobnice u Bosni i Hercegovini' (Application of forensic techniques to mass graves in Bosnia and Herzegovina), *Matemi Reasocijacije* (*Mathemes of Reassociation*) (only one issue published) (2011), 35–9.

39 *Ibid.*

40 E. Huffine, J. Crews & J. Davoren, 'Developing role of forensics in deterring violence and genocide', *Croatian Medical Journal*, 48:4 (2007), 431–6.

41 Jugo, 'Primena forenzičkih tehnika'.

42 Judgment, *Prosecutor* v. *Radislav Krstic* (IT-98-33-T) 'Srebrenica-Drina Corps', Trial Chamber, 2 August 2001, § 260.

43 C. Fournet, *The Crime of Destruction and the Law of Genocide: Their Impact on Collective Memory* (Aldershot: Ashgate, 2007).

44 *Ibid.*, pp. 13–14.

45 L. Ranshaw, 'Missing bodies near-at-hand: the dissonant memory and dormant graves of the Spanish Civil War', in M. Bille, F. Hastrup & T. Flohr Sørensen (eds), *An Anthropology of Absence: Materializations of Transcendence and Loss* (New York, Dordrecht, Heidelberg, and London: Springer, 2010), p. 50.

46 M. Osiel, *Mass Atrocity, Collective Memory, and the Law* (New Brunswick, NJ: Transaction Publishers, 1999).

47 Forensic Science Laboratory, Bureau of Alcohol, Tobacco and Firearms, 'Laboratory report', Report to ICTY, 24 February 2000.

48 A. G. Brown, 'The use of forensic botany and geology in war crimes investigations in NE Bosnia', *Forensic Science International*, 163:3 (2006), 204–10; A. G. Brown, 'Statement of witness – statement of Anthony G. Brown', Report to the ICTY, 26 February 1999; A. G. Brown, 'First report on samples from October 22–24th visit to Glogova', Report to the ICTY, 26 November 1999.

49 D. Janc, 'Srebrenica investigation, update to the summary of forensic evidence – exhumations of the graves and surface remains recoveries related to Srebrenica and Žepa – April 2010', Report to the ICTY, 21 April 2010.

50 Jugo, 'Primena forenzičkih tehnika'; L. Yazedjian & R. Kešetović, 'The application of traditional anthropological methods in a DNA-led identification process', in B. J. Adams & J. E. Byrd (eds), *Recovery, Analysis, and Identification of Commingled Human Remains* (New York: Humana Press, 2008), pp. 271–84.

51 A. Mašović, 'Zalazje je osmadeseta masovna grobnica ubijenih Srebreničana' (Zalazje is the eightieth mass grave of those killed in Srebrenica), *Dnevni Avaz*, 4 December 2009, 5.

52 M. Vennemeyer, 'An analysis of linkages between robbed primary graves and secondary graves related to Srebrenica missing', presented at 21st International Meeting on Forensic Medicine Alpe-Adria-Pannonia, Sarajevo, 30 May–2 June 2012.

53 *Ibid.*

54 Janc, 'Srebrenica investigation'.

55 US Naval Criminal Investigative Service, 'International Criminal Tribunal for Former Yugoslavia – forensic assistance to Srebrenica investigation', Report to International Criminal Tribunal for Former Yugoslavia, 16 January 1998.

56 Judgment, *Prosecutor* v. *Vujadin Popović, Ljubiša Beara, Drago Nikolić, Ljubomir Borovčanin, Radivoje Miletić, Milan Gvero & Vinko Pandurević* (IT-05-88-T) 'Srebrenica', Trial Chamber, 10 June 2010, §§ 421–31; Judgment, *Prosecutor* v. *Radislav Krstic* (IT-98-33-T), 'Srebrenica-Drina Corps', Trial Chamber, 2 August 2001, §§ 205–15.

57 US Naval Criminal Investigative Service, 'International Criminal Tribunal'.

58 Manning, 'Srebrenica investigation', pp. 12–13.

59 Judgment, *Prosecutor* v. *Vujadin Popović, Ljubiša Beara, Drago Nikolić, Ljubomir Borovčanin, Radivoje Miletić, Milan Gvero & Vinko Pandurević* (IT-05-88-T) 'Srebrenica', Trial Chamber, 10 June 2010, §§ 438–42.

60 J. Clark, 'ICTY operations in Bosnia Herzegovina, in 2000, Srebrenica related grave sites', Report to the ICTY, 24 February 2001.

61 R. Wright, 'Report on excavations and exhumations at the Glogova 1 mass grave in 2000', Report to the ICTY, 9 February 2001; J. P. Baraybar, 'Report on excavations at Glogova 2, Bosnia and Herzegovina 1999–2001', Report to ICTY, undated.

62 Baraybar, 'Report on excavations at Glogova 2', p. 20.

63 Janc, 'Srebrenica investigation'.

64 Forensic Science Laboratory, 'Laboratory report'.

65 Brown, 'Statement of witness', First report on samples.

66 Janc, 'Srebrenica investigation'; Jugo, 'Primena forenzičkih tehnika'.

67 Srebrenica Genocide Blog, 'Tertiary mass grave in Zalazje, preliminary work in progress', http://srebrenica-genocide.blogspot.com/2010/06/tertiary-zal-azje-mass-grave.html (accessed 2 November 2012); M. Smajić, 'Očekuje se otkrivanje velikog broja srebreničkih žrtava' (Discovery of a large number of Srebrenica's victims is expected), *Dnevni Avaz*, 29 June 2010, 9.

68 D. Janc, 'Transcript of testimony given on Tuesday, 27 March 2012', transcript, 27 March 2012, www.icty.org/x/cases/karadzic/trans/en/120327ED.htm (accessed 10 November 2012).

69 Judgment, *Prosecutor* v. *Radislav Krstic* (IT-98-33-T), §§ 220–1; S. Wagner, *To Know Where He Lies: DNA Technology and the Search for Srebrenica's Missing* (Los Angeles, Berkeley and London: University of California Press, 2008).

70 Judgment, *Prosecutor* v. *Radislav Krstic* (IT-98-33-T), § 220.

71 Forensic Science Laboratory, 'Laboratory report'.
72 Brown, 'The use of forensic botany'.
73 Manning, 'Srebrenica investigation'.
74 Janc, 'Transcript of testimony'.
75 Judgment, *Prosecutor* v. *Radislav Krstic* (IT-98-33-T), §§ 226–9; Wagner, *To Know Where He Lies*.
76 Forensic Science Laboratory, 'Laboratory report'.
77 Judgment, *Prosecutor* v. *Radislav Krstic* (IT-98-33-T), §§ 226–9; Wagner, *To Know Where He Lies*.
78 Judgment, *Prosecutor* v. *Radislav Krstic* (IT-98-33-T), § 229.
79 Janc, 'Transcript of testimony'.
80 Judgment, *Prosecutor* v. *Radislav Krstic* (IT-98-33-T), §§ 233–6; Verdict, *Prosecutor's Office of Bosnia and Herzegovina* v. *Radomir Vuković & Zoran Tomić* (X-KR-06/180-2), Trial Chamber, 2 July 2010, § 179.
81 Judgment, *Prosecutor* v. *Radislav Krstic* (IT-98-33-T), § 234.
82 Judgment, *Prosecutor* v. *Radislav Krstic* (IT-98-33-T), §§ 237–8.
83 Manning, 'Srebrenica investigation', pp. 15–16.
84 US Naval Criminal Investigative Service, 'Pilica Dom, results of forensic investigation', Report to ICTY, undated.
85 Manning, 'Srebrenica investigation', pp. 12–13.
86 Manning, 'Srebrenica investigation'.
87 ICMP, 'Summary report – Cancari Road 08, BIH', Report submitted to ICTY, 19 February 2009.
88 Jugo, 'Primena forenzičkih tehnika'.
89 Janc, 'Srebrenica investigation'.
90 Janc, 'Transcript of testimony'.
91 Judgment, *Prosecutor* v. *Radislav Krstic* (IT-98-33-T), §§ 249–53; Verdict, *Prosecutor's Office of Bosnia and Herzegovina* v. *Radomir Vuković & Zoran Tomić* (X-KR-06/180-2), § 180; Judgment, *Prosecutor* v. *Vidoje Blagojević & Dragan Jokić* (IT-02-60-A), Appeals Chamber, 9 May 2007, §§ 165–9.
92 Judgment, *Prosecutor* v. *Radislav Krstic* (IT-98-33-T), § 249–53; Manning, 'Srebrenica investigation'.
93 Forensic Science Laboratory, 'Laboratory report'.
94 Manning, 'Srebrenica investigation'; Vennemeyer, 'An analysis of linkages'; Janc, 'Transcript of testimony'.
95 B. Mijatovic, 'Statistical evidence for the investigation of international crimes', *Bulletin de la Société des Sciences Médicales du Grand-Duché de Luxembourg*, 2 (2006), 327–39.
96 C. Katzmarzyk, R. Kešetović, K.-A. Martin, E. Jašaragić, R. Huel, J. Sterenberg, A. Rizvić, M. Skinner & T. J. Parsons, 'The Lukavac Re-association Center: a model for a multidisciplinary approach in the examination of commingled remains', presented at the American Academy of Forensic Sciences Symposium on ICMP's Integrated Forensic Analysis of Srebrenica Event, Seattle, WA, USA, 22–27 February 2010.
97 Yazedjian & Kešetović, 'The application of traditional anthropological methods'.
98 *Ibid.*
99 *Ibid.*

100 H. Memija, *Voices of the Missing – Glasovi nestalih* (Zenica: Studioflaš, 2002).
101 Hajrija Selimović as cited in Memija, *Voices of the Missing*, unpaginated, translated by the author.
102 Wagner, *To Know Where He Lies*.
103 H. Kavazović, 'Address by Husejn ef. Kavazović', Roundtable, Between Truth and Justice – Memories and Hope, Association of Mothers of Srebrenica and Žepa Enclaves, Sarajevo, 2003, cited in Wagner, *To Know Where He Lies*, p. 216.
104 *Ibid.*, p. 217.
105 *Ibid.*
106 Wagner, *To Know Where He Lies*.

Bibliography

Baraybar, J. P., 'Report on Excavations at Glogova 2, Bosnia and Herzegovina 1999–2001', Report to the ICTY, undated

Brown, A. G., 'First report on samples from October 22–24th visit to Glogova', Report to the ICTY, 26 November 1999

Brown, A. G., 'Statement of witness – statement of Anthony G. Brown', Report to the ICTY, 26 February 1999

Brown, A. G., 'The use of forensic botany and geology in war crimes investigations in NE Bosnia', *Forensic Science International*, 163:3 (2006), 204–10

Campbell, D., 'Apartheid cartography: the political anthropology and spatial effects of international diplomacy in Bosnia', *Political Geography*, 18:4 (1999), 395–435

Clark, J., 'ICTY Operations in Bosnia Herzegovina, in 2000, Srebrenica Related Grave Site', Report to the ICTY, 24 February 2001

Connor, M. A., *Forensic Methods: Excavation for the Archaeologist and Investigator* (Plymouth: Altamira Press, 2007)

Dobbs, M., 'Memo to the CIA: Share your secrets', Foreign Policy Blog: Mladic in the Hague – Michael Dobbs Explores the Origins of Evil, 2012, http://dobbs.foreignpolicy.com/posts/2012/01/27/memo_to_cia_share_your_secrets (accessed 28 October 2012)

Forensic Science Laboratory, Bureau of Alcohol, Tobacco and Firearms, 'Laboratory report', Report to the CTY, 24 February 2000

Fournet, C., *The Crime of Destruction and the Law of Genocide: Their Impact on Collective Memory* (Aldershot: Ashgate, 2007)

Haglund, W., 'Forensic investigation of four graves in the area of Nova Kasaba Bosnia and Herzegovina – exhumation: July 20, 1996 through July 26, 1996, examination: August 27, 1996 through September 1, 1996', Report to the ICTY, 15 June 1998

Haglund, W., 'Recent mass graves, an introduction', in W. Haglund & M. Sorg (eds), *Advances in Forensic Taphonomy: Method, Theory and Archaeological Perspective* (Boca Raton, FL: CRC Press, 2002), pp. 243–62

Haglund, W., M. Connor & D. Scott, 'The archaeology of contemporary mass graves', *Historical Archaeology*, 35:1 (2001), 57–69

Huffine, E., J. Crews & J. Davoren, 'Developing role of forensics in deterring violence and genocide', *Croatian Medical Journal*, 48:4 (2007), 431–6

ICMP, 'Summary report – Cancari Road 08, BiH', Report submitted to the ICTY, 19 February 2009

ICTY, 'Special: exhumations', *ICTY-Bulletin*, no. 8, 1996

Janc, D., 'Srebrenica investigation, update to the summary of forensic evidence – exhumations of the graves and surface remains recoveries related to Srebrenica and Žepa – April 2010', Report to the ICTY, 21 April 2010

Janc, D., 'Transcript of testimony given on Tuesday, 27 March 2012', transcript, 27 March 2012, www.icty.org/x/cases/karadzic/trans/en/120327ED.htm (accessed 10 November 2012)

Jesse, E. & M. Skinner, 'A typology of mass grave and mass grave-related sites', *Forensic Science International*, 152:1 (2005), 55–9

Judgment, *Prosecutor v. Radislav Krstic* (IT-*98-33-T*), 'Srebrenica-Drina Corps', Trial Chamber, 2 August 2001

Judgment, *Prosecutor v. Vidoje Blagojević & Dragan Jokić* (IT-02-60-A), Appeals Chamber, 9 May 2007

Judgment, *Prosecutor v. Vujadin Popović, Ljubiša Beara, Drago Nikolić, Ljubomir Borovčanin, Radivoje Miletić, Milan Gvero & Vinko Pandurević* (IT-05-88-T), 'Srebrenica', Trial Chamber, 10 June 2010

Jugo, A., 'Primena forenzičkih tehnika na masovne grobnice u Bosni i Hercegovini', *Matemi reasocijacije* (only one issue published) (2011), 35–9

Juhl, K., *The Contribution by (Forensic) Archaeologists to Human Rights Investigations of Mass Graves*, AmS-NETT 5 (Stavanger: Museum of Archaeology, 2005), http://am.uis.no/getfile.php/Arkeologisk%20 museum/publikasjoner/ams-nett/Mass_Graves2.pdf (accessed 28 October 2012)

Katzmarzyk, C., R. Kešetović, K.-A. Martin, E. Jašaragić, R. Huel, J. Sterenberg, A. Rizvić, M. Skinner & T. J. Parsons, 'The Lukavac Re-association Center: a model for a multidisciplinary approach in the examination of commingled remains', presented at The American Academy of Forensic Sciences Symposium on ICMP's Integrated Forensic Analysis of Srebrenica Event, Seattle, WA, USA, 22–27 February 2010

Kempster, N., 'Photos show mass graves of civilians from "safe areas" U.S. tells U.N: Bosnia: the American ambassador to the United Nations charges "wide-scale atrocities" by rebel Serbs', *Los Angeles Times*, 11 August 1995, http://articles.latimes.com/1995-08-11/news/mn-33948_1_bosnian-serb (accessed 28 October 2012)

Latour, B., *Pandora's Hope: Essays on the Reality of Science Studies* (Cambridge, MA: Harvard University Press, 1999)

Latour, B., *Reassembling the Social: An Introduction to Actor Network Theory* (Oxford: Oxford University Press, 2005)

Manning, D., 'Srebrenica investigation. Summary of forensic evidence – execution points and mass graves', Report to United Nations International Criminal Tribunal for Former Yugoslavia, 16 May 2000

Mant, A., 'Knowledge acquired from post-war exhumations', in A. Boddington, A. N. Garland & R. C. Janaway (eds), *Death, Decay and Reconstruction: Approaches to Archaeology and Forensic Science* (Manchester: Manchester University Press, 1987), pp. 65–78

Mašović, A., 'Zalazje je osmadeseta masovna grobnica ubijenih Srebreničana', *Dnevni Avaz*, 4 December 2009

Memija, H., *Voices of the Missing – Glasovi nestalih* (Zenica: Studioflaš, 2002)

Mijatovic, B., 'Statistical evidence for the investigation of international crimes', *Bulletin de la Société des Sciences Médicales du Grand-Duché de Luxembourg*, 2 (2006), 327–39

Osiel, M., *Mass Atrocity, Collective Memory, and the Law* (New Brunswick, NJ: Transaction Publishers, 1999)

Parks, L., 'Satellite views of Srebrenica: tele-visuality and the politics of witnessing', *Social Identities: Journal for the Study of Race, Nation and Culture*, 7:4 (2001), 561–85

Perera, C. & C. Briggs, 'Guidelines for the effective conduct of mass burials following mass disasters: post-Asian tsunami disaster experience in retrospect', *Forensic Science, Medicine and Pathology*, 4:1 (2008), 1–8

Ranshaw, L., 'Missing bodies near-at-hand: the dissonant memory and dormant graves of the Spanish civil war', in M. Bille, F. Hastrup & T. Flohr Sørensen (eds), *An Anthropology of Absence: Materializations of Transcendence and Loss* (New York, Dordrecht, Heidelberg, and London: Springer, 2010), pp. 45–59

Rhode, D., 'Evidence indicates Bosnia massacre', *Christian Science Monitor*, 18 August 1995, www.columbia.edu/itc/journalism/nelson/rohde/p-8181.html (accessed 25 September 2012)

Ruwanpura, P. R., U. C. Perera, H. T. Wijayaweer & N. Chandrasiri, 'Adaptation of archaeological techniques in forensic mass grave exhumation: the experience of "Chemmani" excavation in northern Sri Lanka', *Ceylon Medical Journal*, 51:3 (2006), 98–102

Schmitt, S., 'Mass graves and the collection of forensic evidence: genocide, war crimes and crimes against humanity', in W. Haglund & M. H. Sorg (eds), *Advances in Forensic Taphonomy: Method, Theory and Archaeological Perspective* (Boca Raton, FL: CRC Press, 2002), pp. 277–92

Sentencing Judgment, *Prosecutor v. Biljana Plavšić* (IT-00-39&40/1-S), Trial Chamber, 27 February 2003

Simanjuntak, H., 'Jainab shuttles between mass graves', *Jakarta Post*, 27 December 2011, www.thejakartapost.com/news/2011/12/27/jainab-shuttles-between-mass-graves.html (accessed 1 November 2012)

Skinner, M., 'Planning the archaeological recovery of evidence from recent mass graves', *Forensic Science International*, 34:4 (1987), 267–87

Skinner, M., D. Alempijevic & M. Djuric-Srejic, 'Guidelines for international forensic bio-archaeology monitors of mass grave exhumations', *Forensic Science International*, 134:2–3 (2003), 81–92

Skinner, M., H. York & M. Connor, 'Postburial disturbances of graves in Bosnia-Herzegovina', in W. Haglund & M. H. Sorg (eds), *Advances in*

Forensic Taphonomy: Method, Theory and Archaeological Perspective (Boca Raton, FL: CRC Press, 2002), pp. 293–308

Smajić, M., 'Očekuje se otkrivanje velikog broja srebreničkih žrtava', *Dnevni Avaz*, 29 June 2010, accessed 2 November 2012

Srebrenica Genocide Blog, 'Tertiary mass grave in Zalazje, preliminary work in progress', http://srebrenica-genocide.blogspot.com/2010/06/tertiary-zalazje-mass-grave.html (accessed 19 February 2014)

United Nations, UN Doc E/CN.4/1993/50, *Situation of Human Rights in the Territory of the Former Yugoslavia. Report on the Situation of Human Rights in the Territory of the Former Yugoslavia Submitted by Mr. Tadeusz Mazowiecki, Special Rapporteur of the Commission on Human Rights, Pursuant to Commission Resolution 1992/S-1/1 of 14 August 1992. Annex I: Summary of the Report of the Special Rapporteur on Extrajudicial, Summary or Arbitrary Executions on his Mission to Investigate Allegations of Mass Graves from 15 to 20 December 1992*, 10 February 1993, www.unhchr.ch/huridocda/huridoca.nsf/0811fcbd0b9f6bd580256673003 06dea/313049964d7549ec802567900054cf88?OpenDocument#more (accessed 28 October 2012)

United Nations, UN Doc S/1994/674/Add.2 (vol. V), *Final Report of the United Nations Commission of Experts Established Pursuant to Security Council Resolution 780 (1992). I. Mandate, Structure and Methods of Work*, 28 December 1994, www.his.com/~twarrick/commxyu3.htm#II (accessed 28 October 2012)

United Nations, UN Doc S/1994/674/Add.2 (vol. V), *Final Report of the United Nations Commission of Experts Established Pursuant to Security Council Resolution 780 (1992). Annex X: Mass graves*, 28 December 1994, http://ess.uwe.ac.uk/comexpert/ANX/X.htm#II (accessed 28 October 2012)

United Nations, UN Doc S/RES/780, *Resolution 780*, http://daccess-dds-ny.un.org/doc/UNDOC/GEN/N92/484/40/IMG/N9248440.pdf?OpenElement (accessed 28 October 2012)

US Naval Criminal Investigative Service, 'International Criminal Tribunal for Former Yugoslavia – forensic assistance to Srebrenica investigation', Report to International Criminal Tribunal for Former Yugoslavia, 16 January 1998

US Naval Criminal Investigative Service, 'Pilica Dom, Results of Forensic Investigation' Report to the ICTY, undated

Vennemeyer, M., 'An analysis of linkages between robbed primary graves and secondary graves related to Srebrenica missing', presented at 21st International Meeting on Forensic Medicine Alpe-Adria-Pannonia, Sarajevo, 30 May–2 June 2012

Verdict, *Prosecutor's Office of Bosnia and Herzegovina* v. *Radomir Vuković & Zoran Tomić* (X-KR-06/180–2), Trial Chamber, 2 July 2010

Wagner, S., *To Know Where He Lies: DNA Technology and the Search for Srebrenica's Missing* (Los Angeles, Berkeley, and London: University of California Press, 2008)

Williams, E. & J. Crews, 'From dust to dust: ethical and practical issues involved in the location, exhumation, and identification of bodies from mass graves', *Croatian Medical Journal*, 44:3 (2003), 251–8

Wright, R., 'Report on Excavations and Exhumations at the Glogova 1 Mass Grave in 2000', Report to ICTY, 9 February 2001

Yazedjian, L. & R. Kešetović, 'The application of traditional anthropological methods in a DNA-led identification process', in B. J. Adams & J. E. Byrd (eds), *Recovery, Analysis, and Identification of Commingled Human Remains* (New York: Humana Press, 2008), pp. 271–84

8

Identification, politics, disciplines: missing persons and colonial skeletons in South Africa[1]

Nicky Rousseau

Locating, exhuming, and identifying human remains associated with mass violence and genocide has come to occupy an important place in the panoply of transitional justice measures. Although such work cuts across the core transitional justice issues of justice, reparation and truth-telling, it has received surprisingly little critical attention from within the transitional justice field.[2] Existing studies, with some exception, can be characterized by an 'inside' literature concerned to document and develop the transitional justice field, often directed towards identifying 'best practice' and refining an appropriate 'tool-kit'.[3] Counterposed to this is a literature often having much in common with the growing critiques of humanitarianism and human rights, in which transitional justice is seen to be a technique of rule, often allied to nationalist and/or a global neo-liberal politics with its associated depoliticizing effects.[4]

In the wider transitional justice literature, the South African Truth and Reconciliation Commission (TRC) – still probably the most well-known and cited truth commission – looms large. It may thus be instructive to examine how the TRC came to exhume bodies, and how an associated practice developed, key features of which continue to characterize post-TRC exhumation work. It is easy to read this practice as comfortably fitting into either the above literatures – in the first, exhumation as an important tool in the transitional justice toolkit; in the latter, how a nationalist nation-building agenda deploys exhumed bodies of guerrilla soldiers, an example of what Katherine Verdery calls the 'political lives of dead bodies'.[5] Rather than pursuing either path, this chapter follows the practice of exhumation as it developed and then left the TRC's door. Such an approach, together with a focus on instrumentalities, interventions, and transformations, works on the borders, rather than situating itself along the dominant and rather well-worn tracks of transitional justice literature.

The chapter also looks at the practice of reburial, with a specific interest in how it came to be figured, and how it featured in debates on the colonial dead as well as in subsequent work of the Missing Persons Task Team (MPTT), a unit established in the TRC's wake. The focus on practice seeks to bring to view, not only the body of exhumation, but a range of other agencies or 'mediating inter-pretants' who do, interpret, and study the work of exhumation – exhumation teams, families, the media, scholars – and to think these *together*. This is part of a growing interest in these latter bodies, the disciplinary knowledge that they bring to bear and the body pro-duced through practices of exhumation and reburial, thus bringing to view the 'disciplines of the dead' – anthropology and archaeology, and more recently the genetics field.[6]

While the politics of dead bodies has come to refer to the potency of dead bodies in articulating certain kinds of politics, 'disciplines of the dead' indexes those scholarly disciplines associated with the dead human body. Rather than counterpose politics and disciplines, my interest here is to extend these concepts to include the politics that arise within and between individuals, disciplines, and institu-tions concerned with exhumation and the ways in which the dead body (or, depending on one's view, those speaking in the name of the dead) compels, 'disciplines', those around it to react in certain ways, calling forth particular practices or rituals. In short, both the body exhumed and the body exhuming is enjoined within and between the terms 'politics of dead bodies' and 'disciplines of the dead'.

The TRC: bodies of evidence and bodies of mourning[7]

Although not included in its mandate, the TRC exhumed a limited number of bodies between March 1997 and June 1998.[8] Many testi-monies to the TRC related to the unjustly buried: funerals banned or disrupted, bodies treated callously or just missing, demonstrating how not even death enabled the raced body to escape apartheid's bounds. Family members, mainly women, expressed their longing for 'just one bone' to bury.[9] In a certain sense, though, the first TRC exhumation arose not in direct response to these pleas but more fortuitously following disclosures by security police, applying to the TRC for amnesty. Over a fifteen-month period, the TRC exhumed around fifty bodies,[10] a tiny fraction of the more than 1,500 persons reported missing to the TRC.[11]

In March 1997, the TRC exhumed the remains of three guerrillas of the African National Congress (ANC) from farms rented by security police in the province of KwaZulu Natal. In the presence of investigators, commissioners, and family members, security police pointed out where they had secretly buried the three, whom they had abducted,[12] interrogated and shot dead on separate occasions. These exhumations drew attention to a significant number of guerrillas killed while infiltrating back into South Africa, but whose remains had not been returned to their families, rendering them missing persons. Further amnesty-related disclosures suggested that these were not always skirmishes as recorded, but planned ambushes in which security forces had no intention to effect arrests. Guerrilla bodies thus came to constitute key examples of the unjustly buried, requiring or calling forth forms of care, restitution, and justice, resulting in TRC efforts to trace, exhume, and identify them.

In most instances, those killed in skirmishes or ambushes were not secretly buried, but entered the legal regimes of the dead body. Accordingly, as is obligatory with unnatural or violent deaths, these bodies were assigned to a police domain. Photographed, fingerprinted, and transported to a police mortuary, the corpse would be recorded in a mortuary register as 'unknown black male' or 'unknown terrorist', and a state pathologist or state-appointed district surgeon would conduct a post-mortem examination. In many instances, even where identity had been established, these 'unknown' bodies were not released to the care of families, but buried in local cemeteries by private undertakers appointed by the state to bury indigent or unclaimed bodies. Here, undertakers recorded receipt of the bodies and provided a coffin deemed appropriate for black indigents by legal regulation. Thereafter the relevant town or city council issued a burial order, assigning the body to a specific gravesite, most often in an area designated for indigents, unclaimed or otherwise unfortunate bodies reliant on the state for burial.

This, then, was how bureaucrats imagined and codified the dead guerrilla, a process that produced a trail of documents for investigators. The practice was often more haphazard – sometimes undertakers took the body straight from the state mortuary for burial; on other occasions undertakers, in an attempt to increase their profit margins, illicitly put more than one body in a coffin, or more than one coffin to a grave; sometimes cemetery officials or grave-diggers, for any number of reasons, would decide to dig a grave different from that assigned by the burial order. In many cemeteries, the graves of those buried as paupers have long since been covered in grass or bush and now resemble desolate fields.[13] Nonetheless, the documentary trail provided important evidence for investigators.

Exhumations took place in something of a legal and forensic vacuum. Nonetheless, exhumations 'spoke' to the TRC's mandate and process in different ways. The TRC's official mandate made no reference to exhumations, nor did investigators follow formal legal procedures, seeking permission for individual exhumations from provincial premiers, rather than from local magistrates. Providing official acknowledgement of human rights violations is an important truth commission function, reaffirming – or, as in South Africa's case, affirming – a rights-bearing citizen, a recognition of which is seen to embody the promise of 'never again'.[14] Although commissioners repeated the ritual of acknowledgement to each victim in every public hearing, the materiality of exhumations and associated images provided a more powerful enactment of this ritual than the symbolic exchange of testimony and words. By returning the physical remains to the care of family, the TRC went beyond recommending reparation, as its mandate prescribed, to *enacting* reparation.[15]

Additionally, the first exhumations occurred shortly before the deadline for perpetrators to apply for amnesty and for the former government to appear before the TRC to answer questions, as part of a shift in gear to a more 'evidentiary paradigm' of determining accountability for human rights violations. Exhumations thus provided dramatic material evidence of police killings and atrocity, bodies rising from their graves, as it were, to accuse members of the former government who continued to deny systematic involvement in gross human rights abuse. Chastising them on the occasion of the first reburials, former President Mandela took 'this opportunity, as president of South Africa, to call on all political parties and organizations, on all soldiers and others across the old political divide – on all among these and other forces who have reason to apply for amnesty – to do so before the 10th of May'.[16]

More widely, TRC exhumations coincided with the internationalization of exhumation and missing persons' work. While work in Argentina, pioneered by the Argentine Forensic Anthropology Team (EAAF), had been ongoing since the mid-1980s, events in the former Yugoslavia and Rwanda in the first half of the 1990s fuelled the growth of exhuming the bodies of mass violence or genocide. Here, too, the body of evidence rather than that of mourning or care drove the expansion of this practice through the work of the International Criminal Tribunals of Yugoslavia and Rwanda. This work brought together different teams, involving a range of experts – physical anthropologists, archaeologists, anatomists, and physicians. Through these interactions and work, debates regarding exhumations and forensic practice came to the fore. One concerned the place of families in exhumation practice; another related to whether DNA testing should routinely be done on exhumed human remains. Rather than being merely a technical question, this latter debate raised important issues regarding resources and expertise.[17]

The TRC was not party to these multiple and unfolding debates about technologies and techniques, authority and power. Notwithstanding contact with the EAAF shortly after the first exhumations,[18] the TRC's exhumation programme operated outside of the forensic frameworks developed by the EAAF and other exhumation experts. Aside from some 'technical advice' provided on one case by the EAAF, no exhumations involved forensic anthropologists or archaeologists: a pathologist oversaw some exhumations in one region, while members of a police forensic laboratory assisted in others, largely to oversee the excavation of the grave, and to take photographs. Most excavations involved a front-end loader, assisted by local grave diggers, who also assisted the police forensic unit to remove the skeletal remains.

Unsurprisingly, then, a subsequent audit of exhumations conducted by the TRC itself in 1999 uncovered serious irregularities, leading to misidentifications and incorrect remains being handed to a number of families.[19] This raised the prospect of causing untold anguish for the affected families, undermining the objectives of a truth commission to provide healing through the techniques of truth recovery and reparation. The reasons for these irregularities were manifold – a cavalier police investigator, inaccurate information arising from a typographical misalignment of columns in a list of guerrilla fatalities supplied by the ANC, the absence of forensic procedures, and, in a few cases, family members who identified skeletal remains according to 'non-scientific' criteria. For example, a news agency reported in 1998 that

[t]he wife of a dead Umkhonto we Sizwe soldier identified his body by his crooked teeth on Monday when members of the Truth and Reconciliation Commission's investigative unit exhumed graves near Louis Trichardt in Northern Province. ... Alice Tati [sic] said the large skull with crooked teeth that was found in a grave at Sekoto cemetery belonged to her husband, Zola Tati [sic], of Port Elizabeth.[20]

A brother-in-law identified a skull by its shape, while a brother claimed one of three skeletons on the basis of a pair of sandals, which he recognized.[21]

This pall cast a wider shadow. Within the TRC, disbelief and distress met the audit's results: the powerful images of exhumed skeletons being returned to families had been counted as some of the commission's uncontested successes. When 'evidentiary proof' was provided – such as that the thirteen partially saponified skeletons exhumed from a farm grave were not guerrillas but elderly people, several of whom still had hospital identification tags around their wrists indicating they had died in hospital beds – some TRC staff responded with anger, suggesting 'They're just bones, why couldn't the matter be left sleeping instead of re-traumatizing families?' The most powerful counter-argument sometimes was not, as may be anticipated, that this was after all the *Truth* Commission, but rather that other families were being denied the opportunity to rebury their dead. This left a strong legacy of the importance of 'best forensic practice', which was emphasized in the TRC's recommendations to government and in the subsequent development of an exhumation unit in the post-TRC period.[22]

Burying the unjustly dead

In May 1997, the public broadcaster provided extensive coverage of the first reburial ceremony, rerunning images of the exhumations themselves, showing scenes of skeletal remains – long bones and, most dramatically, a skull, material witnesses from the grave – emerging from the rich brown earth – scenes that journalist Max du Preez predicted would 'be one of the strongest visual memories of the Truth and Reconciliation process'. The narrative which accompanied this footage spoke of 'uncover[ing] secrets of the past', hinting that more 'secret killings on farms' would be revealed in the coming weeks.[23] It is worth identifying and unpicking some of the threads here, and how they came into being, as this script not only influenced the remaining TRC exhumations, but had a longer life in constituting what is increasingly a normative tradition in South Africa of how to rebury the dead who were unjustly buried.

This script drew on far longer histories of funerary practices, as funeral and burial matters in South Africa have long been political as well as cultural. One strand relates to the practice of state burial for bodies of indigent citizens, which had particular force in South Africa, where it was overlaid with the politics of race. Garrey Dennie has written of African families' long struggles from the late nineteenth century to avoid pauper burials.[24] Dennie traces raced differences in the treatment of corpses: until 1942, coffins for black indigents had detachable bottoms, rendering them recyclable; coffins for white indigents were better constructed, lined with fabric, had handles, and, from the 1940s, a nameplate recording name and date of death. Even after regulations disallowed conveying black indigents on an open truck, they permitted undertakers to convey and bury four black indigents at a time, in contrast to the white indigent's individual hearse and burial. Most injurious for black Christian families was the fact that while a minister of religion was a requirement at white pauper funerals, this was not the case for black paupers, suggesting these bodies fell outside the boundaries of the sacred.[25] The stain of a pauper's burial was so potent that in 1989 an important apartheid functionary buried the mortal remains of his relative, Sabata Dalindyebo, the head of the royal Thembu house to which Nelson Mandela belonged, in a section of a cemetery reserved for female paupers. This gesture of contempt arose from Dalindyebo's strong opposition to apartheid; the gendered aspect served to double the insult.[26]

As a result of such profanities, 'pauper burials' were regarded with abhorrence. To escape such a fate, not uncommon in a population with large numbers of migrants, burial societies were created, mainly by women, as a means to rescue bodies from apartheid's depredations. As Dennie suggests, 'In a life littered with the uncertainties of poverty, burial societies offered Africans a single assurance: the corpses of deceased members would be treated as sacred.'[27] Burial societies provided funds for funerals and transported migrant bodies to rural homesteads, as well as scripting funerals. Under their direction, and as access to refrigeration removed the need for haste, funerals became far larger and more important occasions, thereby '[inventing] a new cultural economy of burial in which … the bodies of their dead [were lavished] with resources unavailable to the bodies of the living',[28] signalling a politics of the everyday.

From the mid-1970s onwards, as youth politics exploded on the scene, funerals were rescripted and came to constitute an important repertoire of political resistance. From initially spontaneous expressions of defiance by young mourners at gravesites of their peers killed during student protests in 1976, and influenced by the visually powerful and emotional funeral of Black Consciousness leader Steve Biko, a more routine script of the political funeral emerged.[29] If burial societies constituted communities of care, which sought to rescue racialized bodies, here funeral committees constituted communities of solidarity, which exemplified the body of resistance. Usurping the role of burial societies, and through often complex and contested negotiations with families, the funeral committee scripted an overtly political funeral from wake to grave – speeches, songs, pamphlets, banners, and flags. The one did not replace the other – many 'struggle songs' were already adaptations of hymns, and such songs were added to more conventional funeral fare; many religious figures supported or participated in the anti-apartheid struggle, injecting a political slant into even the religious rituals of funerals.

The potency of *this* dead body's political life lay in its requiring, in the face of death, not mourning or sorrow, but defiance and resistance, conscripting its peers and families into freedom's struggle – the slogan, 'Freedom or Death: Victory is Certain' worn on T-shirts and painted on banners during the 1980s representing the pledge of those so conscripted. More militarized aspects celebrated the guerrilla – songs from military camps, the famous *toyi-toyi*,[30] and guards of honour in khaki and berets flanking the coffin, fists raised. The funeral, rather than marking a moment of closure, can be seen here to open a ledger of debt, which could only be settled by intensified resistance and further deaths. Indeed, police and mourners regularly clashed at such occasions, generating new fatalities, thus occasioning new funerals. Attempts by the state to control or limit such occasions, deploying armed police, and later by imposing severe restrictions, which included prohibiting political speeches and regalia, never entirely quelled these powerful moments of mobilization.

As the dawn of democracy grew closer in the early 1990s, the funeral script again underwent revisions. In what would be the anti-apartheid struggle's most violent period, the ANC buried two liberation movement icons – former Chief of Staff of the ANC's guerrilla army, Chris Hani, whom white right-wingers assassinated, and Oliver Tambo, president of the ANC throughout its long sojourn in exile and the ANC's public face internationally during Nelson Mandela's incarceration. Here, while many of the earlier accoutrements and rituals were evident, defiance and mobilization gave way to the more sombre and official funeral of a state *to come*. Indeed, for the first time, apartheid police rather than facing off with an enemy escorted and protected mourners, a powerful symbolic moment marking an official, if reluctant, recognition that those regarded as 'bare life', and thus available to be killed,[31] were now citizens, worthy of protection.

Elements of both of these forms of funeral were evident in television footage of the reburial, which followed the first TRC exhumations; a high-profile affair, attended by former President Mandela, other senior government and party officials and several thousand ANC members and supporters.[32] Coffins draped with ANC flags flanked the podium; mourners, many dressed in party colours, sang songs associated with the freedom struggle. Notably, although only three bodies had been exhumed, five coffins were evident: during the earlier investigation, security police had pointed out a spot where the bodies of a further two guerrillas had been thrown, weighted, into the crocodile-infested Tugela River. The ANC symbolically reburied the two alongside their comrades: in this instance, the materiality of the coffins came to constitute the absent bodies cast into the river. In his address, President Mandela proclaimed the five fallen guerrillas 'heroes', who 'did not die in vain' but would be 'inscribed in the nation's roll of honour'. He presented a medal to the young son of Phila Ndwandwe, the single female guerrilla exhumed (one of two in the total of fifty-odd exhumations conducted by the TRC).[33]

In the television footage, vignettes of Phila Ndwandwe and her family interlaced the scenes from the exhumation site and the reburial. Against violent death's body – skull and disarticulated bones – the living, affective, fleshed body, a young Phila, looked out from family photos, including one with her infant son, from whom the abduction would soon separate her. Beyond this, at many levels the scenes unfolding before the camera encompassed the everyday sad rituals and routes familiar to all bereaved families as they prepare for surrendering the beloved body: Ndwandwe's family in the mortuary, looking through a glass window at the skeletal remains, anatomically laid out, and thus constituting a human body; holding a funeral vigil; preparing food for mourners; emerging from the last viewing of the open coffin before the funeral; and the final throwing of handfuls of soil onto the coffin. In some respects, footage drew attention to two different discourses: one of nation and one of family. While the funeral and President Mandela's speech clearly produced Ndwandwe and her comrades as bodies of the new nation, this was not purely a state or party production. Families themselves drew these bodies into this discourse of struggle and nation. Thus

Ndwandwe's sister commented to the television crew that she was 'so proud' of her sister, 'a hero', while an aunt spoke of the family's relief to find out that she was not, as they had been led to believe, 'an askari' (that is, a 'traitor' who had 'sold her people' by going to work for the security police), but instead had been a 'brave person'.[34]

Such images and discourses played a key shaping role, and as further exhumations took place, they began to assume a familiar routine that operated to reverse the ignominious and anonymous pauper burial, restoring individual personhood. Once investigators had located a grave site, the TRC would organize an exhumation; families, local political and government figures (including in many instances provincial premiers) and the media would be informed and invited. After the exhumation, skeletal remains were transported to a mortuary before being handed over to families. Thereafter local or provincial party structures, assisted by government structures, organized or provided financial and logistical assistance. In keeping with their status as guerrillas, reburying the remains generally took the form of a military funeral, replete with folded flags, and twenty-one-gun salutes. Although the political party, not the TRC, shaped the form of the reburial – its function ending when the skeletal remains were returned to families – over time, many of the politically affective aspects seen at the first reburial began to characterize the exhumations themselves. A later TRC *Special Report*, covering an exhumation in 1998, noted that 'Just a few meters away, the scene around the three graves looks more like an ANC rally than a site of an exhumation, but the premier of the North West, Popo Molefe, says the ANC members are here to support the families.'[35] In this instance, several busloads of ANC members, dressed in party regalia, attended, and the work of exhumation was accompanied by songs associated with the guerrilla war.

Exhumations and the associated practice of burial, while restoring personhood, thus placed, not a family member, but the armed guerrilla at the centre of the script. This figure had played an important but primarily symbolic role, rather than the many thousands of youths, armed – if at all – with stones, who by and large used their bodies as weapons and whom police killed in street protests, or the many thousands more killed in inter-civilian violence. This latter violence, much of which security forces encouraged and armed, included civilians targeted because they lived in rival political territory. This centring of the guerrilla was underscored by the fact that, with one exception,[36] all TRC exhumations were of guerrilla bodies, even though they did not constitute the majority of persons reported missing to the TRC.

TRC exhumations can thus arguably be seen to produce both the nationalist discourse and the need for 'best practice', confirming the script suggested by the dominant literature on transitional justice and exhumation noted earlier. This, however, may be too hasty a conclusion. The following section begins to unsettle this seemingly comfortable fit by exploring the ways in which the elevation of the forensic occurred alongside and in the face of other controversies regarding body politics associated with the unjustly dead or buried.

'Skeletons in the cupboard'[37]

As historian Premesh Lalu notes, it 'was not altogether out of place', then, 'in an environment where the return and excavation of dismembered bodies became a national preoccupation through the TRC process',[38] that bones of the earlier dead were said to be restive and, in the TRC's language, demanding repair and restitution. One such instance concerned a quest to locate the head of the Xhosa king, Hintsa, killed and believed decapitated by British colonial forces on 12 May 1835,[39] another a demand to return the remains of Sarah Baartman, whose body parts, including genitalia, and body cast had been displayed as 'the Hottentot Venus' in the Jardin des Plantes and later Musée de l'Homme in Paris;[40] a third instance arose through research by historians on museum collections of skeletal remains in South Africa and Europe.[41] These suggested that, while the TRC had been charged with accounting for human rights abuse during the apartheid period, colonialism's violence remained unresolved.[42]

These bodies spoke to longer histories of dismemberment and dissection, and those of acquisition, whether as war trophies or other means of collection. The skeletal remains in museums, whose afterlives historians Martin Legassick and Ciraj Rassool researched, involved extensive practices of grave-robbing, defleshing, and trafficking of even the newly dead and buried. Moreover, the study of many such bodies was linked to the emerging field of racial science in which scientists read race on the body's surface and interior. Henri de Blainville and Georges Cuvier studied and dissected Baartman's body; Rassool and Legassick documented how British and European scientists competed to gain access to 'bushman bodies' for the purposes of racial science.[43]

Colonialism's violence thus included the violence of knowledge and the agency of the disciplines – with respect to bodies of anthropology, archaeology, and anatomy – in such violence and in elaborating racial science through study of both live and dead bodies. But it was not only the distant past that lay unexamined and unaccounted for: Baartman's body parts had continued to be displayed until 1972 and her body cast until 1974, just as many unethically collected skeletal remains still form part of museum collections, available for further research. Scholarly engagements arising from Rassool and Legassick's research later led to the discovery of two macerated corpses in a collection of one Emil Breitinger, a Nazi sympathizer who had headed the Institute for Human Biology/Anthropology at the University of Vienna; these, named by Rassool and Legassick as Klaas and Trooi Pienaar, had been acquired from the collection of Austrian anthropologist Rudolph Pöch, who had assiduously collected human remains as 'specimens' of 'primitive' or 'inferior' races'.[44]

Some of these controversies spilled into a public debate in Cape Town in 2004 following the exhumation of over 1,000 skeletons, believed to include slaves, from a colonial-era cemetery uncovered during the construction of an upmarket hotel and lifestyle centre in 'Cape Town's glitzy international zone'.[45] Here it was not merely development which had trumped human remains, but the fact that archaeologists and anthropologists, contracted to clear the cemetery, proposed that skeletal remains should not be buried but 'decently reinterred' with privileged access for 'bona fide researchers' to study 'respectfully'. This response by the scientific community was seen to continue, or at the very least to fail to take into account, science's prior legacies of collection and research. For multiple reasons – political, institutional, biographical – this contest and the public activism associated with it was incendiary, with scientists accused of engaging in the 'mass harvesting' of research specimens.[46] For some, these histories have left an indelible stain on the disciplines associated with them; at times, this has included a rejection of all scientific interventions and modes of reading or studying colonial bones, which have been recast as ancestral bones. Thus suggestions that mitochondrial DNA analysis could assist in identifying Sarah Baartman's kin, and later those of the Pienaars, were vigorously opposed.

Zoe Crossland, however, has pointed to more complex distinctions at work in science's encounter with the human corpse in eighteenth- and nineteenth-century Britain. Thus, while the most marginal bodies (criminals, the poor, colonial subjects) were subjected to dissection, post-mortem practices were regarded as different and tended to concern elite bodies.[47] This was precisely the view seemingly taken with regard to Sabata Dalindyebo's body, retrieved from his ignominious pauper's grave, amidst rumours that those who inflicted this insulting burial may also have mutilated his body. Thus, although suggestions of forensic examination were regarded as sacrilegious in the case of Sarah Baartman, in the Dalindyebo matter, as Dennie points out, a post-mortem 'was called to determine whether such sacrilege had taken place …. [here] modern medical science [is] validat[ing] more deeply held notions of the sacredness of the body'.[48] In this case, as in eighteenth- and nineteenth-century Britain, the post-mortem examination was seen to mark the body as human, existing within a community of care, one which acted to prepare it for its sacred ancestral afterlife; in so doing, the post-mortem was marked off from mere dissection, a practice long associated with the animal and the fate of those – paupers, prisoners – who represented only 'bare life'. This suggests that while interventions in and on the dead body perform the function of constructing a line between the living and the dead body, Crossland's work points to finer distinctions, which may operate to draw a line between the dissected and the autopsied body. These are suggestive of different ontologies at work,[49] but also of a certain instability of meaning associated with the dead body (or its remains), which is subject both to continuity and difference.

In several respects, then, the developments associated with the long dead served to interrupt the promise of closure suggested by the TRC and exemplified in the physical acts of exhumation and reburial. By calling attention to longer histories of the dead body and colonialism, they called into question any notion that accounting for apartheid violence alone would be sufficient to address the past's injustices. By pointing to contiguity in the logics governing the dead body of apartheid and those of colonial violence, these developments implicitly suggested a similar contiguity in the modes and techniques of reading dead bodies and skeletal remains associated with these two histories of violence. Indeed, in the post-TRC era, it would be through the same disciplines of anthropology, archaeology, and anatomy that a more professional practice of exhumation would emerge than that which characterized the TRC's practice. Yet, while these disciplines and their associated professionals received such short shrift in the public contests over the long dead, this has not been the case with regard to exhumation practices associated with apartheid's dead.

The missing persons task team

Following recommendations made by the TRC, a unit was established within South Africa's National Prosecuting Authority in
2004–5 to examine unresolved TRC missing person cases, estimated
to be 'some 477'.[50] This figure included instances where the fate of
the missing person was known but the body's fate unknown. To
date, much of the Missing Persons Task Team's (MPTT) work has
focused on tracing, exhuming, and identifying these latter bodies.
Although existing within a government structure, geared towards
the prosecution of political crimes including those arising from the
TRC, the MPTT worked closely with, and largely modelled itself on,
the EAAF, a team that sees the physical and forensic work of exhumation and identification as one aspect of a wider collaborative and
restorative process with families. This has again enjoined the body
of evidence to the body of mourning, although somewhat ironically,
given the MPTT's location in a prosecutorial service, the latter has
dominated.

Forensic expertise, a key issue in tribunals and trials where the
body has been rendered as the 'last witness', has played an important
role where cause of death and individual identification are directed
towards '(ending) the agonising circle of uncertainty' in which the
families find themselves.[51] For the MPTT, misidentifications associated with a number of the TRC exhumations underscored the need
for forensic expertise. However, such expertise was largely non-
existent locally: the police forensic division had no forensic archaeologists or anthropologists in its employ and, in any event, its head
was the wife of a former security policeman responsible for killing the very persons whose remains were among those the MPTT
aimed to locate. Similarly, the University of Pretoria, which had provided the apartheid police with forensic support in cases requiring
anthropological expertise, had also been a key ideological site for
apartheid. Although the MPTT has drawn on expertise from both
institutions on specific cases, it sought to develop an independent
team, contracting the EAAF to conduct the first exhumations and
to assist in developing a local South African team. This has grown
into a longer relationship; a member of the EAAF based permanently in South Africa has trained a group of young postgraduate
students, who have come to constitute a modest exhumation team.
This choice has not been without its own controversies: several team
members' postgraduate training included exhuming the colonial-
era skeletons discussed earlier; a few, under the guidance of their

professor (a key protagonist in those disputes), had sought to conduct further research on the skeletal remains. But here, where physical anthropology has produced cause of death and the individual identities of apartheid's violated and dead bodies in the service of the nation, it has been uncontroversial. Nonetheless, Rassool asserts that the move to human rights work has provided a means to erase the earlier stains from the implicated individuals, institutions, and disciplines.[52] Whether this is so or not, an effect has been to draw a line between colonial- and apartheid-era bones, disrupting their apparent contiguity, rather than the way in which human remains from the colonial era had previously served to interrupt the TRC's language of repair by drawing attention to longer histories of violence and injustice. This is doubly ironic, given that the sanctioned work on skeletal remains of apartheid's dead includes techniques of identification that continue to assign markers of race. Such techniques remain standard and normative within the forensic disciplines, despite resting on notions of measurement and typology, which underpinned racial science, and against a growing lobby, which suggests that at best such markers are predictive and geographical rather than inherent.[53]

Aside from close attention to forensic investigation, the imprint and script developed during the TRC is still strongly visible. At the time of writing, the MPTT has exhumed ninety-four remains, overwhelmingly of guerrillas, with a smaller number of disappeared activists, including at least three persons killed by liberation movement perpetrators. The dominance of guerrillas, the team insists, is not a matter of political preference; while it continues to investigate other cases, such as those who disappeared during pre-transition violence in the early 1990s, it has had little success. Guerrilla bodies were, by and large, almost always political and if killed in ambushes or skirmishes invariably left a documentary trace; the bodies of those killed in protest action or inter-civilian violence were buried in city cemeteries where 'political' bodies are largely indistinguishable from large numbers of deaths arising from criminal or inter-personal violence. Nonetheless, these challenges bring into sharp relief the question of which bodies matter.

While much of the MPTT's day-to-day work happens outside the media's spotlight, exhumations continue to attract media attention. However, the key moments in which the body is scripted still take place after exhumation and forensic examination has been concluded. Here, a further ceremonial aspect has developed: namely, the handover ceremony. The MPTT has a limited role in this, and is not itself directly involved in the reburial. Although its specific format, location, or scale varies, the handover has acquired a status of its own, and in most instances takes place at the premier post-apartheid memorial site, Freedom Park. As with the reburial, it has come to be a moment of celebrating the guerrilla, and inscribing the individual identified guerrilla into the pantheon of heroes: the coffin, draped in the organization's flag, is often guarded by veterans in military fatigues, accompanied by songs of the guerrilla movement. Similarly, the reburial's scale and character depend on a range of factors, both political and more contingent. Thus those organizing or in attendance may be local ANC members, especially military veterans, local or provincial government officials, or, on occasion, important members of the national government.[54]

Such moments are not merely political party celebrations (overwhelmingly ANC), but are framed within a certain nation-building ethos, which continues to place the guerrilla at the centre of memory. Thus although South Africa has not gone the route of a national 'Heroes Acre' for its war dead, nor are these occasions state functions, nonetheless the guerrilla is valorized. This has been accompanied by a quiet revision by of the TRC's more critical stance on the liberation movements, a revision that has gathered momentum under the current President, himself a senior guerrilla commander. It has included how the struggle against apartheid is memorialized, the provision of state pensions and benefits to ex-guerrillas, accompanied by growing mobilization of liberation movement military veteran's associations.

Here again, we seem to be drawn inexorably towards the long-established relationship between nationalism and the dead body.[55] Indeed, by dint of legislation, the National Heritage Resources Act deals with responsibility for the care of graves with historic or national significance, including those who died in the cause of the liberation struggle. These graves, according to this legislation, form part of the 'national estate', transforming the dead into heritage with *national* significance, available for both memorialization and tourism. However, this would be to ignore more complex dimensions at work. Certainly at times the ANC deploys reburials with greater deliberation and intent, as was the case in an election year in a politically contested region when a single exhumation of five activists produced no less than three ceremonies, two addressed by national ministers, while current President Zuma himself gave a eulogy at the reburial.[56] Most often, reburials are far more a local, even community affair, and often represent the endurance of combatant identities. Indeed it is such events that act to solidify this community, whose own access to benefits and opportunities in part relies on the maintenance rather than the dissolution of this identity, and who, by and large, have felt marginalized and unacknowledged in the post-democracy period. It is also clear that these moments are valued and sought after by many family members. Whether or not this is a spontaneous desire or a response to a format offered and institutionalized by the TRC is debatable. Perhaps a more important question to ask is what gives this format such traction? To do so requires further thinking about the particular form and script associated with both TRC and MPTT exhumations, as well as considering the meaning of these in relation to the families of the exhumed. This takes us, in the first place, back to the political funerals of the anti-apartheid struggle.

The impetus to script funerals of those killed during the anti-apartheid struggle as politicized moments of resistance and mobilization often left little room for personal, familial grief. Instead, '[p]ersonal pain and loss become depersonalized into one more death along the path of freedom, one more container of blood emptied to water the tree of freedom, one more statistic in the long saga of the nation's losses'.[57] Political movements themselves took responsibility for organizing many of these funerals, sometimes by mutual agreement with families, but often, too, through considerable pressure, even 'against [the] will' of the family concerned.[58] The sister of a detainee who died in custody recently commented 'we felt overwhelmed by the people organizing the funeral. They wanted to tell us what to say about Neil on the tombstone. My parents kept saying: "But he's our son …" They said: "No he died for us."'[59] Families, in this sense, were constructed as having bequeathed their sons, daughters, husbands, or wives to a nation *yet to come*, a nation few believed lay in their lifetimes.

Yet, today it would seem to be the rescripted political funeral for which families now yearn as an appropriate format – or more particularly the struggle funeral rescripted as official funeral, a more ceremonial and tightly scripted affair of state – in which the nation is enjoined to celebrate those who had lived and died for freedom. But, although desired, the local character of these reburials, which are not formal state functions, means some funerals enjoy more attention (and thus more power) than others. This itself becomes a source of further grievance or pain for families. Insults may be evident in how elaborate a coffin was, the attending crowd's size, whether media were present, how many party or government officials paid their respects, and of course, which funeral the President attended. The wives of one of the first group of guerrillas to be exhumed by the MPTT voiced their dissatisfaction in interviews conducted by Jay Aronson: 'It was like we were burying an old person. We are not happy at all. There were no flags. There were no MKs to march for them to show people that these people have fought for this country. It was like a normal funeral.' Echoing similar sentiments, others suggested their husbands' reburial 'was not proper':

> No matter, they put some stones, the headstones. That doesn't interest us. We wanted these people to be buried as soldiers and respected as people who fought for this country. We are here now, we are free, because of the people like them. Why [are they] not being respected like others? ... So the truth must be said.[60]

The desire for a high-profile political funeral and the accompanying dissatisfaction and disappointment has been understood through two primary and related lenses. The one points to the need for greater acknowledgement of sacrifice. The sister of a combatant killed by the security forces and later exhumed, described visiting parliament in the post-democracy era: 'As I stood there, I thought, this is what Peter died for and who knows his name? He is forgotten.'[61] This forgetting – and this provides the second lens – is materially evident in the inability of transitional justice mechanisms to impact on longer legacies of inequity and structural violence. This is a view frequently expressed by the MPTT, and echoed in Aronson, which points to the inevitable incompleteness of repair where families exist in dire socio-economic circumstances, little changed by political democracy.[62] It is not uncommon for the MPTT to meet families for whom putting a meal on the table is a daily struggle, or who are unable to pay for electricity. In post-democracy, communities are riven by those who are seen to have enjoyed the fruits of democracy and those – the majority – whose materials lives remain largely unchanged. These distinctions are intimate, carefully watched and noted, physical in their visibility.[63] The advancement of a son's, husband's, or brother's peers, often exemplified by employment and possession of the potent symbol of a car, and by association lifting the prospects for their wider families, is a matter of deep sorrow for those whose mainly sons or husbands are missing or killed. And here the notion of the ultimate sacrifice is powerful; here 'the bodies .... serve as a reminder to those in power of the bitter cost of liberation to numerous families, who by and large continue, despite this sacrifice, to live in conditions of deprivation and poverty.'[64]

The politicized and heroic reburial thus addresses a complex amalgam of emotions and needs – on the one hand, it calls for a recognition of freedom's sacrifice, it enacts a proper burial so the missing and unjustly buried now returned to family and community may rest; but in this, it also functions as a reminder (even a protest) that the family bequest to the nation *yet to be* has not been reciprocated in the nation *now present*. Here, the materiality of the remains exemplified in the oft-repeated cry for 'just one bone' is shown to be insufficient; indeed, the insistence on the unfulfilled promise of the nation *now present* is one disabling or refusing closure. For Lizzie Sefolo, the 'sickness was removed [when the bodies were initially recovered], but now it's coming back. Because it's like they were not really people who fought for this country, *it was just remains*' (my emphasis).[65]

This suggests that the issues relating to the family require careful thinking, as well as a more careful disentangling of the seemingly sequential journey from the liminal status of being missing to final reburial, a journey that often engages radically different temporalities. The disappointments expressed in Aronson's interviews assume greater force considering the emphasis that the MPTT, drawing on the EAAF's model, places on the family. This has meant engaging with families, not just as sources of pre-mortem information or persons to whom reports are given, but also as integral to its practice. Encouraged to think of the process as an often lengthy journey, in which they are fellow or co-travellers, family members are often physically present at the site of exhumation, sometimes assisting the team in small ways; at times they will be invited into the laboratory where the skeletal remains will be anatomically laid out and forensic results will be explained and discussed, sometimes family members will touch or hold the bones, and perhaps examine clothing or artefacts found in the grave. On occasion a prayer may be said or a rite associated with the dead will be performed at the scene of death, the exhumation, or in the laboratory, transforming again evidence's body into one of mourning. Family members often speak of the period of investigation and exhumation – as Lizzie Sefolo suggests above – as a healing time, one that often follows a period of silence and official neglect. What is evident from Sefolo's comments is the power of official acknowledgement, one the team provides, but which MPTT head, Madeleine Fullard, suggests needs to be public, indeed 'shouted from the roof-tops'.[66]

At the same time, the interviews conducted by Aronson constitute a small subset of victim families, and it is not at all clear that those he interviewed represent a general view or a particular dissatisfaction

focused on some reburials. There is perhaps a tendency to essential-
ize notions of family, their needs and desires. Those who work with
families are only too aware of complex family dynamics, fault lines
within which the question of who speaks for the family and for the
dead is often disputatious. Exhumations and their associated investigations sometimes reveal explosive family secrets: a combatant's
betrayal to the authorities by a family member, neighbour, or lover;
rivalries within or between families in the same exhumation; revela-
tions emerging during DNA analysis regarding paternity. Nor is the
idea of an exhumation always desired or regarded as healing: the
children of a disappeared activist openly expressed lack of interest
in searching for bones, preferring a focus on the living; news of the
planned investigation and possible exhumation returned a wife to
such a severe depression, that it rendered her physically and psych-
ically unrecognizable to a MPTT investigator between visits over
a few months. Yet despite intimate knowledge of these fractures,
sometimes running along fault lines of gender and generation, the
notion of 'family', often a core rationale for exhumation work, often
remains under-theorized.[67]

Aronson, whose evocative interviews are cited above, proposes
that, in line with the International Commission for Missing Persons,
a 'grave to grave' policy should be implemented, in which families
should not just be co-travellers, but co-drivers helping to shape
policy and identifying priorities, including memorialization.[68] This
would seem to intensify the current script rather than to open it to a
more careful reading.

Conclusion

The TRC privileged recovering, identifying, and returning the material and individual body of the guerrilla and exhumations came to be
scripted through a range of agencies, including the TRC, families,
the media, government, as well as the ANC. Although reburials fell
outside the TRC's purview, being the domain of family and the ANC,
they constituted an important moment, in which the body handed
over to the family now returned to its political community as well
as to a wider nation. Reburials also had the effect of rescripting the
exhumations themselves, becoming dominantly ANC moments.
Through the scripts of exhumation and reburial, the absent and
missing body was produced as evidence, testifying from the grave
to apartheid's atrocity, and later, individually identified, produced as
the nation's hero on whose body freedom rested. The body of grief

and mourning, testified to over and over again in the public hearings, was entangled in these depictions but perhaps overwritten by the larger narratives of what Ciraj Rassool has referred to as a narrative of 'ancestral heroes of the nation'.[69] A further aspect was the misidentification of skeletal remains, a blunder that produced exhumation as a field requiring professionalization, ensuring appropriate expertise and knowledge to remove remains from their improper graves and to conduct the important task of identification.

Even as the TRC was operating, other bodies of the unjustly dead and buried came to the fore and, in the same language of reconciliation and repair, provided something of an interruption, pointing to the failure to account for earlier colonial violence, including the violence of knowledge and racial science. Here attention was drawn to the way in which, even as they may have tried to reckon with this past, scientists continued to regard the body as an object of study requiring the specific expertise of science, while at the same time regarding science's own history as irrelevant or off limits.

In the cases of the colonial dead, all forms of forensic investigation have thus far been refused. Nonetheless, formal handovers accompanied the return of, first, Sarah Baartman from Paris and, more recently, Klaas and Trooi Pienaar, who 'had entered the Natural History Museum (in Vienna) as types' and their reburials strongly echoed those associated with the TRC and MPTT,[70] despite Rassool's prediction in this instance that 'a rehumanisation and privatisation [would be sought] through local reburials, and a retreat from public inscription'.[71] Here it would seem that the imperative to wrest these remains from their object status in museums and research collections resulted in the adoption of the TRC-MPTT script, a script overlaid with longer histories of the political funeral. Indeed, President Zuma addressed the reburial of the Pienaars in 2013, just as former President Mbeki addressed that of Sarah Baartman. An ethos of nation-building characterized both, scripted as restoring the dignity of the victims of colonialism and racial science.

Whereas the coffin in which the exhumed and missing body of the apartheid dead affected a transformation of incomplete and fragmented remains into a mournable body, in the case of Baartman and the Pienaars, the coffin served as well to rehumanize, recuperating the body regarded as first a specimen, then as a museum artefact.[72] If, as Rassool suggested, the mode of exhumation and reburial turned the missing dead of the apartheid era into 'ancestors of the nation',[73] then here one could say that colonial dead have been inscribed not only as citizens but into the pantheon of heroes, those who have sacrificed all, for and on whom the nation rests. Following this, if colonial bodies had initially interrupted the TRC scripts, but the later role of physical anthropology in the MPTT had served to draw a line neatly separating apartheid-era and colonial bodies, then the politics of personhood have tended to erase that line, drawing them ever closer together. These moves signal the ongoing instability of South Africa's bodies of violence.

Notes

1   This chapter, although expressing personal views, draws on experiences of working in the Truth and Reconciliation Commission and in the Missing Persons Task Team (MPTT). Thanks to Ciraj Rassool, Madeleine Fullard, and members of a graduate reading group on the dead body – Riedwaan Moosage, Bianca van Laun, and Aidan Erasmus – for comments and many stimulating discussions.

2   This contrasts with a growing literature on issues of memory and materiality, much of which arises from recent Spanish Civil War exhumations. See, for example, F. Ferrándiz, 'Cries and whispers: exhuming and narrating defeat in Spain today', *Journal of Spanish Cultural Studies*, 9:2 (2008), 177–92, and 'The return of Civil War ghosts: the ethnography of exhumations in contemporary Spain', *Anthropology Today*, 22:3 (2006), 7–12; L. Renshaw, *Exhuming Loss: Memory, Materiality and Mass Graves of the Spanish Civil War* (Walnut Creek, CA: Left Coast Press, 2011).

3   S. Robins, 'Towards victim-centred transitional justice: understanding the needs of families of the disappeared in post-conflict Nepal', *International Journal of Transitional Justice*, 5:1 (2011), 75–98; P. Aguilar, 'Transitional or post-transitional justice: recent thoughts on the Spanish case', *South European Society and Politics*, 13:4 (December 2008), 417–33; J. Aronson, 'The strengths and limitations of South Africa's search for apartheid-era missing persons', *International Journal of Transitional Justice*, 5 (2011), 262–81.

4   See B. Bevernage & L. Colaert, 'History from the grave: politics of time in Spanish mass grave exhumations', *Memory Studies*, 7:4 (2014); I. Kovras, 'Explaining prolonged silences in transitional justice: the disappeared in Cyprus and Spain', *Comparative Political Studies*, 46:6 (2014), 730–56.

5   K. Verdery, *The Political Lives of Dead Bodies: Reburial and Post-Socialist Change* (New York: Columbia University Press, 1999).

6   Z. Crossland, 'Of clues and signs: the dead body's evidential traces', *American Ethnologist*, 1 (2009), 69–76; Renshaw, *Exhuming Loss*; F. Ferrándiz & A. Baer, 'Digital memory: the digital recording of mass grave exhumations in contemporary Spain', *Forum: Qualitative Social Research*, 9:3 (2008), www.qualitative-research.net/index.php/fqs/article/view/1152/2558 (accessed 29 August 2014); C. Rassool, 'Human remains: disciplines of the dead and the South African memorial complex', in D. R. Petersen, K. Guava & C. Rassool (eds), *The Politics of Heritage in Africa: Economies, Histories, Infrastructures* (Cambridge: Cambridge University Press, 2015).

7   T. Laqueur, 'The dead body and human rights', in S. Sweeney & I. Hodder (eds), *The Body* (Cambridge: Cambridge University Press, 2002), pp. 75–93.

8   Truth and Reconciliation Commission, *Truth and Reconciliation Commission of South Africa Report*, vols 2 and 6 (hereafter TRC, *Report*) (Cape Town: Juta, 1998, 2003), pp. 543–54, 550–69.

9   For further discussion, see M. Sanders, *Ambiguities of Witnessing: Law, Literature in a Time of a Truth Commission* (Stanford, CA: Stanford University Press, 2007).

10 For discrepancies in the TRC figures, see TRC, *Report*, vol. 2, p. 543, and vol. 6, p. 556.

11 TRC, *Report*, vol. 6, p. 519. Victim support group Khulumani provides a higher figure of closer to 2000 persons still missing, see www.ediec.org/world-map/map/country/south-africa/ (accessed 29 August 2014).

12 Abduction, more correctly described as an enforced disappearance, was the term employed by the TRC.

13 Personal observations during the period of working with the MPTT.

14 P. B. Hayner, *Unspeakable Truths: Facing the Challenge of Truth Commissions* (New York: Routledge, 2002), pp. 24–7.

15 For the TRC mandate, see the Promotion of National Unity and Reconciliation Act 34 of 1995, available at www.justice.gov.za/legisla-tion/acts/1995-034.pdf (accessed 20 January 2014); for the TRC's interpretation of its mandate see TRC, *Report*, vol. 1, ch. 4, pp. 48–102.

16 SAPA, 'Come clean: Mandela', 26 April 1997, available at www.just-ice.gov.za/trc/media/1997/9704/s970426a.htm (accessed 4 December 2013).

17 This debate disappeared post 9/11. Immense investment in the project to identify individual victims, returning identified fragments to families, led to technical advances, and considerable cost reductions in DNA testing, as well as a far wider pool of expertise, thus removing many previous technical and cost obstacles.

18 Equipo Argentino de Antropología Forense (EAAF), 'Bi-annual report, 1996–7', available at www.eaaf.org/ar_1996_1997/ (accessed 4 December 2013).

19 TRC, *Report*, vol. 6, pp. 550–69.

20 The audit queried whether this was the correct grave. The MPTT subsequently exhumed a further gravesite; DNA tests confirmed those remains as belonging to Zola Tate, while those given to the Tate family by the TRC have been identified as those of another deceased guerrilla.

21 Madeleine Fullard's and Nicky Rousseau's working notes on the audit of the TRC exhumations. In this case our audit verified the graves as being correct for the three guerrillas killed in the same incident, although we were unable to verify whether each family received the correct skeleton.

22 TRC, *Report*, vol. 6, pp. 565–69.

23 SABC, *TRC Special Report*, episode 45, parts 1–4, screened 27 April 1997 by the South African Broadcasting Corporation (SABC), South Africa's public broadcaster, available at www.youtube.com/watch?v=S0zs0LXgNuM (accessed 14 November 2013). See also 'The

breast-feeding warrior', in the DVD series, *Truth, Justice and Memory*, Institute for Justice and Reconciliation, Cape Town, South Africa, 2008.

24 G. Dennie, 'The standard of dying: race, indigence, and the disposal of the dead body in Johannesburg, 1886–1960', *African Studies*, 68:3 (December 2009), 310–30.

25 *Ibid.*, p. 317.

26 K. D. Matanzima, also of the Thembu royal house, served as 'Prime Minister' of the Transkei, declared an independent homeland of South Africa as part of the apartheid government's policy of dividing South Africa into independent ethnic homelands. Dalindyebo, who died in exile in Lusaka, Zambia, was initially buried in Lusaka; his body was returned to his ancestral home following intense negotiations between the exiled ANC and both South African and Transkeian authorities – see G. Dennie, 'One king, two burials: the politics of funerals in South Africa's Transkei', unpublished seminar paper, University of the Witwatersrand, October 1990, p. 7.

27 Dennie, 'The standard of dying', p. 323.

28 *Ibid.*, p. 336.

29 J. Bucher, 'Arguing Biko: evidence of the body in the politics of history, 1977 to the present' (unpublished PhD thesis, University of Minnesota, 2010); see also Special Issue *Drum*, November 1977.

30 A form of war dance, expressing defiance and protest, said to be derived from guerrilla training camps.

31 G. Agamben, *Homer Sacer* (Stanford, CA: Stanford University Press, 1998).

32 SAPA, 'Come clean: Mandela'.

33 SABC, *TRC Special Report*, episode 45.

34 *Ibid.*

35 *Ibid.*, episode 86, part 2, available at www.youtube.com/watch?v=exMp VMcTUDY&list=SPB5E49FFA382FFC46 (accessed 5 December 2013).

36 The TRC also exhumed the body of a former guerrilla in the employ of security police whom they later killed owing to fears about his continued loyalty.

37 C. Rassool & M. Legassick, *Skeletons in the Cupboard: South African Museums and the Trade in Human Remains, 1907–1917* (Cape Town and Kimberley: South African Museum and McGregor Museum, 2000); see also Rassool, 'Human remains'. This section draws on this latter paper and discussions with Ciraj Rassool.

38 P. Lalu, *The Deaths of Hintsa: Postapartheid South Africa and the Shape of Recurring Pasts* (Cape Town: HSRC Press, 2009), pp. 4–5.

39 Lalu, *The Deaths of Hintsa*.

40 Y. Abrahams, 'Colonialism, disjuncture and dysfunction: the historiography of Sarah Baartman' (unpublished PhD thesis, University of Cape Town, 2000); S. Qureshi, 'Displaying Sarah Baartman: the "Hottentot Venus"', *History of Science*, 42 (2004), 233–57.

41 Rassool & Legassick, *Skeletons in the Cupboard*. For an exploration of these themes in Namibia, see M. Biwa, '"Weaving the past with threads of memory": narratives and commemorations of the colonial war in

Southern Namibia' (unpublished PhD thesis, University of the Western Cape, 2012).

42 Lalu, *Deaths of Hintsa*, pp. 1–30.

43 Rassool, 'Human remains'; Rassool & Legassick, *Skeletons in the Cupboard*.

44 Rassool, 'Human remains'.

45 *Ibid.*; N. Shepherd, 'Archaeology dreaming: post-apartheid urban imaginaries and the bones of the Prestwich Street dead', *Journal of Social Archaeology*, 7:3 (2007) 3–28; L. Green & N. Murray, 'Notes for a guide to the ossuary', *African Studies*, 68:3 (December 2009), 370–86; 'Prestwich Place Memorial: human remains, development and truth', 27 July 2010, Archival Platform, available at www.archivalplatform.org/blog/entry/prestwich_place/ (accessed 20 January 2014).

46 Rassool, 'Human remains', p. 18.

47 Z. Crossland, 'Acts of estrangement: the post-mortem making of the self and other', *Archaeological Dialogues*, 16:1 (2009); 102–25.

48 Dennie, 'Two funerals', p. 12.

49 Crossland, 'Acts of estrangement', p. 104.

50 TRC, *Report*, vol. 6, p. 519, para. 37 and note 3.

51 L. Fondebrider, 'Reflections on the scientific documentation of human rights violations', *International Review of the Red Cross*, 84:848 (2002), p. 889.

52 Rassool, 'Human remains', p. 2.

53 See, for example, special issue of *Journal of Physical Anthropology*, 13:1 (2009).

54 These observations are based on my participation in some of these events, discussions with members of the MPTT, as well as media coverage of individual exhumations – see for example, 'Closure for families of MK soldier', available at http://m.iol.co.za/article/view/s/81/a/431085 (accessed 20 January 2014); 'Fallen hero gets apology', available at www.iol.co.za/dailynews/opinion/fallen-hero-finally-gets-apology-1.1534089 (accessed 20 January 2014). See also 'Address by the Deputy Minister of Justice and Constitutional Development', 8 December 2013, available at www.justice.gov.za/m_speeches/2013/20131208-MK-cadres.html (accessed 20 January 2014).

55 B. Anderson, *Imagined Communities: Reflections on the Origin and Spread of Nationalism* (London: Verso, 1983).

56 This funeral was indistinguishable from a guerrilla funeral except for the presence of flags and banners of the 1980s mass democratic movement.

57 M. Ramphele, 'Political widowhood in South Africa: the embodiment of ambiguity', *Daedalus*, 125:1 (Winter 1996), p. 107.

58 *Ibid.*, p. 106.

59 D. McRae, 'History stalks the torturers who drove Neil Aggett to suicide', *Mail and Guardian*, 29 November–5 December 2013.

60 J. D. Aronson, 'The strengths and limitations of South Africa's search for apartheid-era missing persons', *International Journal of Transitional Justice*, 5 (2011), p. 278.

61 Author's notes from family meeting.

62   Aronson, 'The strengths and limitations', pp. 272, 275–7.
63   A. Ashforth, 'Witchcraft, violence, and democracy in the New South Africa', *Cahiers d' Études Africaines*, 38:150/152 (1998), 505–32.
64   N. Rousseau, 'The farm, the river and the picnic spot: topographies of terror', *African Studies*, 68:3 (2009), p. 364.
65   Cited in Aronson, 'The strengths and limitations', p. 278.
66   Personal communication.
67   An exception to this is the significant literature in recent years on tensions between families regarding support for exhumations, especially in Argentina and the current civil war exhumations in Spain. See E. Domanska, 'The material presence of the past', *History and Theory*, 45:3 (2006), 342–4; and Z. Crossland, 'Violent spaces: conflict over the reappearance of Argentina's disappeared', in J. Schofield, W. G. Johnson & C. M. Beck (eds), *Matériel Culture: The Archaeology of Twentieth-Century Conflict* (London: Routledge, 2002), pp. 115–31; L. Renshaw, 'Missing bodies near at hand: the dissonant memory and dormant graves of the Spanish Civil War', in M. Biele, F. Hastrup & T. F. Sørenson (eds), *An Anthropology of Absence: Materialization and Transcendence of Loss* (New York: Springer, 2010), pp. 45–62; and Renshaw, *Exhuming Loss*.
68   Aronson, 'The strengths and limitations', p. 281.
69   Rassool, 'Human remains'.
70   'Reburial of Mr. Klaas and Mrs. Trooi Pienaar, Province of the Northern Cape', www.northerncape.gov.za/index.php?option=com_content&view=article&id=769:reburial-of-mr-andmrs-klaas-and-trooi-pienaar&catid=44:speeches&Itemid=54 (accessed 29 August 2014).
71   Rassool, 'Human remains'.
72   Ciraj Rassool, personal communication.
73   Rassool, 'Human remains'.

Bibliography

Abrahams, A., 'Colonialism, disjuncture and dysfunction: the historiography of Sarah Baartman' (unpublished PhD thesis, University of Cape Town, 2000)
Agamben, G., *Homer Sacer* (Stanford, CA: Stanford University Press, 1998)
American Journal of Physical Anthropology (Special issue on Race), 139:1 (2009), 1–90
Andersen, B., *Imagined Communities: Reflections on the Origin and Spread of Nationalism* (London: Verso, 1983)
Aquilar, P., 'Transitional or post-transitional justice: recent thoughts on the Spanish case', *South European Society and Politics*, 13:4 (2008), 417–33
Aronson, J. D., 'The strengths and limitations of South Africa's search for apartheid-era missing persons', *International Journal of Transitional Justice*, 5 (2011), 262–81
Ashforth, A., 'Witchcraft, violence, and democracy in the new South Africa', *Cahiers d' Études Africaines*, 38:150/152 (1998), 505–32

Bevernage, B. and L. Colaert, 'History from the grave: politics of time in Spanish mass grave exhumations', *Memory Studies*, 7:4 (2014), 440–56

Biwa, M., '"Weaving the past with threads of memory": narratives and commemorations of the colonial war in Southern Namibia' (unpublished PhD thesis, University of the Western Cape, 2012)

Crossland, Z., 'Acts of Estrangement: The Post-Mortem Making of the Self and Other', *Archaeological Dialogues*, 16:1 (2009), 102–25

Crossland, Z., 'Of clues and signs: the dead body's evidential traces', *American Ethnologist*, 1 (2009), 69–80

Crossland, Z., 'Violent spaces: conflict over the reappearance of Argentina's disappeared', in J. Schofield, W. G. Johnson & C. M. Beck (eds), *Matériel Culture: The Archaeology of Twentieth-Century Conflict* (London: Routledge, 2002)

Dennie, G., 'One king, two burials: the politics of funerals in South Africa's Transkei', unpublished seminar paper, University of the Witwatersrand, October 1990

Dennie, G., 'The standard of dying: race, indigence, and the disposal of the dead body in Johannesburg, 1886-1960', *African Studies*, 68:3 (2009), 310–30

Domanska, E., 'The material presence of the past', *History and Theory*, 45:3 (2006), 337–48

Equipo Argentino de Antropología Forense (EAAF), 'Bi-annual report, 1996-7', available at www.eaaf.org/ar_1996_1997/ (accessed 4 December 2013)

Ferrandiz, F., 'Cries and whispers: exhuming and narrating defeat in Spain today', *Journal of Spanish Cultural Studies*, 9:2 (2008), 177–92

Ferrandiz, F., 'The return of Civil War ghosts: the ethnography of exhumations in contemporary Spain', *Anthropology Today*, 22:3 (2006), 7–12

Fondebrider, L., 'Reflections on the scientific documentation of human rights violations', *International Review of the Red Cross*, 84:848 (2002), 885–91

Green, L. and N. Murray, 'Notes for a guide to the ossuary', *African Studies*, 68:3 (2009), 370–86

Hatcher, R., 'Forests of bodies: how exhumations make legible and extend the reach of the state in Guatemala', paper presented at Corpses: Search and Identification in post-Genocide and Mass Violence Contexts conference, University of Manchester, 9–11 September 2013

Hayner, P. B., *Unspeakable Truths: Facing the Challenge of Truth Commissions* (New York: Routledge, 2002)

Kovras, I., 'Explaining prolonged silences in transitional justice: the disappeared in Cyprus and Spain', *Comparative Political Studies*, 46:6 (2014), 730–56

Lalu, P., *The Deaths of Hintsa: Postapartheid South Africa and the Shape of Recurring Pasts* (Cape Town: HSRC Press, 2009)

Laqueur, T., 'The dead body and human rights', in S. Sweeney and I. Hodder (eds), *The Body* (Cambridge: Cambridge University Press, 2002), pp. 75–93

McRae, D., 'History stalks the torturers who drove Neil Aggett to suicide', *Mail and Guardian*, 29 November–5 December, 2013

Qureshi, S., 'Displaying Sarah Baartman: the "Hottentot Venus"', *History of Science*, 42 (2004), 233–57

Ramphele, M., 'Political widowhood in South Africa: The Embodiment of Ambiguity', *Daedalus*, 125:1 (1996), 99–117

Rassool, C., 'Human remains: disciplines of the dead and the South African memorial complex' in D. R. Petersen, K. Guava and C. Rassool (eds), *The Politics of Heritage in Africa: Economies, Histories, Infrastructures* (Cambridge: Cambridge University Press, 2015)

Rassool, C. and M. Legassick, *Skeletons in the Closet: South African Museums and the Trade in Human Remains, 1907–1917* (Cape Town and Kimberley: South African Museum and McGregor Museum, 2000)

Renshaw, L., *Exhuming Loss: Memory, Materiality and Mass Graves of the Spanish Civil War* (Walnut Creek, CA: Left Coast Press, 2011)

Renshaw, L., 'Missing bodies near at hand: the dissonant memory and dormant graves of the Spanish Civil War', in M. Biele, F. Hastrup & T. F. Sørenson (eds), *An Anthropology of Absence: Materialization and Transcendence of Loss* (New York: Springer, 2010), pp. 45–62

Robins, S., 'Towards victim-centred transitional justice: understanding the needs of families of the disappeared in post-conflict Nepal', *International Journal of Transitional Justice*, 5:1 (2011), 75–98

Rousseau, N., 'The farm, the river and the picnic spot: topographies of terror', *African Studies*, 68:3 (2009), 351–69

Sanders, M., *Ambiguities of Witnessing: Law, Literature in a Time of a Truth Commission* (Stanford, CA: Stanford University Press, 2007)

SABC, *Special Report*, episode 86, part 2, available at www.youtube.com/watch?v=exMpVMcTUDY&list=SPB5E49FFA382FFC46 (accessed 5 December 2013)

SABC, *TRC Special Report*, episode 45, parts 1–4, available at www.youtube.com/watch?v=S0zs0LXgNuM (accessed 14 November 2013)

SAPA, 'Come clean: Mandela', 26 April 1997, available at www.justice.gov.za/trc/media/1997/9704/s970426a.htm (accessed 4 December 2013)

Shepherd, N., 'Archaeology dreaming: post-apartheid urban imaginaries and the bones of the Prestwich Street dead', *Journal of Social Archaeology*, 7:1 (2007), 3–28

South African Government News Agency, 'Pienaars reburied in Northern Cape', available at www.sanews.gov.za/south-africa/pienaars-reburied-northern-cape (accessed 6 December 2013)

Truth and Reconciliation Commission, *Truth and Reconciliation Commission of South Africa Report*, vols 2 and 6 (Cape Town: Juta, 1998, 2003)

Verdery, K., *The Political Lives of Dead Bodies: Reburial and Post-Socialist Change* (New York: Columbia University Press, 1999)

9

Bury or display? The politics of exhumation in post-genocide Rwanda

Rémi Korman

The practices and techniques employed by forensic anthropologists in the scientific documentation of human rights violations, and situations of mass murder and genocide in particular, have developed enormously since the early 1990s.[1] The best-known case studies concern Latin American countries which suffered under the dictatorships of the 1970s–1980s, Franco's Spain, and Bosnia. In Rwanda, the first forensic study of a large-scale massacre was carried out one year before the genocide, in January 1993, in the context of a report produced by the International Federation for Human Rights (FIDH) on 'the violations of human rights in Rwanda since 1 October', the date marking the beginning of the country's civil war.[2] Although still comparatively little studied, this period constitutes a link between the pre- and post-genocide context.

Since 1994, however, very few formal forensic investigations have in fact been carried out in Rwanda. Nevertheless, several thousand exhumations have been organized over the last twenty years by survivors of the genocide, churches, and the Rwandan state itself. What accounts for the specific features of the Rwandan case in this respect? In what context are these genocide exhumations carried out and who exactly are the actors organizing them in Rwanda? How are the mass graves to be located, opened, and selected, and how are the exhumed victims identified?

The question of the role of foreign forensic anthropologists in Rwanda since the genocide is particularly important. While the role of foreign specialists in the memorialization and commemoration of the genocide is relatively well known, the activity of forensic anthropologists remains less thoroughly documented.[3] Some of them came to Rwanda in the context of the criminal investigations carried out by the International Criminal Tribunal for Rwanda (ICTR). What techniques did they use? What were their findings, and what relationships did they build with the Rwandan state and the country's population? Latterly, since the early 2000s, several international teams of forensic anthropologists have come to Rwanda in order to assist with the preservation of bodies, as opposed to their forensic examination. How should this new approach be understood? What does it tell us about the links between politics and forensic practices, and is it possible in this respect to talk of 'embedded' forensic anthropology?

In order to answer these questions, we will begin by considering the role of Rwandan actors in the exhumation and (re)burial of bodies of victims of the genocide. We will then re-examine the history of the forensic investigations which took place in Rwanda under the auspices of the ICTR. Lastly, we will consider the question of the political and/or geopolitical dimension of forensic anthropology.

The chronology and geography of exhumations

When the new government of National Unity was set up in July 1994, Rwanda was a country on its knees. Urgency was the order of the day in every ministry, where unpaid staff had the task of imagining a future for the nation, in spite of the genocide and the millions of refugees, both internal and external. Given this context, the question of the bodies from the genocide littering the country was not an urgent priority.

Once they returned to their former homes, survivors attempted to locate the places where their loved ones had been buried by the killers during the genocide. They then set about organizing the first exhumations of bodies which had been buried in small pits or latrines or simply placed in depressions in the ground in order to restore these victims their dignity. However, these exhumations and reburials proved in practice to be very difficult to organize because of the limited physical and economic means at the survivors' disposal. The different logistical methods used by the killers during the genocide posed a particular problem. In some cases the killers had left bodies scattered over a wide area, while in others they had used Caterpillar earth-movers to dig huge mass graves.[4] In the latter case, exhumation would only be possible with a similarly vast logistical effort.

Immediately after the genocide, the resources necessary for this operation were first provided through the assistance of churches, and the Catholic Church in particular. Despite the heavy losses it had sustained during the genocide, it remained, along with the Rwandan Patriotic Army, the only stable institution in Rwanda. Such mass exhumations of bodies were particularly widespread in the Butare prefecture, where the Commission for the Re-launch of Pastoral Activities encouraged debate on the place that should be given to the dead of the genocide and the importance of giving victims a decent burial.[5] Public exhumations were organized, during which survivors would look for any trace of their loved ones' clothes or other objects. Where identification was possible, survivors generally wished to bury the bodies on the family's land, although the Church preferred the creation of dedicated collective cemeteries.

From 1994 onwards, the responsibility for these collective exhumations and reburials was taken over by the state through the emergency decent burial programme. Administered by the Ministry of Work and Social Affairs (Minitraso), the objective of this programme was the collective reburial of victims exhumed from primary mass graves.[6] After being funded for two years by the WHO and UNICEF, in 1996 it was incorporated within the remit of the Genocide Memorial Commission (Commission mémorial du génocide), the official commission within the Ministry of Culture dealing with questions of memory.

Consequently, since 1996, exhumations of bodies from the genocide have taken different forms according to the situation in question. In some places, primary mass graves continue to be discovered and in this case the bodies are exhumed and given a collective burial either in new or existing genocide cemeteries. Further exhumations have also been needed because of the difficult conditions under which the programme of decent burial was originally carried out following the genocide. By the end of the 1990s, many cemeteries were in a poor state. The limited resources available for reburials following the genocide had an impact on the physical stability of the graves. Corruption and the awarding of contracts to the lowest bidder also led to low-quality materials being used. These economic and material problems were compounded by climatic factors, as many collective graves which had been hastily dug in 1994 were subsequently destroyed by landslides during the rainy seasons of the spring of 1995 and that of 1996.

The exact meaning of the concept of decent burial has also shifted over the last twenty years. In the context of the Minitraso programme, reburial most often meant bodies simply being placed in mass graves on top of plastic sheeting, sometimes still clothed and mixed in with the personal effects of the dead.[7] With the improving economic situation of the early 2000s, this type of burial came to be seen as degrading. Some of the new exhumations of secondary mass graves can thus be explained by a desire to give a 'proper' decent burial, involving the washing of bones, the separation of bodies from other objects, and the placing of human remains in draped coffins. In this sense, these new practices mark the reburial with a certain ritualization.[8]

Lastly, this new interpretation of decent burial was accompanied from the mid-2000s onwards by an economic and administrative rationalization of the treatment of bodies. This rationalization was first and foremost economic, owing to the cost of preserving and maintaining the cemeteries and memorials to the genocide. Genocide cemeteries were thus grouped with larger cemeteries and memorial sites. However, administrative rationalization also occurred following a new round of regional reforms. Each district was now required to have its own genocide cemetery, which therefore involved further consolidation. The most contentious matter in this respect concerned bodies being buried by surviving family members on their own land. Following numerous land reforms, in particular in the city of Kigali, large-scale expropriations and population movements have occurred since the end of the 1990s. This new situation has made keeping bodies on private land very difficult. These exhumation policies are often carried out in difficult circumstances. Such repeated exhumations are extremely painful for survivors.[9]

If the burial of a body is commonly considered as a moment of closure in the mourning process, what is one to make of the impact of a second, third, or even fourth official exhumation/reburial of this same body? These various policies of exhumation and reburial cut across one another, sometimes in quite contradictory ways, making the process of burial at a national level difficult to read. Above all, it has become increasingly difficult to be sure of the exact location of the original mass graves.

Identification and display: privacy and collective dimensions of the dead

Although it is important to avoid sweeping generalizations, it does seem to be the case that, since 1994, survivors' organizations and the Rwandan state have taken diametrically opposed views with respect to the identification of victims.[10] For the majority of survivors, the priority since 1994 has been to identify individuals. Every survivor would like to find the body of every member of their family. For the state, the principal concern is the collective identification of victims. Victims are thus identified purely as victims of the genocide, and for the state this anonymity is a reflection of the identity of the crime itself. Genocide does not target individuals but rather a collective, and it is the latter which is identified as the victim. This opposition between individual identification on the one hand and categorized or collective identification on the other is visible in all the debates surrounding the memory of the genocide. It is also manifest in the reports aiming to establish the number of victims. Whereas for the last twenty years the state has been publishing reports focusing on numbers and statistics on a county-wide scale, the IBUKA survivors' association released a report in 1999 entitled *Dictionnaire* nominatif *des victimes du génocide en Préfecture de Kibuye* (Nominal *Dictionary of Victims of the Genocide in Kibuye Prefecture*).[11]

These debates over the individual or collective dimension of bodies were thrown into stark relief during the vote over the 2008 law on genocide cemeteries and memorials, which states that 'memorial sites and cemeteries for victims of the genocide perpetrated against the Tutsi shall be in the public domain' (article 3) and that the 'Remains of genocide victims which were formerly buried shall be transferred to genocide memorial sites and cemeteries as provided for by this Law, upon the initiative of the relatives or upon consultation with the District administration' (article 6).[12]

Historically, this preference for the collective identification of victims has been inscribed within the programmes put in place to preserve and study corpses in Rwanda since 1994. The National University of Rwanda launched a project aiming to preserve evidence of the genocide shortly after reopening and, in 1995, put out a request for assistance from specialists in forensic matters in the Great Lakes region.[13] The assistance in question related to the preservation of bodies and not the analysis of the causes of the victims' deaths. As far as Rwandan actors were concerned, the cause of death was inscribed upon these bodies (cut-marks on skulls, tendons, or other body parts) and thus deemed to have been established by implication. Consequently, whereas the preservation of skeletal remains was central to this project, descriptions of bodies and their injuries are nowhere to be found in official records.

The particular focus on the preservation of bodies can to a large extent be explained by the major role played by Célestin Kanimba Misago in these matters following the genocide. A renowned archaeologist in what was then Zaïre, he came back to live in Rwanda in 1994 after more than twenty years spent in exile. He became director of Rwanda's National Museum in 1996, and this institution was given the official task of advising the government regarding the techniques for use in the treatment of bodies and in exhumations, in partnership with the Commission pour le mémorial du génocide et des massacres ('Commission Mémorial'). Both institutions began working on the mass graves at this time. The Commission Mémorial concentrated principally on locating genocide sites, but also worked on coordinating decent burials as well as organizing commemorations and the construction of memorials. The task of exhuming bodies and preserving bones fell to the National Museum of Rwanda, along with the various prefectures and *communes* (municipalities). These initial actions took place in what was an extremely difficult political and economic context across the country. Under-resourced, they were consequently carried out by actors who did not often have the necessary expertise.

The role of Mario Ibarra, a Chilean who spent two years working in Rwanda as a 'skeletal remains expert' with the Commission Mémorial and the National Museum, is particularly interesting in this respect. He arrived in 1994 as an observer with the UN human rights mission, for which he worked for eighteen months. Interested in the question of the preservation of evidence, he produced a report on the bodies exhumed in Murambi in January 1996, while he was still under contract with the UN. In March 1996 he began working as a volunteer for the Commission Mémorial, and continued to do so until 1997, when he suddenly left the country in some haste. He returned in June 1997 and left for good in July, having been unable to raise the funds needed to finance his work.

Described in Rwandan records and by those Rwandan actors who came into contact with him as an expert on the question of exhumation and the preservation of bodies, Mario Ibarra in actual fact possessed only a degree in sociology.[14] His interest in the question of bodies was in part personal, as a result of his own suffering under the dictatorship in Chile.[15] In the absence of a context that could supply adequate forensic expertise and financial resources alike, workers tried their hand at preserving bodies themselves, occasionally leading to the destruction of the latter. Some employees did receive proper training on the preservation of bones in 1997 during a four-day seminar organized at the National Museum of Rwanda. However, after a year with no salary, they had all left their respective posts. Nevertheless, the work carried out in these early years was the nearest thing there was at this time to the forensic investigations carried out by the staff of the ICTR.

Bodies as evidence of crime: forensic anthropologists in tribunal

The special investigation unit teams

Set up in November 1994 by the United Nations Security Council, the ICTR is dedicated to pursuing and judging those responsible for the genocide. Right from the start, the Office of the Prosecutor decided to focus its efforts on material evidence. For this reason, the use of forensic investigations was encouraged. For the Office of the Prosecutor, such investigations would allow it to counter the classic defence deployed by the accused right from the beginning in 1994, namely to claim that the massacres were committed as a result of 'popular anger' or an 'inter-ethnic war'.

In anticipation of the work that the ICTR would have to carry out, a Special Investigation Unit (SIU) consisting of two teams was formed in 1994.[16] The first would investigate sites of genocide while the second would deal with documentation and search for evidence. During a follow-up mission that lasted from 29 October to 7 November 1994, two forensic science experts provided by Spain studied various genocide sites. While no exhumations were performed owing to a lack of funds and the limited time available, bodies that had not been buried could nevertheless be examined. In the absence of any exhumation, the report published by this mission would give details of locations and any remains and objects found.[17] This report concentrates in particular on the study of the Ntamara church site, where 385 skulls and skeletons were found together. The identification work carried out on the sex and age of the victims was very revealing, as 81 per cent of the victims were shown to have been women or children of less than six years old, attesting to the 'asymmetrical nature of the violence'.[18] The team's report also gave precise descriptions of the injuries to the bodies, demonstrating how the manner of the massacre fitted into the practices of cruelty that are the mark of genocide.[19] Injuries were not just caused by blunt weapons, as the Spanish experts found traces of explosions and shooting in the church, leading them to conclude that at least one automatic weapon was used in the massacre. Once again, the presence at a single site of small arms alongside improvised weapons contradicts the thesis that seeks to explain the genocide as an act of 'popular anger'.

Physicians for Human Rights

Following the official investigation carried out by the SIU and the launching of the first prosecution proceedings against Clément Kayishema,[20] the Prosecutor's Office sought the continuation of forensic investigations in Rwanda. A lack of forensic experts in the ICTR meant that the NGO Physicians for Human Rights (PHR) was given the task of collecting evidence.[21] An official request for assistance was submitted to the director of PHR by the chief prosecutor of the ICTR on 17 October 1995.[22] A suitably qualified individual, Bill Haglund, was assigned to the Prosecutor's Office and set about assembling a team of international experts.[23] Their forensic expertise would in the end be used in two trials: the simultaneous trial of Clément Kayishema and Obed Ruzindana, and subsequently that of Georges Rutaganda.

Between September and December 1995, Dr Haglund made several preliminary visits to Rwanda in order to locate suitable sites for examination. His selection was in the end based on three main criteria: ease of transport and logistics, security conditions on and around the sites, and the lack of any previous excavations of the sites in question. This last point was the most problematic of the three, owing to the disorganized excavations that had already been carried out by survivors. José Paraybar, a member of PHR who was in Rwanda from 1995 to 1996, has described this period:

> I remember the families were coming. Literally, they were like a bulldozer. They were just coming by literally exhuming, you know, as if they were working the fields. They were just like with the shovels and whatever. They were just like exhuming these pieces of people that were coming out.[24]

This situation made finding completely untouched sites difficult, even less than a year after the genocide. Since the three criteria defined by Bill Haglund were fulfilled by the mass graves situated at the Home Saint-Jean in Kibuye, the first forensic investigation was performed here between 6 January and 27 February 1996. Owing to time restrictions, exhumations were only carried out in one of the five pits. However, PHR did examine skeletal remains left on the surface. Over the six weeks of the investigation, 493 bodies were examined.[25] Almost two-thirds of them were women and children under fifteen years old.

The Amgar Garage case

The second and final forensic investigation carried out by PHR took place in Kigali between 30 May and 17 June 1996. This investigation concentrated on the individual murders ordered or committed by Georges Rutaganda in the vicinity of his garage, the 'Amgar Garage', in the centre of Kigali. Over these three weeks of exhuming and identifying bodies, twenty-seven bodies were dug up and studied. In addition to the identification of the bodies by category, DNA tests were also performed in order to establish individual identities.

Following the investigation carried out at the Amgar Garage, the Rwandan government, in a joint decision with the Prosecutor, decided to stop these exhumations and forensic investigations.[26] The majority of the published studies examining this major turning point explain this choice in terms of the 'shock' felt by survivors on seeing these exhumations being carried out, a reaction which formed the focus of a demonstration organized by the Ikuba association in 1996.[27] On balance, however, this hypothesis seems improbably simple. It is more likely that the explanation is to be found in the political climate of this period, the beginning of 1996 having been marked by the ending of the mandate of the second United Nations Assistance Mission for Rwanda (UNAMIR II) in an acrimonious international context.[28] Another hypothesis is that the Rwandan government was unhappy with the preferential treatment given by the United Nations to the International Criminal Tribunal for the former Yugoslavia (ICTY). It is true that several investigators with PHR did split their time between Rwanda and Bosnia. Whatever the truth behind this decision, the absence of forensic studies during the trials conducted by the ICTR after 1996 weakened the cases brought by the Prosecutor's Office, who were thus forced to change their initial strategy.

Lastly, certain criticisms have been made regarding the scientific methods employed by Bill Haglund and the PHR team despatched to Kibuye and the Amgar Garage. These criticisms often emanated from defence lawyers, but also from some expert witnesses called by the defence teams of the ICTR and the ICTY. Indeed, it was at the ICTY that, in order to forestall attacks by the defence on the credibility of the work carried out by Bill Haglund, the prosecution had to remind the court that 'in spite of the management and logistical problems, the scientific validity of his work cannot be questioned'.[29] According to the prosecution, any mistakes were mainly due to the speed with which these investigations were forced to be carried out.[30] When called as an expert witness for the defence during the trial of Georges Rutaganda, however, Kathleen Reichs did nevertheless point out what she perceived as a number of methodological errors.[31] Such methodological debates between forensic anthropologists pose important questions regarding the incorporation of forensic knowledge within historical studies.

From the international circulation of knowledge to embedded forensic anthropology

While in charge of forensic investigations in Rwanda on behalf of the ICTR, PHR did not, however, collaborate with the Rwandan state in any way. As a result, in these early years the memory of the genocide was managed for the most part by local actors. The situation changed after 2000 with the advent of economic growth, more stable institutions, and the internationalization of the memory of the genocide.[32] The arrival of the British AEGIS foundation in Rwanda in 2001–2, in the context of the construction of the national genocide memorial at Gisozi in Kigali, marked a turning point in this process. The latter organization did not simply build monuments, but also became involved with the development of research projects dealing with both the sites of the genocide and the preservation of bodies. It would commission a report into the preservation of these remains from the INFORCE Foundation six years after the last investigations by the ICTR.

However, the objectives here were very different from those of the ICTR trials. The idea now was to use forensic knowledge to help preserve the skeletal remains on display in genocide memorials, along with the mummified bodies displayed at Murambi. A preliminary study was carried out at various genocide sites in November 2002 by Lynne Bell and Margaret Cox.[33] The latter is the founder of the International Forensic Centre of Excellence (INFORCE), which was based at the University of Bournemouth until 2007, when it was transferred to Cranfield University.[34] Cranfield University and its department of forensic sciences have thus been working with the NGO INFORCE in Rwanda since 2007, building on the first study of 2002. In May 2009, at the invitation of the National Commission for the Fight Against Genocide (CNLG), several students from the university, supervised by a member of INFORCE, went to Rwanda to collect data on 300 sets of human remains and twenty mummified bodies located in Murambi. This investigation formed the basis of the human remains conservation project which was presented at the conference on the preservation of evidence of genocide organized in Kigali in February 2010.[35] Staff from the CNLG were then invited to Cranfield University to inspect the equipment that would be sent to Rwanda.[36] This equipment has subsequently been installed on-site in Murambi to be used as a mobile laboratory. According to the INFORCE Foundation, this mobile laboratory will allow bodies to be preserved by placing them in hermetically sealed compartments which should 'last more than 150 years without any deterioration.'[37]

Embedded science?

What can account for the fact that forensic experts have been invited to Rwanda and not specialists in the preservation of human remains? Looking beyond the question of the specific actors involved and the methods they employ, it is important to examine their motivations and also the conditions in which they carry out their work. Since no interviews have yet been conducted with the actors in question regarding these points, the arguments presented here are necessarily embryonic. Nevertheless, what comes across very clearly is that several organizations working in the field of forensic anthropology, including INFORCE, have developed close links with certain political and military institutions.

The debates surrounding 'embedded anthropology' have become particularly important following the wars in Afghanistan and then Iraq in the context of the 'Human Terrain System', which saw the incorporation of anthropologists and other researchers in the social sciences within the armed forces, with a view to gaining a better understanding of the situation on the ground with respect to the populations affected by the war.[38] Generally speaking, 'embedding' refers to the links developed between academics or other researchers and the military. However, this concept can be enlarged. Such a situation raises ethical issues regarding the role and working methods of the researcher, as well as political issues regarding the researcher's involvement in a specific cause. In May 2003, a few days after the fall of Saddam Hussein's regime, the INFORCE Foundation began excavating mass graves in Iraq. The organization's director, Margaret Cox, told a journalist that:

> One of the challenges is to make sure that our goals are not influenced by the political regime. If you are asked to excavate a grave, you have an obligation to make sure it is part of a larger investigative process, so that you know that that grave has been selected for reasons that are about justice and not politics.[39]

The arrival of the INFORCE Foundation in Iraq in direct partnership with the Foreign Office is a clear case of embedded forensic anthropology. In examples such as this, and as stated by Cox, it is vital to underline the importance for critical sociology of retaining a distance from the national and international actors involved in the processes of exhumation.[40]

The situation in Rwanda is not one in which forensic anthropology is so obviously 'embedded'. Nevertheless, it should still be pointed out that Cranfield University, where INFORCE is based, has a Department of Defence and Security with very close links to the UK Defence Academy. The link becomes clear when one considers the collaborative publication between the INFORCE Foundation and a ballistics and ammunition specialist at Cranfield University for the UK Ministry of Defence. This document was published as an annexe to the Mutsinzi report on the causes and circumstances surrounding the deadly attack of 6 April 1994 on the aircraft carrying Rwandan President Juvénal Habyarimana.[41] Commissioned by the Rwandan government, this report raises questions about the institutional cooperation between NGOs, academia, politics, and the military that have not been addressed by academia thus far.

Conclusions on technology, memory, and history

As we have seen, numerous historical, ethical, and political issues are raised by exhumations. The same is true of DNA testing. Given the economic situation in Rwanda directly after the genocide, the latter technique was never given serious consideration. In recent years, however, various actors working in the field of memory have been attempting to change this situation by promoting the virtues of DNA analysis. The NGO DNA for Africa, for instance, despite its somewhat marginal status, is seeking to set up a programme along the lines of the International Commission on Missing Persons established in Bosnia in 1995.[42] More recently, the Canadian researcher Erin Jessee has published a policy report urging the Rwandan government to set up four major projects alongside their work on exhumation and identification.[43] Her proposals include the establishment of a centre for forensic studies, the creation of a database of DNA samples from survivors of the genocide, and an active programme of scientific exhumations in order to ensure the identification of human remains and allow their reburial according to the wishes of surviving relatives. Yet just what would such a country-wide scheme of victim-identification entail in logistical and economic terms? Not only that, such a policy would require a new wave of mass exhumations, which would be contrary to the stated wish of the government to bring closure to the memorial process.

In addition to the political issues raised by these proposals, they pose the question of the historical aspirations of forensic science. The writings of many forensic anthropologists would have us believe that the history of mass killings can be read on the bodies of the victims, which become conflated with the body social as a whole. As a counterpoint to this positivist vision of forensic knowledge, however, the limits of its usefulness for the historian need to be pointed out. How, for instance, does DNA identification or forensic analysis help us to distinguish between massacres committed against Hutus for political reasons and the genocide committed against the Tutsi, given that the bodies of both are more often than not buried in the same places? In fact, forensic analyses can only ever be placed in a more general narrative of the history of events. More importantly, perhaps, in the case of Rwanda, the value which forensic anthropologists ascribe to exhumations and identification in terms of achieving reconciliation and restoring broken relations would seem to be based more on a political desire than on any actual demand from within society.

Notes

1 L. Fondebrider, 'Reflections on the scientific documentation of human rights violations', *International Review of the Red Cross*, 84: 848 (2002), 885–91.

2 FIDH Africa Watch, UIDH & CIDPDD, 'Commission internationale d'enquête sur les violations des droits de l'homme au Rwanda depuis le 1er octobre 1990', March 1993, p. 123.

3 R. Ibreck, 'International constructions of national memories: the aims and effects of foreign donors' support for genocide remembrance in Rwanda', *Journal of Intervention and Statebuilding*, 7 (2013), 149–69.

4 N. Eltringham, 'Exhibition, dissimulation et "culture": le traitement des corps dans le génocide rwandais', in É. Anstett & J.-M. Dreyfus (eds), *Cadavres impensables, cadavres impensés: approches méthodologiques du traitement des corps dans les violences de masse et les génocides* (Paris: Éditions Petra, 2012), pp. 93–105, p. 101.

5 The Commission for the Re-launch of Pastoral Activities, at this time led by Laurien Ntezimana, organized numerous events addressing the issues raised by these commemorations. See C. Vidal, 'Les commémorations du génocide au Rwanda', *Les Temps Modernes*, 613 (2001), 1–46, p. 9.

6 R. Korman, 'Le Rwanda face à ses morts ou les cimetières du génocide comme lieux de mémoire', Université Paris1, Génocides et politiques mémorielles, 2012, available at http://chs.univ-paris1.fr/genocides_et_politiques_memorielles (accessed 20 November 2013).

7 When one such large secondary grave was exhumed in Nyanza de Kicukiro in 2011, the bodies were stilled clothed and mixed in with their personal effects. A grenade was also discovered, the disposal of which required specialist intervention.

8 Regarding this point, see the following films: G. Ndahayo, *Rwanda: Beyond the Deadly Pit*, Ndahayo Films, 2009; E. Kabera (director), *Les gardiens de la mémoire*, Link Media Production, 2004.

9 See the remarks made by Hélène Dumas during the following radio programme: E Laurentin, 'La fabrique de l'histoire', France-Culture (broadcast 26 February 2010).

10 As always, it is necessary to qualify this opposition. One encounters survivors working within state institutions, while other survivors agree wholeheartedly with these policies.

11 IBUKA, *Dictionnaire nominatif des victimes du génocide en Préfecture de Kibuye* (Kigali: IBUKA, 1999). Emphasis added.

12 République rwandaise, 'Loi portant organisation des sites mémoriaux et cimetières pour les victimes du génocide perpétré contre les Tutsi au Rwanda', *Journal Officiel*, 2008, pp. 62–77.

13 In this period, university lecturers were mainly drawn from the Tutsi diaspora, who were returning from Zaïre and Burundi. Faced with the challenge of preserving traces of the genocide, several academics formed an informal committee tasked with preserving and documenting evidence of the genocide. This committee, led by the archaeologist Célestin Kanimba Misago, included the historian Joseph Jyoni Wa Karega and the anthropologist Aloys Rufangura. It brought together researchers from the CERCOSH (Centre d'Études et de Recherches Contemporaines en Sciences Humaines) of the National University of Rwanda, based in Butare. For more information, see the correspondence between professors Vincent Mubiligi and Vénérand Bigirimana: V. Mubiligi & V. Bigirimana, 'Conservation des restes humains', CNLG Archives, November 1995.

14 Interview with Louis Kanamugire (former director of the Commission Mémorial), Kigali, 14 September 2010.

15 It has not been possible to find details of his personal history in the records of the Valech Commission, which has the job of listing the victims of the Chilean dictatorship.

16 High Commissioner of the United Nations for Human Rights, Field
    Operation for Human Rights in Rwanda. Groupe des enquêtes spéciales,
    'SIU, rapport final d'enquête sur le génocide', Kigali, 4 December 1995.

17 Nations Unies, Haut Commissaire aux Droits de l'Homme *et al.*, 'Mision
    en Ruanda. Informe medico-forense', Madrid, 22 November 1994.

18 These remarks on forensic investigations are drawn heavily on the thesis
    recently submitted by Hélène Dumas. See H. Dumas, 'Juger le génocide
    sur les collines: une étude des procès gacaca au Rwanda (2006–2012)'
    (unpublished thesis, Paris, EHESS, 2013), p. 40.

19 C. Vidal, 'Le génocide des rwandais tutsi: cruauté délibérée et logiques
    de haine', in F. Héritier (ed.), *De la violence* (Paris: Odile Jacob, 1996),
    pp. 325–66.

20 See trials ICTR-95-1 and ICTR-96-3.

21 PHR defines itself as an organization which seeks to use medicine and
    science in order to 'stop mass killing and human rights violations'.

22 M. Seutcheu, 'Working together to prosecute human rights criminals:
    an insider account of the relationship between human rights organisa-
    tions and the International Criminal Tribunal for Rwanda', for the work-
    shop on 'Human Rights: Issue Linkages and the New Human Rights
    Agenda', for the Visiting Fellows Program of the Human Rights Program
    at Harvard Law School, 2003, p. 35.

23 A social history of the investigators working for PHR would be particu-
    larly interesting. Many of them originally come from Latin America or
    have worked on the crimes committed in Latin America in the 1970s–
    80s. By taking their histories into account, some nuance may be brought
    to the idea of the Holocaust's omnipresence with regard to memory
    models.

24 Listen to the audio podcast 'Uncovering the evidence', in *Voices on
    Genocide Prevention* (Washington, DC: United States Holocaust
    Memorial Museum, 2009).

25 It is not possible here to describe in more detail the importance of the
    voluminous report (700 pages long) published following this investiga-
    tion. It nonetheless constituted the main piece of evidence used in the
    trial of Clément Kayishema.

26 O. Adede, 'Statement of the registrar of the international criminal tribu-
    nal for Rwanda, Ictr/info-9-2-06', ICTR, 29 April 1996.

27 T. Cruvellier, *Court of Remorse inside the International Criminal Tribunal
    for Rwanda* (trans. C. Voss) (Madison: University of Wisconsin Press,
    2010), p. 13.

28 This included the expulsion of dozens of NGOs in December 1995, the
    slow pace of the ICTR's work, and the meagre financial assistance pro-
    vided to the new regime in contrast to the aid given to refugee camps.

29 M. Klinkner, 'Forensic science expertise for international criminal pro-
    ceedings: an old problem, a new context and a pragmatic resolution',
    International Journal of Evidence and Proof, 13 (2009), 102–29.

30 *Ibid.*, pp. 102–29.

31 K. Reichs, 'Report on the forensic investigations at the Amgar Garage
    and nearby vicinity, Kigali Rwanda by William Haglund, PhD', report to

Giroud, Peris, Pappas, Sutton, Prihoda & Dickson (defence lawyers of Georges Rutaganda, ICTR-96-3-T), 1999.

32 H. Dumas & R. Korman, 'Espaces de la mémoire du génocide des Tutsis au Rwanda', *Afrique Contemporaine*, 238 (2011), 11–27.

33 M. Cox & L. Bell, 'An initial assessment of the condition and requirements for conservation of human remains at six genocide memorial sites in Rwanda', Inforce Foundation Report, series 1, 2003.

34 The INFORCE Foundation has four main objectives: to respect the human needs of families regarding the return of bodies and the choice of burial site, to help in the prosecution of those responsible for these crimes by collecting evidence, to set and disseminate professional standards in forensic science, and to train local staff in forensic science methods.

35 G. Muramira, 'Genocide experts meet in Kigali', *New Times*, Kigali, 2 June 2010.

36 The members of this mission included Ildephonse Karengera, director of the Memory and Genocide Prevention department, Martin Muhoza, who was in charge of the conservation of human remains at the CNLG, and the Rwandan MP Evariste Kalisa, then president of the Rwandan parliamentary commission on national unity, human rights, and the fight against genocide.

37 The bodies will be placed in acrylic coffins, with around twenty bodies being preserved on each site in the first instance.

38 J. Assayag, 'L'anthropologie en guerre', *L'Homme*, 187–8 (2008), 135–67.

39 J. Wallace, 'Seeker of truths digging for justice', *Times Higher Education Supplement*, 24 September 2004.

40 Such a study could follow the model of the work produced by Nicolas Guilhot. See N. Guilhot, *The Democracy Makers: Human Rights and the Politics of Global Order* (New York: Columbia University Press, 2013). It should be noted that what few studies do exist tend to fall into the realm of speculative conspiracy theories or even genocide denial.

41 M. C. Warden & A. McClue, 'Investigation into the crash of Dassault Falcon 50 registration number 9XR-NN on 6 April 1994 carrying former president Juvénal Habyarimana', Defence Academy of the United Kingdom Cranfield University, 27 February 2009, p. 112.

42 See www.dna4africa.org/ (accessed 20 November 2013).

43 E. Jessee, 'Promoting reconciliation through exhuming and identifying victims in the 1994 Rwandan genocide, Cigi-Africa initiative policy', 17 July 2012, p. 12.

Bibliography

Assayag, J., 'L'anthropologie en guerre', *L'Homme*, 187–8 (2008), 135–67

Cox, M. & L. Bell, 'An initial assessment of the condition and requirements for conservation of human remains at six genocide memorial sites in Rwanda', Inforce Foundation Report, series 1, 2003

Cruvellier, T., *Court of Remorse inside the International Criminal Tribunal for Rwanda* (trans. C. Voss) (Madison: University of Wisconsin Press, 2010)

Dumas, H., 'Juger le génocide sur les collines: une étude des procès gacaca au Rwanda (2006–2012)' (unpublished thesis, Paris, EHESS, 2013)

Dumas, H. & R. Korman, 'Espaces de la mémoire du génocide des Tutsis au Rwanda', *Afrique Contemporaine*, 238 (2011), 11–27

Eltringham, N., 'Exhibition, dissimulation et "culture": le traitement des corps dans le génocide rwandais', in É. Anstett & J.-M. Dreyfus (eds), *Cadavres impensables, cadavres impensés: approches méthodologiques du traitement des corps dans les violences de masse et les génocides* (Paris: Éditions Petra, 2012), pp. 93–105

FIDH, Africa Watch, UIDH & CIDPDD, 'Commission internationale d'enquête sur les violations des droits de l'homme au Rwanda depuis le 1er octobre 1990', March 1993

Fondebrider, L., 'Reflections on the scientific documentation of human rights violations', *International Review of the Red Cross*, 84: 848 (2002), 885–91

Guilhot, N., *The Democracy Makers: Human Rights and the Politics of Global Order* (New York: Columbia University Press, 2013)

High Commissioner of the United Nations for Human Rights, Field Operation for Human Rights in Rwanda, Groupe des enquêtes spéciales, 'SIU, rapport final d'enquête sur le génocide', Kigali, 4 December 1995

Ibreck, R., 'International constructions of national memories: the aims and effects of foreign donors' support for genocide remembrance in Rwanda', *Journal of Intervention and Statebuilding*, 7 (2013), 149–69

IBUKA, *Dictionnaire nominatif des victimes du génocide en Préfecture de Kibuye* (Kigali: IBUKA, 1999)

Jessee, E., Promoting reconciliation through exhuming and identifying victims in the 1994 Rwandan genocide', Cigi-Africa initiative policy, 17 July 2012

Kabera, E. (director), *Les gardiens de la mémoire*, Link Media Production, 2004

Klinkner, M., 'Forensic science expertise for international criminal proceedings: an old problem, a new context and a pragmatic resolution', *International Journal of Evidence and Proof*, 13 (2009), 102–29

Korman, R., 'Le Rwanda face à ses morts ou les cimetières du génocide comme lieux de mémoire' Université Paris1, Génocides et politiques mémorielles, 2012, available at http://chs.univ-paris1.fr/genocides_et_politiques_memorielles/?Le-Rwanda-face-a-ses-morts-ou-les (accessed 10 November 2013)

Korman, R., 'The Tutsi body in the 1994 genocide: ideology, physical destruction, and memory', in É. Anstett & J.-M. Dreyfus (eds), *Destruction and Human Remains: Disposal and Concealment in Genocide and Mass Violence* (Manchester: Manchester University Press, 2014), pp. 226–42

Laurentin, E., 'La fabrique de l'histoire' (radio programme), France-Culture (broadcast 26 February 2010)

Muramira, G., 'Genocide experts meet in Kigali', *New Times*, Kigali, 2 June 2010

Nations Unies, Haut Commissaire aux Droits de l'Homme, Ministerio de Justicia, E. Perez Pujol & J. M. Abenza Rojo, 'Mision en Ruanda. Informe medico-forense', Madrid, 22 November 1994

Ndahayo, G. (director), *Rwanda: Beyond the Deadly Pit*, Ndahayo Films, 2009

Reichs, K., 'Report on the forensic investigations at the Amgar Garage and nearby vicinity, Kigali Rwanda by William Haglund, PhD', report to Giroud, Peris, Pappas, Sutton, Prihoda & Dickson (defence lawyers of Georges Rutaganda, ICTR-96-3-T), 1999

République rwandaise, 'Loi portant organisation des sites mémoriaux et cimetières pour les victimes du génocide perpétré contre les Tutsi au Rwanda', *Journal Officiel*, 2008, pp. 62–77

Seutcheu, M., 'Working together to prosecute human rights criminals: an insider account of the relationship between human rights organizations and the International Criminal Tribunal for Rwanda', taken from the workshop on 'Human Rights: Issue Linkages and the New Human Rights Agenda', for the Visiting Fellows Program of the Human Rights Program at Harvard Law School, 2003

'Uncovering the evidence', *Voices on Genocide Prevention*, audio podcast (Washington, DC: United States Holocaust Memorial Museum), 2009

Vidal, C., 'Les commémorations du génocide au Rwanda', *Les Temps Modernes*, 631 (2001), 1–46

Vidal, C., 'Le génocide des rwandais tutsi: cruauté délibérée et logiques de haine', in F. Héritier (ed.), *De la violence* (Paris: Odile Jacob, 1996), pp. 325–66

Wallace, J., 'Seeker of truths digging for justice', *Times Higher Education Supplement*, 24 September 2004

Warden, M. C. & A. McClue, 'Investigation into the crash of Dassault Falcon 50 registration number 9XR-NN on 6 April 1994 carrying former president Juvénal Habyarimana', Defence Academy of the United Kingdom Cranfield University, 27 February 2009, p. 112

10

Remembering the Japanese occupation massacres: mass graves in post-war Malaysia

Frances Tay

The violence visited upon British Malaya during the Japanese occupation of December 1941 to August 1945 has prompted several historians to evoke comparisons with the atrocities that befell Nanjing.[1] During this time, numerous civilians were subjected to mass killings, summary executions, rape, forced labour, arbitrary detention, and torture. In particular, the *shukusei* (cleansing) or *daikensho* (big inspection) operation of February to April 1942 – known locally as the *sook ching* (purge through cleansing) massacres – has become symbolic of Japanese brutality. The death toll from these massacres remains contested; estimates range from 5,000 to 50,000.[2] As a result, multiple mass graves scar the territory's landscape. While these serve as physical testament to this dark period in the country's history, many of these sites remain relatively unknown and scarcely remembered.[3] Often, documented cases of exhumations – be it Bergen-Belsen in Germany, Vinnytsia in Ukraine, or Priaranza in Spain, to name but a few sites where mass graves have been excavated – have sparked social and political debates.[4] In marked contrast, the response of the Malaysian general public has been largely muted, except in cases where the reinterment of remains has threatened state-sponsored dominant narratives. The reasons for this seeming ambivalence are manifold. In the first instance, the main ethnic groups in the territory – comprising indigenous Malay and migrant Chinese and Indian minorities – experienced the occupation differently. As such, there is no shared collective memory that can be harnessed to fashion a mutually cohesive narrative. Rather, 'sectional narratives' predicated upon these varied communal experiences have emerged.[5] This divergence in experience resulted from the occupiers' practice of race-specific policies, where the Chinese community in particular bore the brunt of Japanese aggression.[6] In contrast, Japanese occupation policy was relatively supportive of the Malays and encouraging towards the Indians.[7] The lack of an inclusive past is exacerbated by the continued marginalization of minority histories from official historiography of the occupation. This state of affairs emerged from the confluence of socio-political forces and events which shaped the territory's path towards independence and beyond. Very briefly, post-war independent Malaysia was born amidst inter-racial strife; a fragile union forged from the fires of the Malayan Emergency – a decade-long post-war insurrection instigated by a largely ethnic Chinese communist guerrilla force.[8] Intent on preventing the development of 'another Palestine' or 'Balkans of Asia', the reoccupying British colonial administration enshrined the privileged status of the ethnic Malay majority in the fledgling nation's new constitution.[9] Thus, the historiography of the Japanese occupation accords primacy to the Malay ethnic majority's collective memory of the war. This dominant narrative promotes the occupation as a catalyst in the awakening of Malay nationalism, leading to decolonization and self-determination.[10] Experiences that diverge from the national narrative are marginalized, including the suppression of Japanese atrocities during the occupation.

This chapter explores three selected exhumations dating from the immediate post-war context to more recent times. What is revealing about these cases, despite the passage of time and progressive improvements in the field of forensic investigation, is the lack of protocol or application of scientific procedures.[11] As such, these cases contribute little to furthering the science of forensic excavations of mass graves. However, what they do emphasize is that exhumations are not straightforward affairs of search, discovery, and identification. Forensic investigators often tout the nostrum that exhumations can 'give voice to the dead'; though what is revealed usually does not begin nor end with the excavated physical evidence.[12] The evidence selected for interpretation is dependent upon the actors involved and their guiding motivations; while the historical narratives or 'truths' which emerge are influenced by socio-political and cultural contests of the present. In these contests, the symbolism attached to exhumed human remains take on what Katherine Verdery describes as 'social, political and cultural afterlives'.[13] By engaging in a cross-sectional comparison, we can detect the evolving 'afterlives' of victims of the Japanese occupation, evident through the ever-changing symbolism attached to their remains in response to changing socio-political contexts. The cases examined amplify the processes involved in the manipulation of exhumed remains to serve the needs of the living, rather than reclaim the stories of the dead. Further, in serving the needs of the present, these cases illustrate that exhumations may inadvertently obfuscate the past rather than recover history.

Bukit Dunbar, Penang, 1946

Shortly after the reoccupation of Malaya in September 1945, the British military administration launched investigations to gather evidence to bring war crimes charges, not only against Japanese army personnel but also against civilian collaborators. These took the form of identity parades and public displays of photo line-ups of potential war criminals, the gathering of testimonies and affidavits from survivors and witnesses, as well as several exhumations at known killing sites. The authorities were compelled to proceed with the impending trials quickly, influenced in part by the need to assuage the vengeful mood pervasive among the Chinese community at that time, and in part by the need to address pressing issues, from food shortages and rehabilitation of essential industries to general reconstruction efforts. The sheer scale of the task was challenging amidst the confusion and chaos left by war; some Japanese army personnel had escaped or could not be located from nearby theatres of war, Indian National Army conscripts – who had been recruited by the Japanese ostensibly for an offensive against the British in India – had blended in with other civilian prisoners and PoWs, while potential witnesses or survivors were not always forthcoming. Against this backdrop, investigators appear to have relied heavily upon testimonies, more so than physical evidence, to secure convictions. For example, in a study of selected war crimes trial cases relating to Japanese atrocities in Malaya, it is evident that the opening of mass graves was conducted only sparingly.[14] For example, among the forty-seven cases examined by this researcher, only one trial introduced photographic evidence and supporting testimonies relating to an exhumation.[15]

In this singular case, a mass grave at Bukit Dunbar on Thien Eok Estate near Gelugor town was excavated. The exhumation appears to have been conducted merely to provide supplementary evidence that multiple deaths had indeed taken place in Penang Gaol, and that bodies had been disposed of in mass graves on the site. The process was rudimentary; no medical officers or forensic scientists were involved. Further, testimony provided by Major Douglas Hayhurst, the second officer-in-charge of the No. 6 War Crimes Investigation Team, indicates that the exhumation was not exhaustive. For example, Major Hayhurst witnessed the opening of one mass grave measuring 50 feet in length and 3 feet wide. Though he estimated that its depth was probably 10 feet or more, the excavation work had stopped at 6 feet deep. When asked by the prosecuting officer how many remains were unearthed, he answered, 'I counted 232 skulls.' When asked if there were other corpses in that mass grave, he answered, 'Yes, you could see them in layers.' When asked if there was evidence of other graves, Major Hayhurst replied, 'there were three or more in the same area, though these were not disturbed'. There was no further investigation into the probable ethnicity, gender, and age of the victims or causes of death. It appears that the authorities merely assumed that since the majority of known victims were indeed Chinese, they were accountable only to the Chinese community. Local Chinese associations were consulted about the discovery, and upon their request, the remains were reinterred *in situ*. Arguably, such actions have compounded the myth of the 'Chinese as victim' to the exclusion of suffering experienced by all other ethnic groups.[16] And as the other graves were not opened, collectively how many were buried there was not determined. Instead, a host of local prison guards, undertakers, drivers, hospital staff, and other witnesses were cross-examined to establish that civilians had indeed been incarcerated, tortured, killed, or died while in custody and that they had been disposed of at Bukit Dunbar.

Why, then, was the mass grave at Bukit Dunbar excavated? In retrospect, it is clear that the exhumation was not so much concerned with the minutiae of the crimes committed, but in the site's value as both a visual and physical testament of Japanese atrocities. It is telling, for example, that during the trial, the presiding court official asked if photos of the exhumations had been released to the press. The response by the prosecuting officer is equally revealing: 'I believe one of the exhibits was released to the Chinese Press.' Why was there concern in ensuring that images of the exhumation were made public? And why in particular were the Chinese media favoured? Perhaps the British were anxious to demonstrate to the Chinese community – the loudest segment of the local populace in demanding retribution – that the wheels of justice were indeed turning.[17] Or perhaps the British were intent on exposing the wanton cruelty of the Japanese occupiers, so as to contrast the relatively benign nature of British colonialism. And what became of the nameless, unknown mass found at Bukit Dunbar? Some of the remains were collected, along with others in various sites throughout the island by the local China Relief Fund chapter.[18] These were reinterred at Air Itam, beneath an obelisk commemorating 'Penang Overseas Chinese war victims, compatriots and transport workers'.[19] Omitted were details of how they had met their fate or the contexts in which they had lost their lives. Instead, the Luguo Bridge Incident of 1937 which had sparked the Second Sino-Japanese War was given prominence. Clearly, this was a memorial to commemorate *tongbao* – a Chinese term that can be read alternately as 'compatriot' or 'siblings from the same bloodline'.[20] In this final resting place, the remains were now transmuted into symbolic representations of the Chinese fallen, not in Penang or even Malaya alone, but martyrs in China's 'War of Resistance to Japan'.[21]

However, it was only in 1951, in the midst of the Malayan Emergency, that this memorial was 'officially' unveiled to the larger public. The date chosen for the occasion was 11 November, to coincide with Remembrance Day, which marks the end of the First World War. Local Chinese community leaders re-dedicated the site as a Chinese anti-war memorial. Was this a deliberate attempt to 'neutralize' Chinese nationalism and to downplay historical links with the motherland, especially in light of the recent establishment of the communist People's Republic of China? Or perhaps it was to emphasize that the Chinese migrant community aspired towards being peaceful, law-abiding citizens of a future Malaya, quite separate from the wayward communist 'bandits' who were threatening peace in the territory.[22]

In the decades following independence in 1957, and partially in response to the communist threat of the Malayan Emergency, large numbers of the Chinese migrant population were granted citizenship in an effort to domesticate them. Did the conversion of this minority group to Malayan citizens change how the Chinese viewed their war dead? In the next section, we examine an exhumation conducted in 1982 to explore this question.

Parit Tinggi, Negeri Sembilan, 1982

Xiao Wen Hu was seven years old in 1942 when Japanese soldiers arrived at Parit Tinggi village in Kuala Pilah district. The villagers were asked to assemble in a clearing, ostensibly to register for 'safe passes'. Unbeknown to the villagers, Captain Iwata Mitsugi had received orders from Seremban Headquarters to conduct a *shukusei* and that 'any Chinese found in [his] area were to be summarily executed'.[23] The assembled men, women and children were segregated into groups of about twenty, marched into the surrounding areas and killed. In total, 675 civilians lost their lives before the village was razed to the ground.

Xiao sustained five bayonet wounds but was among thirty survivors who lived to bear witness to this massacre. Like many other displaced persons, Xiao became a refugee; he eked out a living on the streets and was eventually sold into child labour before being adopted by an Indonesian Chinese family. When he reached adulthood, Xiao made his way back to Malaya. Each Qing Ming, the annual day for honouring ancestors, Xiao returned to the mass grave at Parit Tinggi, where he would make contact with other survivors and their relatives. With each passing year, the wish to honour the family he had lost grew in him. He vowed he would someday build a memorial so that the events of that tragic day would not be forgotten.

In 1981, Xiao's wish came true. The impetus to exhume and reinter the remains was prompted by the revelation that the mass grave was located on government land. It would only be a matter of time until this land would be redeveloped and the grave disturbed. Survivors and relatives, Xiao included, were concerned that they would no longer be able to visit and pay their respects on Qing Ming. With the support of local Chinese community associations, a committee was established in May to raise funds for exhumation works and to erect a memorial. Xiao led the committee as chairman.

The importance of being able to worship at the graves of ancestors at Qing Ming is rooted in tradition. According to Chinese beliefs, those who died 'bad' deaths, for example through suicide or murder, are destined to wander aimlessly as 'hungry ghosts' or 'beggar spirits' if they are forgotten by their descendants.[24] If unappeased, these spirits can wreak havoc upon the prospects of living relatives. To counter this, rituals have to be performed to ease their way in the underworld. In Malaysia, Buddhist rites, Taoist rituals, Confucian teachings, and local pagan customs have melded into a unique Chinese religion of sorts.[25] Despite this, the conduct of funeral and post-funeral rites continue to uphold many of the cultural traditions transmitted by the early generations of migrants.

The exhumation at Parit Tinggi in 1982 bore the hallmarks of a traditional Chinese funeral. A Buddhist priest offered prayers for the deceased before excavation works began. Again, as at Bukit Dunbar, no forensic scientist was involved. Hired labourers set to work with basic tools – *cangkul* (hoe) and baskets – while some volunteers sifted through the earth with their bare hands. There was no protocol involved in documenting the exhumation nor was there any attempt to reassemble the bones into complete skeletons. The remains gathered – tibia, femur, and rib bones in recycled cardboard boxes, skulls in gunny sacks and plastic pails – were relocated to a temporary tomb at the Kuala Pilah Chinese cemetery, even as construction works on a permanent memorial continued apace on the same site. The use of makeshift containers to hold the remains may seem haphazard, even callous and disrespectful. However, the handling of remains does not represent a significant aspect of the burial process. According to Chinese custom, in the absence of a body, what matters is that the spirit is saved from 'homelessness' through a proper burial and the allotment of a physical resting place. In this way, the deceased are restored to their 'proper position as ancestral ghost'.[26]

In August 1984, the permanent memorial was unveiled. Survivors, relatives, the Chinese media, and representatives of various local Chinese organizations turned out *en masse*. Fruit, a roast pig, 'hell money', incense, and other gift offerings were presented to ease the afterlives of the dead, while monks from a local Buddhist association chanted prayers. This was clearly a communal affair and in some respects, also a private one; for survivors like Xiao, they had fulfilled their filial obligation in ensuring their ancestors spirits would not be in limbo. The main inscription on the monolith, in Chinese characters, states that this is a memorial for Chinese *tongbao*. In a similar way to the remains reinterred at Air Itam, the loss of these lives was consecrated to the larger Chinese collective memory of sacrifice and martyrdom at the hands of the Japanese invaders. In contrast, a plaque in the Malay language states rather simply: 'To remember those lost in the events of Parit Tinggi, Kuala Pilah on 16th March 1942'. Above it, in Chinese, there is a similar though more explicit message: that those killed included Chinese men, women, the elderly, and children. A smaller plaque explains that the victims' remains were reinterred at this memorial so that members of the community can continue to pay their respect. In rescuing these remains from potential future desecration, communal sentiment has been strengthened through a narrative of common victimhood. By erecting a memorial, they have reinserted their collective memory into the historiography of the occupation. It is evident that

Figure 10.1 Workers using rudimentary tools to excavate the mass grave at Parit Tinggi.

Figure 10.2 Excavated remains from the Parit Tinggi mass grave are placed at a temporary tomb awaiting burial at Kuala Pilah Chinese Cemetery.

by omitting any mention of the Second Sino-Japanese War on any of the inscriptions at this site, the survivors and descendants who participated in the exhumation and reinterment of the Parit Tinggi remains have asserted their personal and communal identification with their adopted land. The victims have been recast as part of a larger Malayan collective who were lost in one terrible chapter in the wider catalogue of Japanese aggression on Malayan soil.

In the next section, we examine a more recent exhumation conducted in 2002. Given the passage of time, and with each successive generation, especially among those without firsthand experience of the war and who know no other home than Malaysia, what meaning or resonance can the war dead conjure for the settled Chinese minority?

Batu Caves, 2002

On 11 November 2002, Liew Yew Kiew, eighty-nine, formerly a villager of Sungai Tua, Batu Caves, led a contingent of Chinese press, Chinese association members, and Quek Jin Teck, secretary-general of the Malaysian Chinese Cultural Society, to a clearing amidst the thick undergrowth. They arrived bearing eighteen ceramic urns, adorned with lion heads. They were there to retrieve the remains of the '9-1 Martyrs' whose mass grave was threatened by state land redevelopment. Liew had witnessed the events of 1 September 1942, when a clandestine meeting of thirty Malayan People's Anti-Japanese Army (MPAJA) resistance members had been set upon by a Japanese army battalion. In the ensuing clash, many of the villagers were also massacred. Eighteen of the guerrillas were captured and beheaded; several of their heads were displayed afterwards at a roundabout in Ampang to serve as a public warning.[27]

However, on that day in November, there was not a trace of human remains or material remnants to be found. In a symbolic gesture, handfuls of earth from the site were gathered instead into the urns. These were placed in hearses and ceremoniously driven to Nilai Memorial Park, a Chinese cemetery on the outskirts of the capital. At Nilai, the urns were buried in a ceremony attended by a gathering of about 100 Chinese community leaders and politicians. The reason for the relocation, Deputy Minister Tan Chai Ho explained, was 'to let the younger generation know that the 18 martyrs were heroes. Their sacrifices showed they were patriots who fought for the country. Such nationalistic attitude should be emulated.'[28] To that end, a permanent memorial, it was envisaged, would also be erected on the site of the reinterred remains.

A year later, in December 2003, the completed 9-1 Memorial was unveiled at an official ceremony attended by press, Chinese political and community leaders, as well as 100 visiting former MPAJA and Communist Party of Malaya (CPM) veterans from China. The message propagated was once again unabashedly political; this was an event to commemorate fallen heroes of the 'Resist Japan-Defend Malaya War of Resistance'.[29] The emphasis was clear: these were Malayan/Malaysian martyrs; their sacrifice was not limited to the Second Sino-Japanese War cause, but they had also acted out of patriotism for Malaya. There was no mention of the post-war communist insurrection, of forced deportations of communists by the British colonial administration to China, or of the connections between the MPAJA and the CPM leadership. Instead, what was clearly a Chinese communal affair was transmuted into a universal anti-war message, reminiscent of that propagated by Chinese leaders in 1951 in front of the Air Itam Memorial in Penang. 'We are a peace-loving nation', Deputy Minister Datuk Donald Lim was quoted as saying, 'and the idea behind this memorial is more of an anti-war stance, which is fitting, considering that at this juncture there are wars going on around the world, like Afghanistan for instance'.[30] In the mainstream press, the event was reported as a nostalgic reunion of former resistance fighters. In the alternative media, the opportunity was taken to remind the public that MPAJA fighters, who had sacrificed for the nation, had once been hunted as communist terrorists and bandits. Readers were also reminded that this same 'Chinese resistance was aided and supported by the British and the Allies'; further, that 'the resistance was actually quite multiethnic'.[31] The latter observation was a pointed reminder that not all wartime resistance fighters were communists or Chinese; there were Malay communists and resistance fighters as well.

Surprisingly, the reinterment and commemoration of the 9-1 Martyrs sparked little public debate. However, when it was revealed that an additional monument would be erected on the same site to remember 'Malayan heroes' of all ethnicities in the 'War of Resistance against Japanese Invasion', there was public outcry. The Information Minister, Zainuddin Madin, of ethnic Malay origin, decried the plans as a 'monument for Communists' and called for its demolition.[32] A retired lieutenant-colonel, also of Malay ethnicity, wrote to the *New Straits Times* broadsheet asking, 'How do you justify building monuments to commemorate those who fought the Japanese when there is proof that a large number of them actually committed all kinds of atrocities against the people of this country under the communist banner?'[33] The leader of the opposition Democratic Action Party, Lim Kit Siang, released an open letter deriding Zainuddin's claims that all anti-Japanese fighters were communists and mocked the minister's earlier recorded statement that just because he was Information Minister, 'he knows history, he understands history, he is part of history and that he bears witness to history'.[34] Despite the controversy, the new monument was unveiled officially in September 2007. Beneath the obelisk, the message that this is 'a monument for Malayan heroes' is repeated in four languages – English, Malay, Tamil, and Chinese. As before, attendance at the commemoration ceremony comprised primarily Chinese community leaders, politicians, and MPAJA veterans. Curiously, Zhan Gujing, a political attaché of the Embassy of the People's Republic of China in Malaysia, led the commemoration proceedings. There was no coverage in the mainstream press and if there were any dissenting voices, they were silent.

Today, the two monuments still stand on opposing sides at the Anti-War Memorial site in Nilai Memorial Park. Despite exhortations by Chinese politicians that school trips should be organized so that the young can 'learn about the sacrifices made by those who fought for the country', the site receives few public visitors.[35] It is not included on any tourist map and ambitious plans to build a museum on the grounds appear to have been abandoned. On a recent visit in 2012, this researcher noted that even though it was Qing Ming, and the cemetery was busy with visitors engaged in the annual ritual of remembering the dead, the memorial site was eerily desolate. Despite its professed *raison d'être* to honour martyrs of the Japanese occupation, the memorial appears to hold little resonance for the Malaysian public – Chinese or otherwise – at large. If the intention of the memorial was to be a political manoeuvre to insert Chinese collective war memory into the national historiography of the war, that attempt also appears to have failed.

Conclusion

Exhumations often resurrect ghosts from the pasts. As Verdery posits, the emotions, narratives, and commemorations they trigger often result in a reassessment of an uncomfortable past within society.[36] In Malaysia, however, exhumations – especially those conducted since independence – have not resulted in such opportunities. These exhumations have not promoted much empathy or sparked much interest among the general public, largely because the mass graves, the victims contained within, and the events that produced these mass corpses have been perceived (rather mistakenly) to have affected only the Chinese segment of the population. As such, the history of the Japanese occupation of Malaya, as it is propagated in contemporary Malaysia, remains partial and distorted. Thus, sensitive and thorny issues arising from the occupation remain unexplored and neglected – among them, questions of collaboration and complicity with the Japanese occupiers, and the deepening of inter-ethnic divisions between the Malay and Chinese communities in the aftermath of the occupation.

The conduct of exhumations and reinterment in more recent times demonstrates a desire on the part of the Chinese community to insert their collective communal war memory into the national historiography of the occupation. This is evident in the recasting of Chinese victims as Malayan martyrs and patriots; an overt attempt perhaps to minimize the community's migrant origins and to emphasize the community's participation in the liberation and decolonization of the nation. Rejection by the Malay political elite of these overtures indicates that national history and historiography remain in service to the national teleology of Malay supremacy. Under these circumstances, as Blackburn and Hack have observed, minority war histories are 'left to themselves, without the sponsorship of the state, to write their own histories, to nurture their own cultures, and to commemorate their own wartime past'.[37]

Notes

1 Christopher Bayly and Tim Harper characterize the Japanese invasion as a 'Rape of Malaya'. See C. Bayly & T. Harper, *Forgotten Armies: Britain's Asian Empire and the War with Japan* (London: Penguin, 2005), p. 208; Geoffrey C. Gunn argues that the planning and coordination of the *sook ching* massacres summon comparisons; G. Gunn, 'Remembering the Southeast Asian Chinese massacres of 1941–45', *Journal of Contemporary Asia*, 37:3 (2007), 273–91.

2 For various estimates, see M. Shinozaki, *Syonan: My Story* (Singapore: Marshall Cavendish, 2006); H. Hirofumi, 'Massacre of Chinese in Singapore and its coverage in postwar Japan', in Y. Akashi & M. Yoshimura (eds), *New Perspectives on the Japanese Occupation in Malaya and Singapore, 1941–1945* (Singapore: NUS Press, 2008), pp. 234–49; B. K.

Cheah, 'Japanese army policy toward the Chinese and Malay-Chinese relations in wartime Malaya', in P. H. Kratoska (ed.), *Southeast Asian Minorities in the Wartime Japanese Empire* (London: Routledge Curzon, 2002), pp. 97–110; 'War death: plea for payment is being studied', *Straits Times*, 9 March 1962, cited in W. K. Kwok, 'Justice done? Criminal and moral responsibility issues in the Chinese massacres trial Singapore, 1947', Genocide Studies Program, Working Paper 18, Yale University, 2001.

3 There is no consensus on how many mass graves exist in Malaysia. In 2009, Professor Nobuyoshi Takashima of Ryukyu University reportedly claimed that his researchers had located seventy mass graves with an estimated death toll exceeding 100,000; see S. Ahmad, 'One man's fight against Japan's historical amnesia', *New Straits Times*, 18 February 2009, 24.

4 M. Z. Rosensaft, 'The mass-graves of Bergen-Belsen: focus for confrontation', *Jewish Social Studies*, 41:2 (1979), 155–86; I. Paperno, 'Exhuming the bodies of Soviet terror', *Representations*, 75:1 (2001), 89–118; M. Elkin, 'Opening Franco's graves', *Archaeology*, 59:5 (2006), 38–43.

5 The term 'sectional narrative' emphasizes that these narratives are not entirely absent from public discourse but are suppressed as they are incompatible with existing parameters of official memory; T. Ashplant, G. Dawson & R. Michael (eds), *The Politics of War Memory and Commemoration* (London: Routledge, 2005), p. 20.

6 For discussions on why the Chinese were targeted see Y. Akashi, 'Japanese policy towards the Malayan Chinese 1941–1945', *Journal of Southeast Asian Studies* 1:2 (1970), 61–89; and Hirofumi, 'Massacre of Chinese'.

7 This statement is not meant to negate the suffering experienced by other ethnic groups during the occupation. However, as historian Henry Frei points out, 'the Chinese reminisce as the prime victims of Japanese reprisals and revenge; and Malay and Tamil sources reflect fewer problems with the Japanese who sought to woo these peoples'; H. Frei, *Guns of February: Ordinary Japanese Soldiers' Views of the Malayan Campaign and the Fall of Singapore 1941–42* (Singapore: NUS Press, 2004), p. xix.

8 In 1963, Malaya was reformed as Malaysia, incorporating Peninsular Malaya, Singapore, and the Borneo island states of Sabah and Sarawak. It was hoped that this union would stem communist influence in the region. On the impact of the communist insurgency of 1948–60 on Malay–Chinese race relations and how this affected British policy towards Malayan self-determination see F. G. Carnell, 'Communalism and communism in Malaya', *Pacific Affairs*, 26: 2 (1953), 99–117; V. Purcell, *Malaya: Communist or Free?* (Stanford, CA: Stanford University Press, 1954); G. Means, 'Malaysia: a new federation in Southeast Asia', *Pacific Affairs*, 36:2 (1963), 138–59; F. H. H. King, *The New Malayan Nation: A Study of Communalism and Nationalism* (New York: Institute of Pacific Relations, 1957); and A. Lau, 'Malayan union citizenship: constitutional change and controversy in Malaya, 1942–48', *Journal of Southeast Asian Studies*, 20:2 (1989), 216–43.

9 I. Morrison, 'Aspects of the racial problem in Malaya', *Pacific Affairs*, 22:3 (1949), p. 251; T. Silcock, 'Policy for Malaya 1952', *International Affairs*, 28:4 (1952), p. 447.

10 For an exploration of how state-sponsored national war narratives have shaped Malaysian historiography of the Japanese occupation, see K. Blackburn & K. Hack, *War Memory and the Making of Modern Malaysia and Singapore* (Singapore: NUS Press, 2012), pp. 255–91.

11 In the last two decades especially, the field of forensic investigation involving mass graves has led to the adoption of specific protocols, much of which has been established through experience by organizations such as the Physicians for Human Rights. In 1991, the United Nations introduced an examination protocol in its 'Manual on effective prevention and investigation of extra-legal, arbitrary and summary executions'. See N. Collins, 'Giving a voice to the dead', *Human Rights*, 22:1 (1995), p. 48; and W. Haglund, M. Connor & D. Scott, 'The archaeology of contemporary mass graves', *Historical Archaeology*, 35:1 (2001), 57–69.

12 Forensic investigators appear to attach much significance to the power of human remains to testify to 'the truth', 'give voice to the victims', or 'impart their stories from the grave'; see for example: Collins, 'Giving a voice to the dead'; Haglund *et al.*, 'The archaeology of contemporary mass graves'; W. Haglund, 'Archaeology and forensic death investigations', *Historical Archaeology*, 35:1 (2001), 26–34. However, Slavicist Irina Paperno argues eloquently that the body as forensic evidence is not infallible; historian Nanci Adler concurs. Both have written about the Soviet terror and how 'facts' culled from exhumations have been manipulated depending on how social and political actors ascribe meaning and interpret these evidence; see Paperno, 'Exhuming the bodies of Soviet terror'; N. Adler, 'The future of the Soviet past remains unpredictable: the resurrection of Stalinist symbols amidst the exhumation of mass graves', *Europe-Asia Studies*, 57:8 (2005), 1093–119.

13 Exhumations inevitably lead to fraught contests of meaning-making and memory-building; the latter is intrinsically linked to the present, where the past is mediated through existing political and cultural struggles within contemporary society. See K. Verdery, *The Political Lives of Dead Bodies: Reburial and Postsocialist Change* (New York: Columbia University Press, 1999), p. 7.

14 The war crimes trial cases examined by this researcher are from the following collections at the Public Records Office, Kew, London: WO235, Judge Advocate General's Office: War crimes case files, Second World War, and WO311, Judge Advocate General's Office: War crimes files – Japanese war crimes – monthly summaries and results of trials.

15 WO235/931: 'Penang Gaol case': War crimes trial of Major Higashigawa Yoshinobu and thirty-four others, Penang, 30 August–2 September 1946.

16 As Kevin Blackburn and Karl Hack have pointed out, apart from memories of everyday victims and war heroes, Chinese memories of the occupation are intrinsically rooted in the *sook ching* ('purge through cleansing') massacres of 1942. As the primary victims of these massacres, the Chinese community continue to emphasize victimhood in their commemoration of the occupation; a claim that has not been challenged by other ethnic groups. See Blackburn & Hack, *War Memory*, pp. 135–73.

17 There was a palpable mood among the Chinese populace that British justice was not being dispensed quickly or severely enough; for example, Tay Koh Yat, chairman of the Overseas Chinese Appeal Committee, submitted a public demand for more death sentences and public executions, see Kwok, 'Justice done?'.

18 China Relief Fund chapters were established throughout the territory in response to the Japanese invasion of China in 1937. Ostensibly, their function was to raise funds for humanitarian needs, though remittances also supplemented the war chest of the nationalist government in China. Contributions from Malaya to China were reportedly C\$30.4 million between November 1938 and December 1940. For more details on the role of the China Relief Fund in Malaya and the Second Sino-Japanese War, see S. Leong, 'The Kuomintang-Communist United Front in Malaya during the National Salvation Period, 1937–1941', *Journal of Southeast Asian Studies*, 8:1 (1977), 31–47; and S. Leong, 'The Malayan overseas Chinese and the Sino-Japanese War, 1937–1941', *Journal of Southeast Asian Studies*, 10:2 (1979), 297–9.

19 The reference to 'transport workers' refers to volunteers who participated in building and maintaining the Burma Road between 1937 and 1938. This was a vital supply route from Burma to southern China used by the Allies to supply the nationalist forces in China during the early years of the Second Sino-Japanese War. For more details, see C. Hendershot, 'Burma's value to the Japanese', *Far Eastern Survey*, 11:16 (1942), 176–8.

20 The term *tongbao* consists of two characters, tong (同) meaning 'same', and bao (胞) meaning 'womb'.

21 The Second Sino-Japanese War is remembered in China as the 'War of Resistance to Japan' or simply 'War of Resistance'; R. Mitter & A. Moore, 'China in World War II, 1937–1945: experience, memory, and legacy', *Modern Asian Studies*, 45:2 (2011), p. 225.

22 At the height of the Malayan Emergency, Chinese elites were at pains to illustrate to the British that the migrant Chinese community could become loyal future Malayan citizens. In collaboration with the authorities, 'education for citizenship' programmes were implemented to 'make Malayans' out of the Chinese by providing a counter-ideology to communism. See Morrison, 'Aspects of the racial problem', pp. 250–1; and E. H. G. Dobby, 'Resettlement transforms Malaya: a case-history of relocating the population of an Asian plural society', *Economic Development and Cultural Change*, 1:3 (1952), 163–89.

23 'Abstract of evidence in war crimes trial of Colonel Watanabe Tsunahiko, Captain Iwata Mitsugi and Second Lieutenant Goba Itsugo, WO311/543', Judge Advocate General's Office: War crimes files – Japanese war crimes – monthly summaries and results of trials.

24 For discussions on the consequences of 'bad deaths' or 'bad burials', and the part played by ancestral worship to mitigate the wrath or displeasure of the dead, see M. L. Cohen, 'Soul and salvation: conflicting themes in Chinese popular religion', in J. L. Watson & E. S. Rawski (eds), *Death Ritual in Late Imperial and Modern China* (Oxford: University of California Press, 1990), pp. 180–202; see also S. Harrell, 'The concept

of soul in Chinese folk religion', *Journal of Asian Studies*, 38:3 (1979), 519–28.

25 C.-B. Tan, 'Chinese religion in Malaysia: a general view', *Asian Folklore Studies*, 42:2 (1983), 217–52.

26 Cohen, 'Soul and salvation', p. 189.

27 For more details on the events of 1 September 1942, see J. Wong, 'Chuán song liè shì de jīng shén' (Commemorating the spirit of the 1 September martyrs), *Malaysiakini*, 5 August 2005.

28 M. Liu, 'Tribute to war martyrs', Asiawind, 14 December 2002, www.asiawind.com/forums/read.php?f=1&i=3084&t=3082&v=f (accessed 19 February 2014).

29 J. Wong, 'Remembering the martyrs', *Malaysiakini*, 12 December 2003.

30 'Emotional trip for ex-members of anti-Japanese force', *New Straits Times*, 8 December 2003.

31 J. Wong, 'War museum to commemorate fallen heroes', *Malaysiakini*, 5 December 2003.

32 'MB: demolish "communist" monument', *Malaysiakini*, 20 December 2006.

33 M. I. Hassan, 'This is definitely not appropriate', letter to *New Straits Times*, 28 December 2006.

34 K. S. Lim, 'Media statement', *DAP Malaysia*, 22 December 2006.

35 'Pay tribute to war heroes', *The Star*, 24 August 2009.

36 Verdery, *The Political Lives of Dead Bodies*, p. 7.

37 Blackburn & Hack, *War Memory*, p. 257.

Bibliography

Adler, N., 'The future of the Soviet past remains unpredictable: the resurrection of Stalinist symbols amidst the exhumation of mass graves', *Europe-Asia Studies*, 57:8 (2005), 1093–119

Ahmad, S., 'One man's fight against Japan's historical amnesia', *New Straits Times*, 18 February 2009

Akashi, Y., 'Japanese policy towards the Malayan Chinese 1941–1945', *Journal of Southeast Asian Studies*, 1:2 (1970), 61–89

Ashplant, T., G. Dawson & R. Michael (eds), *The Politics of War Memory and Commemoration* (London: Routledge, 2005)

Bayly, C. & T. Harper, *Forgotten Armies: Britain's Asian Empire and the War with Japan* (London: Penguin, 2005)

Blackburn, K. & K. Hack, *War Memory and the Making of Modern Malaysia and Singapore* (Singapore: NUS Press, 2012)

Carnell, F. G., 'Communalism and communism in Malaya', *Pacific Affairs*, 26:2 (1953), 99–117

Cheah, B. K., 'Japanese army policy toward the Chinese and Malay-Chinese relations in wartime Malaya', in P. H. Kratoska (ed.), *Southeast Asian Minorities in the Wartime Japanese Empire* (London: Routledge Curzon, 2002), pp. 97–110

Cohen, M. L., 'Soul and salvation: conflicting themes in Chinese popular religion', in J. L. Watson & E. S. Rawski (eds), *Death Ritual in Late Imperial and Modern China* (Oxford: University of California Press, 1990), pp. 180–202

Collins, N., 'Giving a voice to the dead', *Human Rights*, 22:1 (1995), 28–48

Dobby, E. H. G., 'Resettlement transforms Malaya: a case-history of relocating the population of an Asian plural society', *Economic Development and Cultural Change*, 1:3 (1952), 163–89

Elkin, M., 'Opening Franco's graves', *Archaeology*, 59:5 (2006), 38–43

Frei, H., *Guns of February: Ordinary Japanese Soldiers' Views of the Malayan Campaign and the Fall of Singapore 1941–42* (Singapore: NUS Press, 2004)

Fujitani, T., M. White & L. Yoneyama (eds), *Perilous Memories: The Asia-Pacific Wars* (Durham, NC: Duke University Press, 2001)

Gunn, G., 'Remembering the Southeast Asian Chinese massacres of 1941–45', *Journal of Contemporary Asia*, 37:3 (2007), 273–91

Haglund, W., 'Archaeology and forensic death investigations', *Historical Archaeology*, 35:1 (2001), 26–34

Haglund, W., M. Connor & D. Scott, 'The archaeology of contemporary mass graves', *Historical Archaeology*, 35:1 (2001), 57–69

Harrell, S., 'The concept of soul in Chinese folk religion', *Journal of Asian Studies*, 38:3 (1979), 519–28

Hendershot, C., 'Burma's value to the Japanese', *Far Eastern Survey*, 11:16 (1942), 176–8

Hirofumi, H., 'Massacre of Chinese in Singapore and its coverage in post-war Japan', in Y. Akashi & M. Yoshimura (eds), *New Perspectives on the Japanese Occupation in Malaya and Singapore, 1941–1945* (Singapore: NUS Press, 2008), pp. 234–49

King, F. H. H., *The New Malayan Nation: A Study of Communalism and Nationalism* (New York: Institute of Pacific Relations, 1957)

Kwok, W. K., 'Justice done? Criminal and moral responsibility issues in the Chinese massacres trial Singapore, 1947', Genocide Studies Program, Working Paper No. 18, Yale University, 2001

Lau, A., 'Malayan union citizenship: constitutional change and controversy in Malaya, 1942–48', *Journal of Southeast Asian Studies*, 20:2 (1989), 216–43

Leong, S., 'The Kuomintang-Communist United Front in Malaya during the National Salvation Period, 1937–1941', *Journal of Southeast Asian Studies*, 8:1 (1977), 31–47

Leong, S., 'The Malayan overseas Chinese and the Sino-Japanese War, 1937–1941', *Journal of Southeast Asian Studies*, 10:2 (1979), 297–9

Lim, K. S., 'Media statement', *DAP Malaysia*, 22 December 2006

Liu, M., 'Tribute to war martyrs', Asiawind, 14 December 2002, www.asiawind.com/forums/read.php?f=1&i=3084&t=3082&v=f (accessed 19 February 2014)

Malaysiakini, 'MB: demolish "communist" monument', 20 December 2006

Means, G., 'Malaysia: a new federation in Southeast Asia', *Pacific Affairs*, 36:2 (1963), 138–59

Mitter, R. & A. Moore, 'China in World War II, 1937–1945: experience, memory, and legacy', *Modern Asian Studies*, 45:2 (2011), 225–40

Mohd, I. H., 'This is definitely not appropriate', letter to *New Straits Times*, 28 December 2006

Morrison, I., 'Aspects of the racial problem in Malaya', *Pacific Affairs*, 22:3 (1949), 239–53

New Straits Times, 'Emotional trip for ex-members of anti-Japanese force', 8 December 2003

Paperno, I., 'Exhuming the bodies of Soviet terror', *Representations*, 75:1 (2001), 89–118

Purcell, V., *Malaya: Communist or Free?* (Stanford, CA: Stanford University Press, 1954)

Rosensaft, M. Z. 'The mass-graves of Bergen-Belsen: focus for confrontation', *Jewish Social Studies*, 41:2 (1979), 155–86

Shinozaki, M., *Syonan: My Story* (Singapore: Marshall Cavendish, 2006)

Silcock, T., 'Policy for Malaya 1952', *International Affairs*, 28:4 (1952), 445–51

The Star, 'Pay tribute to war heroes', 24 August 2009

Tan, C.-B., 'Chinese religion in Malaysia: a general view', *Asian Folklore Studies*, 42:2 (1983), 217–52

Verdery, K., *The Political Lives of Dead Bodies: Reburial and Postsocialist Change* (New York: Columbia University Press, 1999)

Wong, J., 'Chuán song liè shì de jīng shén', *Malaysiakini*, 5 August 2005

Wong, J., 'Remembering the martyrs', *Malaysiakini*, 12 December 2003

Wong, J., 'War museum to commemorate fallen heroes', *Malaysiakini*, 5 December 2003

Index